MW00477855

FUTURE
VISION

The 189 Most Important Trends of the 1990s

FROM THE EDITORS OF
RESEARCH ALERT

SOURCEBOOKS TRADE
NAPERVILLE, ILLINOIS

Sourcebooks Trade

A Division of Sourcebooks, Inc.
P.O. Box 372
Naperville, Illinois, 60566
(708) 961-2161

Design and Production: Monica Paxson, Emily Friel
Cover Design: Creative Mind Services/Concialdi Design

In cooperation with the Partners in Publishing Program

 KENDALL/HUNT PUBLISHING COMPANY
2460 Kerper Boulevard P.O. Box 539 Dubuque, Iowa 52004-0539

0-8403-6439 hardcover; 0-8403-6438 paperback

Library of Congress Cataloging-in-Publication Data

Future vision: the 189 most important trends of the 1990s / from the
    editors of Research alert.
        p.   cm.
        Includes bibliographical references (p.)
        ISBN 0-942061-17-9:hardcover -- ISBN 0-942061-16-0: paperback
        1. Social prediction--United States. 2. Economic forecasting-
-United States. 3. United States--Social conditions--1980-
4. United States--Economic conidition s--1981-   I. Research alert
(Long Island City, New York, N.Y.)
HN59.2.F88   1991
303.4973--dc20   90-49474
                                                          CIP

10 9 8 7 6 5 4 3 2 1

Dedication:
This work is dedicated to those who
will use it to make a positive con-
tribution to tomorrow's America.

Acknowledgments:

I would like to acknowledge three kinds of assistance provided for this book.

First, I would like to thank all the sources that provided the information we have reviewed in these pages. We never underestimate the amount of work, care, and expense it took to bring all these reliable findings to light. I wish to express particular gratitude to the publications the *Public Pulse* (from The Roper Organization), and *American Demographics* whose excellent work has served not only to illuminate trends, but also to educate us along the way. Special gratitude also to the *Wall Street Journal*, the *New York Times*, and *USA Today*, whose accurate trend coverage has been invaluable. Many thanks also to the hundreds of other companies who regularly send *Research Alert* their fine research..

Second, I wish to thank the current and former editors at *Research Alert* who worked so hard to create this book; particularly Ann Loughlin, Elisa Nudelman, and Dan Thomas. Thanks also to Dominique Raccah at Sourcebooks, who had the future vision to make this book a reality.

Finally, a few notes of personal thanks to my wife, the actress/psychotherapist le Clanché du Rand, for her patience with the many months of 70-hour work weeks; to my parents for the habits and genes that make me able to enjoy 70-hour work weeks; and to the subscribers of *Research Alert*, whose loyalty foots the bill for those 70-hour work weeks.

Eric Miller
Editor/Owner of *Research Alert*

Note: All the research findings in this book come from the sources cited throughout. The source of each finding is listed adjacent to each fact; where no source is listed, the finding is the opinion of the editors. *Research Alert* neither commissioned nor performed any research cited herein.

Table of Contents

Introduction
Putting Trends into Perspective

"Vision is the art of seeing things invisible," Jonathan Swift reminds us.

Like any art, vision requires discipline and expertise. If performed well an art looks easy; in hindsight, the future seems obvious. Future vision is the art of seeing the invisible future. And like other arts, it opens up a whole new world.

It *is* possible to see into the future. By analyzing past and present facts, the careful futurist can envision trend lines extending forward into the future. These trends map out the probable routes and likely landmarks we all will experience in America's journey to the end of the century and beyond.

Any of a thousand unforeseeable things may occur to influence the specific roads we travel, but trends based on facts usually hold true, and the directions they give us are reliable. Of course, at any moment cataclysmic events could change the course of history, making trend predictions as obsolete as a map of a flat earth, but making predictions on that level is better left to those with divine gifts.

Future vision is important. Wise parents instinctively caution their children as they face major life decisions, "Think about your future." The same advice serves all of us who are re-creating America—the social and political leaders and workers, the business people, the informed citizens who contribute their thoughts and opinions, their taxes and votes, to our evolving society. Future vision enables the nation's leaders to plan for the needs of the nation; it equips business leaders with necessary information to anticipate future markets; it empowers informed citizens to take command of the world in which we live. Future vision presents America with its probable tomorrow, giving us all a chance to roll up our sleeves and fulfill our greatest potential.

Accurate future vision may be *possible*, but it isn't *easy*. Even the President of the United States admits he has trouble with his future vision—"the vision thing" is the way Mr. Bush refers to the difficulty.

Pundits are often less humble. Many seem more than willing to express their visions of the future—whether those visions are based on facts or just conjecture. Future visionaries are everywhere—on TV talk shows, lecture circuits, in magazines, on bookshelves. It frustrates me, personally, that the accurate ones are mixed in with the blowhards. Future vision is too important to be abused with bad thinking. To differentiate between clear and cloudy sight, check out the posture of the visionary. Make sure the trend tracker has:

- both feet on the ground,
- head held high and screwed on straight,
- eyes forward.

Too many current visionaries are presenting pictures of tomorrow while in a risky posture.

- Many let their feet lift off the ground. They present rosy, cloud-nine pictures of how great it is going to be. However, the ozone is pretty thin up there (and getting thinner), and, however pleasant the view, sooner or later the vision will be brought down to earth by reality. If you have made plans according to these visions, you're in for a crash.

- Others have their ears too close to the ground. They are too concerned with the small shifts in attitudes and opinions reflected in surveys that appear every day in the media. Keeping an ear to the ground while you are standing is hardly a position that enables you to see the future with clarity. Try to move forward in that posture and you are heading for embarrassment, if not real trouble. As Harry Truman said, "How far would Moses have gone if he had taken a poll in Egypt?"

- Some pundits do have feet on the ground, and head held high, but they don't have their eyes straight ahead or their heads screwed on straight. They have an agenda to promote. They pick the facts that serve their point of view. If you move into the future with your eyes following their line of vision, reality is going to walk you into a wall sooner or later.

A Different Future Vision

This book is going to present you with a different future vision. It is grounded in fact—all the trends are based on and expressed with facts. This vision stands tall—our analysts see hundreds of thousands of pages of research every year, and can distinguish among fads, fluctuations, and genuine trends. It looks straight ahead—we have no ax to grind; the only point of view we want to promote is a clear line of vision that gives you the specific information you need to anticipate tomorrow's America.

This future vision is different in another way, too; it paints with a small brush. Rather than giving you a dramatic, abstract-impressionistic picture of tomorrow, we will paint a realistic, detailed canvas of trends. The U.S. is a complicated entity; there is no simple set of trends that can capture the direction of the entire nation. So multifaceted is this country, that one can apply the following rule of thumb: for most general trends, their opposite will also be true.

For example, it is true that environmentalism is catching on with Americans and changing their lifestyles. It is also true, however, that the majority of the nation has yet to make any significant adjustment in its everyday living. Also, statistics can be presented in different ways to substantiate dramatically different conclusions—any student of U.S. politics has seen this practice in action a thousand times. So, we use a fine brush to paint America by micro-trend.

Real trends take time. They gestate under the surface for years, even decades. Their first appearances are subtle. Their growth into the daily lives of average citizens takes additional years or decades. In fact, the development of real trends is so natural that we generally don't notice their emergence until we look back to the way it was before. For example, can you remember the kind of adjectives used to describe a woman who sought a big business career in the 1950s? Few of the words back then would have been assessments of her skills; today virtually all the words would appraise her talents, not her sex. The change is tremendous, yet it appeared incrementally over decades. If you are going to bet on trend announcements, choose the tortoise over the hare.

Our future vision demands that we be:

Factual. Instead of presenting large, catchy-but-difficult-to-put-into practical-terms trends, we give you facts.

Specific. The story of tomorrow's America cannot be told accurately in general terms; the true, complicated tale must be laid out piece by piece.

Unbiased. Some of the actual trends contradict popular thinking (for example that Baby Boomers spend and don't save), others show no movement in areas (such as racism)where we all hope for some. We report what is happening and what is likely to happen; no hidden agendas.

Broad in perspective. Some of the most interesting trends occur in small corners of the American scene; others are major social shifts. We feel you must know them all.

Aware of hype. Throughout these pages you will find small sections that we call Hype Alerts. These draw your attention to claims you may have seen or heard that are based on shallow thinking, inadvertent or intentional hype, or just plain boneheadedness.

The Problem of Hype

Our information age has spawned a demon. There is so much information presented to us that hype has become a preferred mode of cutting through the clutter. It works—it grabs attention. More insidiously, hyped trends *seem* true because they are usually *based* in fact; they lodge in the mind because they are clever. Hype is troublesome when you mistake it for reality.

The artifice of hype is practiced in three basic ways:

- reporting a false fact;

- taking an actual fact, framing it, shining a spotlight on it—thus removing it from context or overemphasizing it;

- citing an inclination as an actuality.

Here are a few examples:

False fact. This is not the most common form of hype, but it is one of the most difficult to deal with.

Here's an example. In 1987, a major business magazine reported that "By 1990, 75 percent of the U.S. population will live within 50 miles of the shore, compared with 40 percent in 1984." I remember reading that sentence and being impressed. It was used in a cover story about the growing dangers of ocean pollution, and the statistic stayed in my mind. It wasn't until I was working with a Census Bureau study two years later that I stumbled into the realization that the fact was just plain wrong. The truth is that today slightly more than half (53 percent) of the U.S. population lives within 50 miles of the shore. This percentage is unchanged since 1984, and has *decreased* slightly since 1970.

The false fact was presented to millions of readers; I've seen it printed in the literature of environmental organizations and heard it used elsewhere. It created a false impression of crisis in my mind, and *my* work is dedicated to dealing with such facts. Certainly, we must attend to ocean pollution; we have to plan and take action. But crying wolf with false facts, whether intentionally or inadvertently false, is counterproductive.

And this is just one fact in one article. None of us can examine all the facts we encounter; we take them in and retain general impressions—in this case, and in too many others, a false impression.

An actual fact overemphasized into hype. Overemphasis of a small temporal shift in opinion is a more frequent danger. Genuine trends take time to emerge; a modest one-year shift in attitude does not warrant the claim of its being a new trend. You've seen this kind of thing often, though you may not realize it.

Gerald Celente points out a classic example of trend-by-hype in his book *Trend Tracking*. During and after the hostage crisis in Iran, there was a surge of patriotic fervor in the U.S. It looked like a genuine trend, trickling down from the White House into every level of the nation; headline after headline announced it as a trend. People believed it. Businesses made plans based on it. However, nothing happened. There were no significant results—Americans didn't start "buying American." The percentage of oil that is imported climbed back to extravagant levels; flag sales subsided. It was a fad. If you bet the bank on it, you lost.

A fact can be hyped by removing it from context too. Not long ago, I saw an announcement that this was the era of the sensitive man.

The claim was substantiated with the fact that more than 200 colleges and universities now offer courses that study the male experience. That's true. The report "forgot" to mention that more than 70 percent of the enrollees in those courses are females.

Announcement of intentions as actualities. If you believe that intentions are reality, then you will find the U.S. to be the Garden of Eden. That sounds silly, yet many trend mavens announce inclinations as if they were actualities. Expressed ntentions would have you thinking that most Americans are sorting their household garbage; that dads are spending more time with the kids and doing a lot more of the housework; that materialism is passé; that today's youth is politically conservative.

These hyped trends are not true trends. Fathers have been telling pollsters ever since there were pollsters that they want to spend more time with their kids. Yet while they have added an average of a few minutes a week to pitch in with the housework, they have added almost no time in their schedules to spend with the kids. And, at the same time, they have predictably increased their work hours as soon as a child comes into the family. While 90 percent of Americans share pro-environmental attitudes—solid majorities respond to surveys supporting the ecological point of view—only 20 percent live in areas where they have to sort their trash.

Don't believe the hype. Both the doomsayers and the cheerleaders are hype mongers. Generally, the facts don't warrant either position. There is precious little reason to think that homelessness, the underclass, racism, abuse of women, children, and the elderly, and so forth are likely to become substantially less pervasive in this decade. Similarly, there is little reason, based on the facts, to think that the economy is going to go into a serious depression in the 1990s, that the number of homeless will double, or that America will dramatically lose its influence on the world—all of which I have seen claimed. America is entering a future more complex than that; one replete with shadings of good and bad news. Few of the trends are at the extremes.

Let me add a personal note. The fact that hyped trends are not true, that there is little reason for grinning optimism or brow-furrowing despair, does not make the business of future vision based upon the facts any less exciting. On the contrary, the actual changes in America today are more exciting than trend fiction. The prodigious effort required to separate fact from fluff is indeed worthy detective work.

The Semantic Quagmire

In addition to hype, words themselves have become tricky for the future visionary. Trends have changed America, but we haven't changed the words we use to describe these new Americans. Definitions have blurred, meanings have become vague—all of which can lead to vague thinking and seeing. For example: who exactly are the old, the mature, the seniors, the elderly in this era of longer, active lives? Today's "seniors" live lifestyles previously associated with the middle-aged. There are at least three different lifestyle groups within what is vaguely called "seniors"—each with its own attitudes, self-perceptions, and needs, but without a word to name it. My mother spent her 68th birthday trekking in Antarctica—is she old? A marketer who addresses her as an "old" consumer will permanently lose her as a customer. A son who addresses her as old will have to catch up with her to apologize.

What is leisure? The amount of activity now crammed into leisure makes much of it look like the old definition of work. Consumer researchers have been getting disparate answers to questions about leisure in recent years, because Americans now define it in so many different ways. Some surveys find a decrease in the amount of U.S. leisure, others find an increase. I have concluded that this confusion is largely semantic. To some of us, leisure means feet up in a hammock; to others it constitutes morning golf, an afternoon making a home movie for America's Funniest Home Videos, dinner out, and a night at the theater. Yet, the word for all of this is leisure.

What does traditional mean? Most of us have seen the phrase "The New Traditionalist" bandied about. What does it mean? If it means a June Cleaver household, fewer than 9 percent of Americans are traditional. If it means valuing home and family, almost all of us are traditional. If it means women want families *and* work, you will have to define what you mean by family, what you mean by work, and so on.

Boundaries have blurred. Work doesn't automatically mean nine to five anymore. Family doesn't necessarily mean parents and kids. Old doesn't mean old. Home has become a place where we work and exercise, as well as a place where we retreat from work and effort. Work is becoming a place where we take care of the kids and undertake education. Other boundaries have blurred as well. Journalism and entertainment are sometimes barely distinguishable; advertising and journalism have met in advertorials; education, journalism, entertainment, and advertising have met in the classroom on Channel One.

We all must be more precise in the words that we use, or try to create new ones. The fragmenting marketplace, with its smaller moving targets, requires precision. That is why we rely so heavily on facts; they are the scope for taking more accurate aim.

John Q. Pundit

I believe in consumers—they are better trend predictors than experts. Time and again consumers have pointed a clear path toward America's future as the experts gave informed opinion pointing in every direction.

For example, consumers have proven themselves to be the best forecasters of future economic trends. The government spends untold millions collecting statistics to point to the future. Experts analyze and pronounce. The media puts out the word. But, as Fabian Linden of the Conference Board puts it, "Unfortunately, the economic forecasting fraternity's performance has been less than inspiring. The nation's consumers have a far better record in foretelling our economic fortunes."

A few examples: In early 1986, economists were predicting strong growth while consumer confidence was low; consumers were right. The inverse was the case in 1988, and again consumers were right. Just after the stock market's 1987 Black Monday, pundits were doom-saying (recession predictions and warnings of disastrous Christmas '87 sales). Consumers noted the trouble, but didn't feel a recession coming. Result? No recession, and Christmas sales were up from the previous year.

Richard Curtin, who directs the University of Michigan monthly *Index of Consumer Expectations* (which was adopted by the U.S. Commerce Department in 1989 as one of its leading economic indicators) pinpoints the reason that consumers are the best trend predictors: "Even though they may be unsophisticated in economics or may show little little fiscal practicality, consumers know their interests. They may not know the latest figures for, say housing starts or gross national product, but they know that a neighbor has lost his job or that paychecks aren't stretching as far as they did." If there is a difference between experiential and intellectual knowing, go with the gut.

A study that recently came out of Wharton School of Business confirms the point. Predictions about consumer behavior were elicited from experts, academics, and novices. None of the three groups performed better than chance. Consumer research leaders had predicted that academics would have an 80 percent accuracy score; they got 51 percent—significantly worse than chance.

Follow the people, study them, note their actions, learn how to think what they think, feel what they feel. That is the basis of 20/20 future vision. The people will point you toward tomorrow's America.

Eric Miller
Owner/Editor of *Research Alert*

The 1990s
Overview of the Coming Decade

The world as you know it no longer exists.

The world you will know is unlike anything you've ever seen.

America is moving. Its people and its institutions are transforming basic self-definitions—it is no wonder Americans feel they live in a time of change.

I would like to present you with an overview, a context of trends, within which to use the specific trends that comprise the remainder of this book. This chapter comes perilously close to the very trend-hyping I've just been alerting you to. Here, however, the intent is different—this overview willshow you the five biggest rivers flowing toward the future; the succeeding chapters will point out all the tributary trends that make these rivers possible. These are general trends, and like big rivers, contain currents that flow against the prevailing movement. The remainder of the book will indicate all the specific eddies, swirls, rapids, and navigation channels you will need to know about to sail forward.

These are the five primary trends reshaping America.

1. the redefinition of family

2. changing forces of influence

3. the end of the mass market

4. outgrowing the youth culture

5. a new American point of view

The Redefinition of Family

The basic unit of society, "family," evolved as a social arrangement that served to perpetuate our particular species. In the West's civilized human family of recent centuries, blood has been thicker than anything. Blood lineage defined family.

In 1990s America, even the way we begin families—marriage—has changed. There used to be many reasons for marrying, love being one of the foremost. Social acceptance of alternative lifestyles has reduced the marital-imperative. "Why not just live together?" is a serious question in many, if not most, committed relationships. This used to be an option for only an unconventional few.

With women feeling that they can earn their own livings, the financial necessity of marriage has also diminished. So, with diminishing social and financial pressure to marry, having children is becoming the primary reason, often the sole reason. Even getting-married-to-have-a-child will decrease as a marital imperative in the 1990s as single-parenting-by-choice becomes more common and more socially acceptable. As a result of this transformation in the reasons we start families, and the network of changes within existing families, we will have very different families appearing in the 1990s.

Family size is smaller than at any time in U.S. history (now averaging about 3.15 members). This is particularly significant in light of the fact that birth rates are edging up faster than expected (1989 birth rates were the highest since 1972). Higher birth rates + smaller families at the same time = fragmented families.

For the first time, a majority of American families have no children living at home. Singles and unmarried people living together now outnumber married couples with children. In just eight years (1980 to 1988) the percentage of U.S. families with two parents present fell by more than 7 percent, while the number of couples without dependent children increased by 18 percent.

The trends that change the definition of a social structure as basic as the family take time to develop. In this case the trends have been active for decades, but have intensified in the last 10-15 years, and will present new connotations of the word family in the 1990s. Such major trends are born from the convergence of many influences. The following is a partial list of the key tributary trends, which together are phasing out the former family and creating the new. They come from demographic, social, and political, as well as economic fields.

- delayed marriage

- high divorce rates (though dropping slightly recently)

- delayed childbirth

- record numbers of singles (now almost a quarter of all U.S. households)

- high teenage pregnancy rates (increasing for whites and Hispanics, not for blacks)

- record-high out-of-wedlock births

- record numbers of single-parent families

- record numbers of families with stepchildren (now one-fifth of all families with kids, and the number is rising)
- high rates of mobility, (though now slightly lower than in the 1950s through 1970s)
- acceptance of alternative lifestyles, such as cohabitation, homosexual couples, asexual couples, group living
- fewer small-farm families
- less religious influence
- persistent unemployment in underclass areas

The "family" of the 1990s will continue to grow smaller, and there will be an increasing percentage of non-traditional types of families. The proliferation of household types is finding much greater acceptance, allowing the exceptions to old rules to become the new norms.

As the old definition phases out, a new definition is emerging. This new definition is, of necessity, one that answers the needs of the time. As we approach the end of the century, "being there" is becoming as thick as blood. Those who give care are "family." Child care, eldercare, and just plain taking care in general are becoming progressively more important as a result of the fragmented family structure. The structural answers to these basic needs may come to embody the new definition of family.

Of course this new definition includes the Cosby family and Roseanne's family, but it will also come to include several older people living together, cohabiting couples in their 40s, single parents, lesbians with a child, and so forth, as family. This is the "family" you will find on your block by the end of the century. Indeed, several state legislatures have already redefined the term family to extend "family" benefits to once-excluded arrangements. For example, in 1989, New York State changed the definition of family to enable the surviving gay mate to keep the rent-controlled apartment of a deceased partner.

Actually, the gay community provides a good example of the evolving concept of family. Largely as a result of the impact of AIDS, a care network has appeared to answer the needs of the 9 percent to 14 percent of Americans who are gay (since 1948 Kinsey data is still the basis of most counts, no one is sure how large the gay population actually is). The structures within the gay support family couldn't look less like the Cleaver household, yet they also constitute "family." As it often does, the gay community is pointing to a future social direction. Gays have undertaken a widespread education campaign, and have developed household arrangements to serve the needs of community members—the 1990s' emerging definition of family.

Changing Forces of Influence

White, western-European-lineage men. That is the briefest description of the history of America's leaders. This hegemony is in the grip of unprecedented change. The social and economic clout of two groups in particular is going to redirect your future. This redirection will affect your life on every level, from the laws you obey to the lamp you buy for the study. And because of these changing influences, your grandchildren's senior years will take place in a society you'd barely recognize.

Women

Women have, of course, made tremendous contributions to leading America, and their influence behind the scenes cannot be overestimated. Now, however, they are moving from "behind every good man ..." into direct, primary influence alongside men.

The women's movement has been more successful than most of us realize. The remaining hurdles may be great, but in three areas the success has been steady.

1. Choice. Marketers call it life phasing; women call it choice. Women have claimed the right to do what they want in life, when they want to do it. And they have claimed the right to make different choices at different times in their lives. Social stigmas against having children or not having children have been reduced.

Both staying home with the kids and not staying home with the kids are acceptable choices. Being career-driven for a period of years and then focusing on family for a period of years and then changing careers is an acceptable and common pattern. Starting a new career in mid-life is not only looked upon favorably, it is admired.

Where "tradition," "duty," and "responsibility" have been the essential elements of women's life choices (along with other factors such as money), money is becoming a more important factor. In the leaner, meaner economic climate of the 1990s, almost all of women's life choices (family, work, marriage, leisure, and so on) will pit personal choice against financial factors; there will be fewer other issues to weigh.

Women's freedom to make their own life choices (and then change them) will have a tremendous impact on all U.S. institutions. This influence will begin to be felt strongly in the 1990s. Business and government will create viable day care to enable those who want to go back to work to do so easily. You will see colorful onsite day care centers in many of those glass office building complexes. Corporations will expand flextime and an array of benefits ("cafeteria plans") to accommodate the personal needs of workers. You may even see breast-feeding breaks replacing some coffee breaks. Corporate leaders will not offer these career amenities as a generous expression of support for the values of the women's movement, they will *have* to offer them to keep the skilled young (and not-so-young) workers upon whom they will be more dependent in the 1990s.

Working at home has become an alternative for many. Women are starting businesses at a record rate—women now own a third of U.S. businesses, and may well own close to 40 percent by the year 2000. There are more female entrepreneurs than male.

Men are also adjusting to women's choices. Men are doing more housework (though the larger change has been that women are doing less and seem willing to live in a slightly less tidy house). Men are doing more of the family errands, including shopping. By the end of the century they will begin to take a greater hand in childrearing—the beginning of a change in an age-old pattern.

2. Money. The wage gap persists—working women earn about 66 percent of what men earn—and the gap is unlikely to close more than another six or seven percentage points in the 1990s. The wage gap was at 59 percent in 1980, and closed only one percentage point in the decade of the '70s.

However, the working wife has become a fixture in the U.S. economy—her emergence is arguably the single most important change of the 1980s. There was a dramatic increase in the number of affluent Americans in the 1980s; that was not a hyped trend, it was a fact. However, don't picture legions of cigar-smoking male moguls entering the ranks of the upscale. Middle-class couples were the ones who moved up, and they did so primarily on the strength of the wife's increased income. Men's earnings remained relatively flat through the '80s; women's earnings were the engine for the rocketing affluence. Families are now more dependent on a wife's earnings to maintain their standard of living than at any time in history. And working women will fuel the engine of affluence in the 1990s.

Don't let me mislead you with a rosy picture of easy money. Most of these working women are not the confident, career-driven Supermoms of media mythology. Most women are working less for the fulfillment of a career than because it now takes two incomes to meet the household budget without a setback in standard of living. They are working in addition to running the household, and then are experiencing the stress that results from juggling countless balls of responsibility at any given time. This widescale stress is the reason that convenience will continue to be a growing concern to most American families in the 1990s.

With their increasing financial clout on the most local level of government (the home), women's influence will continue to increase. They now have more influence on major family purchases than at any time in U.S. history; more major purchase decisions are made jointly than ever before. The pattern used to be, the man made most of the major decisions. Some were made jointly, and a few (home- and education-related items) were made by the wife. Now, and increasingly in the 1990s, most decisions are and will be made jointly, with a few made by the man or woman individually. By the end of the century, women will actually buy more than half of all the cars that are sold in the country, possibly as many as 60 percent of the cars sold in the year 2000.

And the '90s look bright for women's increasing influence. Smart business persons that they are, women have been investing in their futures with record levels of education. Women now earn more bachelor's degrees than men (the unprecedented switch happened in the mid-1980s). As recently as 1970, women got only 75 percent as many sheepskins as men. Also, business has become women's first choice as a major. Women's isolation in pink-collar jobs is decreasing. Thirty percent now hold managerial/professional jobs (the same percentage as men); half of America's accountants are women. With the labor shortage in the 1990s, women are in a very strong position to continue the rate of gain they enjoyed in the '80s.

Let me note, however, that I don't hear the "glass ceiling" shattering in the 1990s. As we enter the decade, fewer than half of the largest 1,000 firms in the U.S. have females comprising more than 5 percent of their senior management; only 3 percent of senior execs at Fortune 500 corporations are women. The invisible barrier that keeps women out of the top echelons of corporate power will recede in the '90s as more women with the requisite number of years of experience rise toward the top. Women will manage at higher levels, but may not gain fair access to the very top by the end of the century. Surveys show that stereotypes of women as management risks still persist, and such prejudices disappear only with experience and over time. There may be a few celebrated cases where we hear the glass shatter, but they will be isolated. It will be a decade of slow gains.

3. Politics. The '80s brought America the first woman on a national ticket (Geraldine Ferraro); the '90s will probably present the first woman in the top slot—at the least, we will probably see a woman launch a credible presidential campaign.

Although women's gains in holding elective office have brought them to record levels of representation, they remain far below male rates. Females now comprise only 5 percent of the U.S. Congress (up from 4 percent in 1975); 14 percent of statewide elective offices (up from 10 percent in '75); 17 percent of state legislators (double the 1975 representation); and more than 14 percent of mayors/municipal governing board members were females in 1985 (up from 4 percent in 1975). The 1990s will bring more gains. However, they will be the same kind of slow, incremental kinds of gains the nation has been generating in recent history.

Minorities

It is not just women who will join white men in leading America to the end of the century and beyond; minority groups also will dramatically increase their influence. In fact, by the year 2088, "minority" populations will become the U.S. majority. This is already true in major cities such as New York and Los Angeles. California will be the first state to have a minority majority, about a generation from today.

Immigration rates are exceeding expectations. The Census Bureau puts together "middle," "high," and "low" series projections to allow for future variables—the middle series is commonly used as the basis of many predictions. However, current immigration (legal and illegal) is running along the "high series" projection lines. If this rate continues, it means that almost half of all population growth in the U.S. will be from immigration as soon as one generation from now. It also means a faster increase in demographic influence for Hispanics (particularly of Mexican origin) and Asians. And these new arrivals will continue their pattern of urban concentration—three-quarters of 1989 immigrants were relatives of current U.S. residents, and tend to move into housing nearby. This pattern is expected to hold through the 1990s.

A specific example of the influence of minority population growth: The Big Apple is still seen as America's foremost urban center. It now has a white plurality; in just one generation it will be 35 percent Hispanic, 27 percent white and 27 percent African-American; in two generations it will be 14 percent to 15 percent each white and Asians, 30 percent African-American, and 41 percent Hispanic. And these estimates are based on "middle series" projections, so the growth of Hispanic and Asian populations could be even faster if it continues at the present rate.

Sheer demographic power increases influence. With the African-American population growing faster than the white, the Hispanic population increasing at 4 times the rate of the white population, and the Asian-American population at 8 times the white rate, the minority population is going to wield substantially greater clout. Not only will this growth translate into electoral presence for minority leaders, it will disseminate into the fabric of the culture. It is no coincidence that tacos surpassed spaghetti and pizza to become the most popular ethnic food for the first time in 1990.

Each of the three major minority groups exerts a different kind of influence.

African-Americans are the largest minority group and will continue to be until the year 2015, at about which time the number of Hispanics is expected to surpass them. Although they suffer disproportionate amounts of social strain, African-Americans exert great cultural, political, and economic influence. For example, their television viewing is well above average; they watch almost an hour a day more TV/cable than do white consumers. There has been a tremendous increase in the number of TV programs featuring African-American characters in the 1980s, in response to their heavy TV viewing. Look for more of the same in the 1990s.

The media doesn't shine much publicity on the increases in wealth among many African-American households—more than a third of all African Americans live at middle-class income levels or above, and in these households, educational and income attainments continue to increase at a faster than average rate. While poverty levels have been increasing for whites and Hispanics, they have changed very little among African-Americans. Incidentally, contrary to popular hype, the teenage pregnancy rates are increasing for white and Hispanic young women, but not among African-Americans.

Hispanic-Americans are exerting influence through numbers (high immigration and birth rates) as well as through assimilation. As there are fewer young people in school and in the work force in upcoming decades, Hispanics will provide a larger proportion of all young people. They will comprise a growing share of both skilled and unskilled job entrants.

As Hispanics are assimilated into the mainstream, their language barrier will decrease (this is their single largest hurdle, along with low educational attainments), and their incomes will rise. Current research doesn't provide much optimism for significant decreases in the Hispanic poverty level (it has been increasing in recent years), but does suggest that even as poverty persists there will be strong increases in the number of middle and upper-middle class Hispanic families.

While most Hispanic-Americans will continue their pattern of slow assimilation (that accelerates with each generation away from immigration), the 1990s will witness a new phenomenon— the emergence of a unique kind of Hispanic-American culture. As the economic importance of the highly concentrated, Spanish-speaking market has increased, governments and marketers have addressed more of their efforts in Spanish, thereby decreasing the need to learn English to get jobs and get by. With this diminishing motivation, a hothouse of cultural influences will begin to generate a distinct culture of its own—neither traditional American, nor identical to the country of origin. This unique culture will be heard throughout the nation—literally. Its music is likely to transform pop music tastes; its food will find its way into your kitchen; its language will be heard in more of your kids' classrooms.

Asian-Americans. Although the total number of Asian-Americans is and will remain substantially less than that of other minority groups, the influence they wield will not. Why?

Their numbers are increasing faster than any other minority segment's. More immigrants come from Asia than from any other region. Although they now comprise less than 3 percent of the population, their share will triple in just two generations.

They earn more. Asian-American households earn more on average than those of other groups: the average Asian-American household earns $23,000 per year, the average white, $21,000, the average Hispanic, $16,000, and the average African-American, $14,000.

They are more educated. Not only do Asian-American students have a deserved reputation for academic achievement, but Asian-American immigrants (with the exception of Vietnamese) enter the U.S. with unprecedented levels of education.

They assimilate into the mainstream faster than other ethnic groups. They pick up English faster than other non-English speaking immigrants, they arrive with more financial support, they earn more money and faster than other groups, and they have higher rates of successful entrepreneurship than other ethnic groups. Their priorities are akin to the values of the American Dream: hard work, tightly knit families, education as a top priority, financial conservatism, and buying the best. You will see Asian-Americans move into leadership positions in the U.S. in the 1990s. They will succeed particularly visibly in business and education in the decade of the 1990s. In the early 2000s, you will see a substantial cultural and electoral presence for Asian-Americans, especially on the West Coast.

End of the Mass Market

The old mass market just ain't what it used to be—and it never again will be. Markets have fragmented, permanently, and this will create a new business climate for the 1990s. In fragmented markets, the mandate to find as many customers as possible becomes the need to find as many of the *right* customers as possible.

The middle class is smaller. Economists debate the statistics regarding the size of the population living in poverty, but there is general agreement that there has been a movement toward both income poles.

There are certainly more on the upscale end of income. By some counts, one-fifth of the population lives in upscale households, while almost the same number live poised on the edge of poverty or in poverty (almost a quarter of the nation's children do live in poverty). More rigorous definitions put roughly 13 percent each into the affluent and poverty categories. But by general agreement, the middle is shrinking, migrating toward the income extremes, and it will continue to do so throughout the rest of this decade. The former mass market, located in the center of the spectrum, is shrinking.

Fewer new households. The rate of household formation will slow substantially during the 1990s—to just slightly over the overall population growth rate. The population will grow at less than 1 percent per year, while the household formation rate will grow at less than 2 percent per year.

Households formed at substantially faster rates than the population grew throughout the 1980s. Because new households purchase disproportionately more of many household items, the consumer economy enjoyed a kind of artificial consumption high in the 1980s, disguising the harder consumption facts of slower population growth. In the 1990s, the household formation rate will slow to almost that of the population growth rate, and household consumption (particularly of durables) will demonstrate this. The continuing fragmentation of families into more non-traditional households can be expected to alleviate this problem somewhat, stimulating enough formation of new households to keep the rate slightly above the population growth rate.

The fragmenting market. As discussed above, the variety of family types will encourage fragmenting families. Lifestyle and life phase are becoming more important targeting tools than demographics. The old techniques will be less effective. An ad on network TV will still reach a lot of consumers. But with the shrinking share of viewers of which the networks can boast, and the increasing clutter of 15-second spots, there may well be less bang for the network ad buck.

In the 1980s, consumer products "discovered" promotion, and coupons, sweepstakes, and tie-ins were successful tools. In the 1990s the game is likely to move more to the retail level. In a fragmented market, one place you can be sure to reach consumers is in the stores. What home-shopping and promotion was to the 1980s, retail will be to the 1990s. The competition will square off in the store.

Marketers will rely on ever more sophisticated target marketing to find the niches and segments that have split off the once-mainstream market. Geodemographic and psychogeodemographic targeting can guide marketing efforts to the level of exact addresses to reach your best prospects. The TIGER file from the Census Bureau puts street-level mapping within the reach of any business in the U.S., enabling them to target markets with an accuracy that would have been unthinkable just a decade ago. Businesses have been used to targeting with the use of binoculars; they have now been given a microscope.

What this will mean to you is that *in addition to* the current barrage of advertising that you see (some reports tally the exposure at one thousand ad messages a day for the average urban dweller), you will receive more targeted product messages. You will be addressed more on the phone, through your personal computer, in your already stuffed mailbox. You will see more high-tech advertising devices in stores—video screens are already appearing on super-market carts. You will be enticed by aromas in the food aisles, by audio channels in stores, by exclusive TV programs (with ads) played in your gynecologist's office; you will use video catalogs to shop.

The increasing importance of affluents. It can almost be claimed that affluent markets, which now earn over half the nation's income and have over two-thirds of all discretionary dollars, will become a sort of new mass market. The affluent market will wield the kind of influence that the mass market once did. It will set the tone for the nation's consumption as the mass market did in the past. It has spurred what the Roper Organization has called an *aspiration inflation* among the public. It is likely that affluents, old-money families, and upscale entrepreneurs will be the style-leaders of the 1990s—the new images of emulation, replacing the Milkens and Trumps of the '80s.

Expect to see trickle-down marketing in the 1990s—mass market products launched for the upscale, with reliance on the trickle-down effect to bring them to the rest of the markets. And I'm not talking BMW—I'm thinking laundry detergent and canned soup.

However, don't make the mistake of equating the affluent market with a mass market; it is every bit as fragmented as the rest of the population. Not only is it composed of widely differing groups with different needs, but it is more accurately targeted as a mind-style than as a demographic. The little old lady with $500,000 in tens stashed in her mattress lives little of the affluent lifestyle, and certainly doesn't spend like there's no tomorrow. The just-out-of-school phenom earning $28,000 as an assistant editor on a national magazine may live affluence fully, driving a Prelude with the CD blaring, and up to the ears in debt. Lump both consumers into the same category and a marketer will never find a way to reach them both effectively with ad messages. The affluent market is just as fragmented and hard to find as other fragmented markets, but its overall cultural clout is increasing.

The affluent mind-style has certain characteristics that will grow in importance in the 1990s. The affluent-minded bore easily. They are experience-oriented. They are pragmatic. They will pay for time saving. They seek quality. They are price-aware and look for "good values." They are media-hip and wary of hype.

This mindset is a real problem for market researchers. The tedious task of filling out a lengthy questionnaire is exactly what the affluent-minded do not have patience for. So, surveys often have small samples of affluent respondents, and deliver contradictory and less-reliable results.

Two general media trends, seemingly at odds. Reaching fragmented markets is progressively more difficult. The increasing expense of doing so has caused the first of these trends, and the opportunities presented by fragmented markets is causing the second.

1. There is a consolidation of major media into fewer primary outlets—fewer newspapers, fewer sources of information, less in-depth reporting, greater need for entertainment value in information.

2. There is an increase in targeted media—an explosion in the number of cable channel viewers (cable penetration is now just under 60 percent of U.S. homes, and will rise to 70 percent in 1994). There are many more specialty magazines, VCRs (penetration now at 71 percent, rising to over 73 percent in 1992), and so on. Home shopping, by catalogue and cable, succeeded in the '80s because it answered the needs of niches and convenience—though both will endure an inevitable shakeout (the result of their over-extension and competition). Both are here to stay and to succeed.

A new medium. Look for explosive growth in an underused medium that is as close as the kitchen wall—the telephone. The 1980s brought us cordless phones, cellular phones, fax machines, fiber optic cables and a $500-billion worldwide telecommunications industry whose gross earnings may well double in the next decade. Videotext (which requires a computer and modem) has not yet lived up to its hyped promises (though Prodigy now claims 25 percent annual growth), but telephone information and entertainment services are leaping their way into the 1990s—"audiotext" (particularly 900 and 800 numbers) is expected to double its 1990 $500 million + gross within four years. Currently, more than two-thirds of 900 number use is for entertainment, but marketers will make significant usage of it for product introductions, target marketing, and billing in the 1990s. Videotext is also expected to grow steadily in the 1990s. About 25 million households now have a computer, and this number will increase substantially in the 1990s, as will the one-sixth of PC homes that have a modem, making them videotext possibilities. Video- and audiotext will be hot media in the 1990s. Consumers will enjoy the convenience and the novelty; marketers will find new, creative ways to reach niche markets.

The business climate of the 1990s will be mixed clouds and sun—steady (if slow) growth in the GNP, less pronounced business cycles, but a decreasing rate of growth in consumer spending (partly as a result of increased savings). As a result of slower growth in overall spending, the 1980s will come to look like a love-fest compared to the competitive nature of the 1990s. There will continue to be a tremendous increase in new consumer products introductions. In 1985, there were 7,300 new products put into U.S. supermarkets; in 1989, there were 12,000 new products, two-thirds of them food items. And these numbers are rising, even as more than 80 percent of new products fail. Talk about competitive—more than 200 new oat bran products appeared in 1989 alone; more than 1,700 condiments, and more than 1,300 new candies and snacks.

Many of the new offerings will wisely aim for a target market, chipping away at established products. Product manufacturers will respond with targeted extensions of their current product lines. Consumer loyalty will be challenged by products tailored to specific needs and wishes of target segments. The difficulty in reaching consumers through traditional vehicles will intensify the battle for the consumer's attention. And on the retail front, there are already far too many products for the finite amount of super-market shelf space; the display battle at the point-of-purchase will intensify.

Business will also face labor shortages (and consequent higher costs) while it picks up a larger share of the tab for solving social problems. This is the climate in which corporations will encounter fragmented markets. The value of information will increase, as will the speed of its obsolescence.

Computers will be the weapon of competitive business wars. Technology gains will facilitate information use, as well as increase productivity through the growing use of robotics. The amounts of available information will grow exponentially in the 1990s, and the company that handles it and uses it the fastest will have an edge in finding customers.

I've told you that I put my trust in consumer wisdom—so what do consumers say about the U.S. economy and business climate for the 1990s? They are guardedly optimistic. They foresee only slow gains on most fronts: slow economic growth, and modest improvement in their own personal financial picture; but they don't anticipate downturns in their own or national prospects. They don't expect much improvement in solving economic crises (such as the budget deficit, the S&L bailout), and then don't put much faith in government's ability to fix economic problems. Still shy about the stock market after Black Monday and the black eyes from ethics violations, they are looking for safer investments; the quick millions syndrome is slowing. There is a "back to basics" feel to their overall perspective; pulling back from extremes.

Outgrowing the Youth Culture

Research shows us that when foreign visitors leave the U.S., they have two main impressions of us as a people: how young and active we seem, and how hard we work. They cite Disneyworld as the quintessence of America.

We are and always have been a young culture. Throughout history all societies have had a preponderant young population. Graphically, the age distribution of all societies has looked like an isosceles triangle—a wide base with many young people at the bottom and a few elderly at the top. Within the next couple of decades, in America, this triangle will come to resemble a rectangle standing vertically—with near-equivalent numbers of people in the age groups from young to old. Individually, many may accept aging with grace or denial, but its increase is going to have profound impact on all aspects of society.

As a nation, we have never been as old as we are now, and we're still aging. In the 1970s, America was in its twenties—the median age was 28 in 1978. In the 1980s, America turned thirtysomething—the median age rose from 30 to 33. In the 1990s, America will pass through the mid-thirties—the median age will be over 36 in 1999. In the first decade of the new century, America will be hitting the near-forty crisis with a median age over 39 years. In the new century's second decade, America will pass 40 and continue to climb. We will no longer be a youth culture.

We all get a general sense of the age wave and its influence on the population. However, a specific look at the changes it will bring in just this decade point to the dramatic shapes the wave will take as it passes over the 1990s. In this decade alone, there probably will be:

- an 8-percent decrease in the number of small children (under 5 years);

- a 7-percent increase in the number of other children (5 to 17 years);

- an 11-percent decrease in the number of young adults (18 to 34 years);

- a 28-percent increase in the number of middle-aged (35 to 54 years);

- a 7-percent increase in the young-old (55 to 74 years);

- a 26-percent increase in the elderly (age 75+).

The fastest growing ten-year age group will be the 45-54 group, which will increase by 46 percent. This is significant not only because it is the standard image of middle age, but also because this is a peak-earning period, and suggests a continuance of the trend toward affluence, which is often especially concentrated in those years.

The 1990s will be about the middle-aging of the nation. Assuming that middle age can roughly be bracketed at 35 to 54 years, the U.S. will become more middle aged than ever during the 1990s. In 1980, 21 percent of the population was middle aged. In 1990, 25 percent is middle aged; by the year 2000, more than 30 percent will be middle aged.

The media attention to the age wave has created a general impression of crisis in issues relating to the elderly. Certainly, there will be demands placed on elderly services. But the Social Security crunch will not hit hard in this decade; the number of workers per Social Security recipient will decline only slightly in the 1990s, to about 4.7 workers per retiree (from just over 5 in 1990). The real crunch will hit in the early decades of the 21st century, when the number of workers per retiree will plummet to just over 2.6 by 2030. The retiree crisis is not the agenda of the 1990s; it will hit in 2012 when the eldest Baby Boomers reach the traditional retirement age of 65. (Don't bank on that date, however. There are too many changes going on in Boomer retirement plans and too many legislative actions on the horizon to expect a crisis will drop from the sky in 2012.)

In the year that the Baby Boomers entered their forties, the first magazine targeting women over forty (*Lear's*) made a dramatically successful appearance, followed by another winner in *Mirabella*. The numerical clout of the Boomers (whose social influence is almost impossible to underestimate) will bring middle-aged priorities to the nation.

A middle-aging nation will:

Value time almost above all. Time may be the most precious currency for the 1990s. Those in their middle years will have substantial amounts of discretionary money, but will *not* have substantial amounts of time—they will happily trade one for the other. Good news for service and convenience industries. Good news for nannies.

Spend more on health—both prevention and cure. This is in the country that *already* spends far more per capita than any other on health care. Fitness will become middle-aged by decreasing its impact, but not its pervasiveness. Jogging will slow to the speed of fitness walking. Nutrition consciousness will grow. You'll see less drastic dieting (but plenty of concern about weight) and more healthy eating. There will also be a growing market for splurge food. There will be more attention to labels, freshness, ingredients. There will be greater call for natural foods and an insatiable appetite for convenience.

Want quality—in everything, from TV entertainment to bank services. Extra features on the VCR will be less appealing than easy-use and a reputation for quality. But middle-aged consumers are sophisticated consumers, and quality claims alone will not create a quality image. They demand quality in performance, and will shun a product that doesn't deliver it—not to mention shunning the store that doesn't deliver the goods with quality service.

Be more concerned about security. This concern comes with the middle-aged turf, and crops up not only in fancy burglar proofing systems, but in values. Investments become less risky, savings become more important, the retirement nest egg becomes a more active concern.

Ask for information. Middle-agers are sophisticated, feel sophisticated, and want to wield their smarts in the marketplace. To do this they demand information: on food labels, in brochures about cars they are interested in, about the environmental impact of lawn sprays, about political candidates—and so on, inexhaustibly. Provide all the information you can. Don't shortchange them in this regard, or short change is what they will give you.

Place personal comfort as a higher priority. Traditionally a growing priority for middle-agers, this trend will appear not only in apparel and furnishings, but also in cars, travel, even electronics—user-friendliness will be very popular.

Demand less clutter. The MTV-mindedness of the '80s will slow in the '90s to please a middle-aged nation. Not only will the speed of entertainment slow, but the plot lines will have to deepen because shallow stimulation will not hold this audience. Involvement will replace stimulation as the key to TV success in the 1990s, and it may extend somewhat to the movies as well. It is no coincidence that the slowest-paced network show in recent memory was also the first surprise upscale hit of the 1990s—ABC's "Twin Peaks."

Save more. This is a much debated issue, because there are so many ways to calculate it. The no-saving/spendthrift images of the '80s were exaggerated, and the move to savings in the '90s will probably be slow and sustained. But savings rates will increase. Housing rose sharply as a share of the household budget in the '80s and will subside in the '90s. If healthcare's share of the household budget holds steady (as it may), or increases less dramatically (as it probably will), there will be an increase in savings. The Boomers' bad rap about savings has been hyped; all factors considered, their savings rate has not been far below that of prior generations.

Decrease partisanship. Political labeling will decrease, pragmatism will increase—the image of being a doer will attract more enthusiasm than any party affiliation.

Be more experience-oriented. Middle-agers traditionally turn inward. They express greater interest in interpersonal values, and turn toward intangible acquisitions like experiences, learning, and gratification from helping others. Of course, this doesn't mean they won't consume; it is more of a directional tilt for their passion.

Foster activist consumers. Middle-agers are more secure within themselves and know their power. They will exert more of that power as consumers in the 1990s. Environmentally-harmful products will feel consumers vote no with their wallets; offensive advertising will feel and hear the response. Controversies and boycotts will be more popular, and effective.

Consumer activism doesn't always hurt the bottom line. The much-publicized flap over the "offensive" material in the TV show "Married with Children" gave the show a bigger boost in the ratings than any advertising they ever did. Consumer activism parallels decreasing trust in institutions. Confidence in government is low and business is being blamed for all manner of ills— including being the number-one environmental enemy.

Have more home computers. Fantastic early-'80s images of PC screens adjacent to TV screens in most American homes have not been realized; fewer than one-quarter of U.S. households house a personal computer. Yet the picture is brighter for the 1990s. Computer-familiar Boomers and their younger cohorts will see that a PC can do more for them than play games. As software and network services expand, the PC will make their lives easier and save them time.

Move less. Middle agers move much less often than do younger people—the average 45-to 54-year old hasn't moved in the last eight years, while a young person in his or her twenties moves every year (on average). Less moving means less purchasing of durables and less start-up housing spending, with less discretionary money going to basics.

Look to prolong youth. Young people know they will never die, and older people resign themselves to the reality. Middle-aged people, however, begin to suspect that they might not live forever, and work to prolong life. This motivation is ancient, of course, and expresses itself in fitness, nutrition, and environmental trends. The search for the fountain of youth will have America increasingly fitness-walking, going to plastic surgeons, staying very active—and this will only increase through the 1990s as Boomers occupy the forties and move into their fifties.

A New American Point of View

We are the world—America's long-standing self-focus is broadening.

I write this section more on gut feel from emerging statistics than from the findings themselves. We are in the early stages of broadening our national peripheral vision. I think this change comes from three major influences:

- Environmentalism—America and the rest of the nations have finally met an enemy that is larger than any one country or block of countries. Environmental degradation is this common enemy. Its threat to the health, and even survival, of the human race is forging a supra-national peacetime alliance that will demand (and get) greater awareness of the issues, greater cooperation among countries, and sacrifices in everyday lifestyle.

  Begun in Europe, the Green movement has moved to the U.S. While industrial and governmental institutions have resisted the changes demanded by environmental activists, acceding only to go-slow changes in the status-quo, consumers have grabbed the lead on environmental issues. They are pushing for change wherever possible, and have brought this trend to the surface far faster than usually happens. Consumers are joining the world view, realizing that they must think globally as they strive to act locally. And they are creating local action. A majority of the public now feels that we must improve the state of the environment, even at the cost of economic growth. There are no two ways about it, and there won't be in the 1990s.

- Much has been written about "the global village," the increase of international contact through communications and travel. But that is only the means, not the result. The result will be a broadening of our national point of view. In the days when limited communications kept the local newspaper filled primarily with local news, the perspective tended to be local. Now that the media and transportation put worldwide experience in our daily lives, we are beginning to include worldwide points of view into our local thinking.

Turn on the TV news any evening, read the paper, and you realize that at this time America is not at the center of the action. With the globalization of markets, the mind-bending changes in international politics, the emergence of the European Community as a superpower in 1992, and the impact of Asian countries on the U.S., Americans attend to the world as if it mattered. We are beginning to get the idea that the U.S. is not the center of the planet, and because the foment seems to be going in directions compatible with our national values, Americans seem to be taking it in stride. Americans are admiring the courage of foreign politicians more than that of their own. There will be a continued opening of American eyes to the world. More travel, more trade, more idea sharing, more international joint undertakings in the 1990s. And let me note that the U.S. is not about to lose its place of influence in the world—it won't run the show, but will share the leading role.

- There is a subtle evolution in values—the American Dream is changing. The change has a lot to do with the middle-aging of the nation. People in their forties and fifties predictably turn away from their external values toward more inner values—their expressions of self become less materialistic and more experiential and interpersonal. I think a similar adjustment is just beginning in our national values.

To put it in Californianese, we are mellowing out. The we-are-the-best boosterism of the Reagan years has subsided. As the standard of living increased only slightly overall in the 1980s, the dream began to change from exceeding the lifestyle of one's parents to living a decent lifestyle. Americans no longer expect to live better than their parents did; they just want to live as well. Maybe it is more accurately said that they just want to live well—no comparisons.

Some decades ago, a diminishment in our standard of living or quality of life would have incited angry reaction; it would have struck at the heart of our national identity. Instead of the expected throw-the-bums-out response, there has been a surprisingly mature acceptance of the situation. It is a middle-aged, affluent wisdom. It is very like the America of the 1990s.

In a number of research studies I see Americans defining themselves more as individuals and less as members of institutions or organizations (religious, political, business, and so on). Also, there is an increasing sense of alienation from power structures. It is at this individual level that the national perspective is broadening. It is in the living room, not the boardroom or hearing-room, that the new point of view is dawning. It is over coffee tables, not computers, that the American family is being redefined. Women and minorities are exerting their growing influence not from the top down, but from the bottom up. The mass market is fragmenting, reducing the importance of generalized thinking, and raising the importance of smaller groups.

In the 1990s, America will be led by individualism—the very trait that has always been our national strength. Trends will emerge from the smallest units of society, from committed individuals and families and neighborhoods, upwards to our institutions. The very spirit that pulled Americans across the dangerous plains in wagons 150 years ago will recreate the nation that meets the new millennium.

That is a satellite view of the five major trend-rivers of the 1990s and beyond. Now, let's come back down to earth. I invite you to discover the 189 tributaries that are flowing into the future, and the hundreds of smaller trends that are nourishing this complex, marvelous land.

Population
A Middle-Aged Mosaic

The turbulence of change in family structure has been great in recent decades. However, it now appears that this upheaval is subsiding, giving way to a stabilization of new norms rather than a return to old standards. Later marriage, fewer children, later childbirth, high divorce rates—these will form the American family of the 1990s. Overall, the U.S. population growth rate will steadily slow, with 10 percent growth during the 1980s, dropping to 7 percent in the 1990s, to 5 percent in the first decade of the new century—all-time lows except for during the Great Depression.

Zero population growth will be reached in the 2020s, with only immigration accounting for increases in the population. However, recent increases in immigration are speeding the scenario, making it possible that immigration will account for half of all U.S. population growth as soon as the year 2015. After the total peaks at just over 300 million about the year 2038, U.S. population will begin to decline for the first time ever. Volatile birth, death, and immigration rates could change this prediction, but the overall trends are reliable.

Households

Population and household growth rates slowing. The rate of growth of new households softened the market blow of a slowing population growth throughout the 1980s—household formation has been running at twice the rate of population growth. But no more. In the 1990s, the household formation rate will be parallel to the population growth rate. This will have a direct impact on household purchasing, which has only been sideswiped in the collision with the slow population growth of the '80s, but will now begin to feel the full impact. The average household size is decreasing too—hitting an all-time low of 2.62 persons per household in 1989 (in 1970 it was 3.14). *Census Bureau.*

U.S. household types 1960-1988
(figures rounded)

	1960	1970	1980	1988
Married couples with children	44%	40%	31%	27%
Married couples without children	30%	30%	30%	30%
Other families with children	4%	5%	8%	8%
Other families without children	6%	6%	5%	6%
Men living alone	4%	6%	9%	10%
Women living alone	9%	12%	14%	14%
Other non-family households	2%	2%	4%	4%

Source: Census Bureau

Non-traditional households are now the norm:

- Just over a third of U.S. households are families with children. *Census Bureau.*

- Only 5 percent to 10 percent of U.S. households (by different estimates) now fit the traditional model of a working Dad and housekeeping Mom raising 2+ kids. *Census Bureau.*

- The '80s saw a steep decline in the number of young (under 25 years) married couple households—down 46 percent during the decade. In the 1990s, the decline will continue but will slow to an estimated 32 percent. At the same time there will be a 7-percent increase in the number of non-family (mostly those living alone) young households in the 1990s—the number of these households declined 21 percent during the 1980s. *American Demographics, January 1989.*

- Non-family households accounted for 29 percent of all households in 1989 (up from 19 percent in 1970). Most of those non-family households (84 percent) are made up of singles living alone. *Census Bureau.*

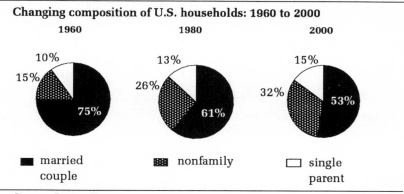

Changing composition of U.S. households: 1960 to 2000

Source: Census Bureau

- Almost a quarter of all children under 18 live with a single parent; almost half will at some time in their childhood. *Census Bureau.*

- Young people are living with their parents longer. In 1960 only 43 percent of 18- to 24-year-olds lived with their parents or in a dorm; 54 percent did in 1985, and the numbers are rising. The stay-home young adults are much more likely to be male (60 percent of males and 48 percent of females age 18 to 24).

Females in this age group are more likely to head their own households or be married than are males. *U.S. Department of Education.*

- Stepfamilies are the fastest growing family type in the U.S. By the turn of the century stepfamilies (including those with adult children) will be the most common kind of American family. *Stepfamily Association of America.*

- Out-of-wedlock births continue to rise; now 40 percent of all U.S. births. *Census Bureau.*

- There will be the appearance of and growth of two-generation geriatric families—seniors caring for their parents in their '90s. *The Futurist.*

Marriage/divorce

Marriage rates keep dropping. Married couples now comprise 56 percent of U.S. households, down from 75 percent in 1960. *Census Bureau.* In 1988, the marriage rate dropped another two percentage points to its lowest point since 1967. *National Center for Health Statistics.*

Later marriage. The median age for men at first marriage is now 26 (it was 24 in the 1950s). For women it is now 24—the highest ever. And both are rising, but not so rapidly for men—the age difference between brides and grooms continues to narrow. *Census Bureau.*

Hype Alert: "Divorce remains at record high levels."
Nope, the divorce rate is at its lowest point since 1975, at 4.8 people per thousand. The record high was reached in 1981. *National Center for Health Statistics.*

Hype Alert: "Half of all U.S. marriages end in divorce."
Maybe yes, maybe no. The divorce rate for the nation can also legitimately be called 13 percent. In 1988, there were 2,389,000 weddings and 1,183,000 divorces—these numbers produce the widely quoted 50 percent figure. However, not all those people who divorced in 1988 were also married in that year. To get

another estimate, take the percent of the total adult population who are currently or ever have been married (72 percent) and look at the number of these people who are currently divorced (9 percent), and you'll find a 13 percent current divorce rate. *Census Bureau.*

Influences on Divorce

- The divorce rate among the elderly is increasing. It's now increasing three times as fast for the elderly as for the U.S. population as a whole. Fewer than 3 percent of all married couples will see a 50th anniversary. There are fewer than 40 men for every 100 women age 85+, and this group is the fastest-growing age segment in the country. *Age Wave.*

- Women who live with a man before marrying him have an 80 percent greater chance of divorce than those who don't. *Neil Bennett, Yale University.*

- Women who marry younger husbands have a greater chance of getting divorced than those who marry men their own age or older. Divorce rates are also higher in marriages in which the woman has a higher level of education than the man, and in marriages mixing different religions. *Susan Loiselle, Yale University.*

- The presence of a son reduces the likelihood of divorce by 9 percent over the presence of a daughter. *University of Pennsylvania, Population Studies Center.*

- Lack of commitment is named as the number-one reason for failed marriages (53 percent), way ahead of other reasons such as immaturity (32 percent), finances (17 percent), and adultery (11 percent). *Better Homes and Gardens.*

Births

Unexpected birth boom. For the first time since the Baby Boom, there were four million births in one year (1989 saw the highest birth rate since 1964, near the 1957 Baby Boom peak), a surprise to the Census Bureau. The unexpected birth boom derives from three factors: the sheer number of Boomer mothers (even though the fertility rate has dropped by 50 percent since 1960, from 3.8 children to 1.8 children per woman), delayed childbirth that is clumping births together, and a lower than expected rate of childlessness among Boomers. The Census Bureau had projected a rate as high as 25 percent. It now appears to be closer to 15 percent. Look out for a wave of demand for services, starting with childcare and rippling though elementary school classrooms at the end of the century. *National Center for Health Statistics, Census Bureau.*

Changing patterns of future births. The Baby Bust generation will bring fewer workers to the job market, and these will be better educated than any past generation. This will result in earlier financial security. Many demographers predict that this will encourage women to have children younger, particularly in their late 20s—so the mother's average age at giving birth— now at 23.7 years and rising (up 9 percent in 25 years) may begin to level or even drop by the mid-1990s.

Later births. Roughly one-third of all U.S. births are to women in their 30s, vs. 19 percent in 1976. There may not, after all, be a drop in births as predicted, since there is evidence that the postponement of births may not mean the limiting of the number of births. In 1975 only a third of women in their early 30s planned to have a baby in the future; now that percentage is approaching 55 percent. *Census Bureau.*

Child care demand soars. Continuing large numbers of late births will create even greater child care problems. Mothers in their 30s go back to work sooner, so there will be greater-than-anticipated numbers of 1- to 3-year-olds needing daily care. Add to this the current overall surge in births (approximately 70 percent of births are still to women in their 20s), plus the anticipated decrease in the age at which Baby Bust mothers will give birth, and you have an equation for a child care crisis in the early 1990s. Bear in mind that 13 percent of U.S. children live in California, 8 percent in Texas, and 7 percent in New York. *Census Bureau.*

Moms' rate of going back to work slows. The rate of new mothers going back to work within a year of a baby's arrival has risen sharply in recent years—31 percent in 1976, now over 52 percent. This rise will slow, however, in the 1990s, after perhaps rising as high as 60 percent by the turn of the century. The current level of 65 percent of all mothers (with kids under 18) in the workforce is approaching its peak. *Census Bureau.*

The baby month. More babies are born in September—7 percent more—than any other month. Why? It's not the cosiness of the Christmas season (because the same pattern is true in India and Israel); the latest hypothesis suggests the aberration has something to do with temperature and light cycles. *Jeffrey Miron, University of Michigan, as cited in the New York Times.*

Aging

Rapid increases among the old-old. Until the Boomers reach their senior (65+) years just after 2010, the growth in the number of seniors will be slow, with the number of old-old (85+) growing much faster. From 1985 to 1995, the total senior population will grow about 18 percent. This will slow to about 7 percent in the post 1995-decade. *Census Bureau.*

In 1950, just 10 percent of the population was over age 65. Two generations from now, it will be double that percent. In 1950 there were 13 elderly for every 100 workers; in 2040, this ratio will triple to 37:100. *Population Reference Bureau, Inc.*

Will the increases be more dramatic? Some predict that the growth in the elderly population will be far greater than Census Bureau predictions. The CB sees the current three million who are 85+ quintupling to 15.3 million by 2050 (5 percent of the U.S. population). Other demographers, however, foresee much greater growth. The National Institute on Aging predicts an 870-percent increase, and others predict as much as 1,000-percent increases, to 30 million (10 percent of the U.S.) or higher. Look at Census Bureau figures as low estimates.

Global aging. The age wave is breaking over more than the North American continent. Japan is facing a huge age wave—in the next 40 years, Japan's elderly population will increase by 20 million, a 160-percent increase over current levels. Sweden now has the oldest population in the world, with 17 percent over the age of 65 years. *Population Reference Bureau, Inc.*

Projections of age structure of OECD nations' populations
(figures rounded)

	1950	1990	2010	2030	2050
United States					
under 14	27%	22%	18%	19%	19%
15-64	65%	66%	68%	62%	62%
65+	8%	12%	13%	20%	19%
United Kingdom					
under 14	22%	19%	20%	19%	19%
15-64	67%	66%	66%	62%	62%
65+	11%	15%	15%	19%	19%
West Germany					
under 14	24%	15%	13%	15%	17%
15-64	67%	69%	67%	59%	59%
65+	9%	16%	20%	26%	25%
Canada					
under 14	30%	21%	17%	18%	19%
15-64	63%	68%	68%	60%	60%
65+	8%	11%	15%	22%	21%
Japan					
under 14	35%	18%	18%	17%	17%
15-64	60%	70%	63%	63%	60%
65+	5%	11%	19%	20%	22%
France					
under 14	23%	20%	17%	17%	18%
15-64	66%	66%	66%	61%	60%
65+	11%	14%	16%	22%	22%

Source: Organization for Economic Cooperation and Development

Hype Alert: "Mature Americans have mind-sets similiar to their parents."

Actually, older people are more like their kids than their parents. The group that is currently in their 50s has educational levels, incomes, and consumer attitudes much closer to their children's patterns than to their parents' patterns. *Find/SVP.*

Rethink two old saws about the elderly: people do not generally become more conservative (politically and socially) with age, and older people are not more set in their ways than are young people. Their thinking evolves at much the same rate as that of younger people. *Steven Cutler, University of Vermont.*

Life expectancy continues to grow. A full year was added to U.S. life expectancy in the 1980s—now at an average of about 75 years (still only average among industrialized nations, and we spend more per capita on health care than any other country). However, life expectancy for African-Americans is decreasing, while it is increasing for other groups. *National Center for Health Statistics.*

Whether the mortality rates go up or down, 83 percent of Americans expect to meet God in heaven; 74 percent expect humor there, and only 6 percent predict they are headed the other way. *Newsweek.*

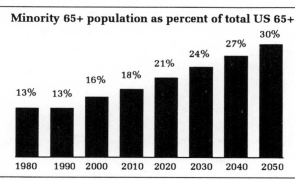

Minority 65+ population as percent of total US 65+

Source: Census Bureau

Singles

Growth in childless single person households, with projections to 1990 and 2000, in millions
(figures rounded)

	1970	1980	1990	2000
Single person households	10.9	18.3	24.2	31.1
Total households	63.4	80.8	94.0	105.5
Share of total	17%	23%	26%	29%

Source: Harvard University Joint Center for Housing Studies

A singular nation. One-quarter of all U.S. households (22.7 million) are composed of people living alone. *Census Bureau.* Over a third (37 percent) of adult Americans (18+ years) are now single, up 74 percent since 1970. *Adweek's Marketing Week.* Young (and not so young) people are staying single longer. You've heard this before, but maybe you didn't know how dramatic the trend was. Since 1970:

- the percentage of women in their early 20s who remain single has risen from 36 percent to 61 percent, and still-single men has risen from 55 percent to 71 percent;

- the percentage of women in their late 20s remaining single has risen from 11 percent to 30 percent, men 19 percent to 43 percent;

- in their early 30s, the percentage of female singles has risen from 6 percent to 16 percent, men from 9 percent to 25 percent. *Census Bureau.*

More males. There are 12 percent more young (ages 20 to 39) single men in the U.S. than women. *Census Bureau.* Young singles present a good market for travel, entertainment, consumer electronics, kitchen appliances, home furnishings, self-help products, gourmet foods, and computers.

Regions

Growth in the South and West. The top five fastest growing states in the latter 1980s were all Sunbelters (in descending order: California, Florida, Georgia, Texas, Arizona). *Census Bureau.* The Midwest seems to be coming out of its early '80s population growth slump; its growth rate now approaches that of the Northeast. In the 1990s, nine states will grow at twice the rate of the rest of the nation—eight of those nine are in the West or South. *Population Reference Bureau, Inc.* In 20 years, a majority of the nation (60 percent) will live in the South or West. Texas will pass New York as the second most populous state within two years (California remains tops). Population growth is down for the fifth straight year in energy-producing states; rebounding upwards in some industrialized states. *Census Bureau.*

South Atlantic growth. The South Atlantic region has just become the largest in the nation, surpassing the East North Central. The Pacific region will pass the East North Central in 1990 to become the third-largest. Florida is the population hotspot, largely because of internal migration. In the first decade of the new century, Florida will have more than two million new residents move in from other states—over five times the internal migration of the entire Western region. This growth rate is eight times higher than Florida's growth from foreign immigration.

Regional distribution of whites and blacks, 1980 and 2010
(projected)

	1980		2010	
	White	*Black*	*White*	*Black*
New England	6.0%	1.9%	5.7%	2.0%
Middle Atlantic	16.3%	16.8%	13.4%	15.9%
East North Central	18.8%	17.1%	14.9%	15.5%
West North Central	8.3%	3.0%	7.1%	2.7%
South Atlantic	14.8%	28.7%	18.2%	31.3%
East South Central	6.0%	10.8%	5.7%	9.2%
West South Central	10.2%	13.2%	11.8%	12.7%
Mountain	5.5%	1.0%	6.9%	1.3%
Pacific	14.1%	7.5%	16.3%	9.4%

Source: Census Bureau

Regions: old, young, and coastal. Now the most populous, the South Atlantic will become the oldest region by 2000. California means youth. Currently, one out of nine American children lives in California. By the turn of the century one in eight will, with a 20-percent increase in numbers in the 1990s. As the century turns, 42 percent of California children will be Caucasian, 36 percent Hispanic, 13 percent Asian, and 9 percent black. *Stanford University/University of California Berkeley.*

Hype Alert: "Three-fourths of Americans live within 50 miles of the coastline."

This is a bogus stat, and we've seen it used several times. It dramatizes coastline crises, and so has found its way into more than one environmental flyer. The fact is that 53 percent of Americans live within 50 miles of a coast—23 percent by the

Atlantic, 12 percent by the Pacific, 12 percent by the Great Lakes, 6 percent by the Gulf of Mexico. Not much of a trend here, either—in 1970, 54 percent of Americans lived within 50 miles of the coast. *Population Reference Bureau, Inc., Population Today.*

The most popular cities to move to, and from, in 1988

To	From
1. Orlando	1. New York
2. Tampa	2. Los Angeles
3. Atlanta	3. Hartford
4. Norfolk	4. Philadelphia
5. Jacksonville	5. Denver
6. Nashville	6. Chicago
7. Houston	7. Miami
8. Seattle	8. Boston
9. Las Vegas	9. Providence
10. Phoenix	10. Detroit

Source: Ryder Truck Rental

Metros/Cities/Rural

Hype Alert: "The death of U.S. metropolitan areas."
While there may be out-migration population losses from some cities, particularly in the Midwest (Detroit went down 324,000 and Chicago 256,000 between 1980-87), most metros are growing.

- The share of total U.S. population in metropolitan areas continues to rise (from 56 percent in 1950 to 77 percent in 1987).

- The majority of all the nation's population growth was in metro areas (86 percent from 1980 to 1987, the latest year available). In those years, metro population rose twice as fast as non-metro (8.5 percent vs. 4.1 percent).

- The growth of metro areas has not been from increases in central cities, even though minority populations (which tend to predominate) have higher than average population growth rates. Almost 60 percent of metro dwellers now live outside central cities—in the suburbs. *Census Bureau.*

The southern and western regions continue to drive the metro population growth, with both net migration and natural increases ahead of the rest of the country. The Sunbelt is hot—population growth rates continue at almost four times the non-sunbelt rate. Annexation of territory into metro areas also supports the strong metro growth in these regions—the rate of annexation in the South and West is double that of the rest of the nation. (Hey, not fair— what can New Jersey do with 100 percent of its population already *in* metro areas? Six of the top nine states in percentage of population in metro areas are Northeastern states).

- Only about a third of the cities in the North have increased in population in the 1980s, while 80 percent of those in the South and West did. In fact, between 1980 and 1987, no cities in the Northeast or Midwest enjoyed large population increases, while 35 in the South and 26 in the West did.

- Population decreases were seen in 12 cities in the Northeast, 29 in the Midwest, 10 in the South, and 3 in the West. To look at it another way: 61 MSAs are now growing at twice the national rate or faster (all are in the South or West). Fifty-four MSAs have lost population since 1980, 41 of them are in the Northeast of Midwest, and 46 are under 500,000 in population. *Census Bureau.*

---

10 largest metropolitan areas in 1988
(1980 rank in parentheses)

	population in 000s	change 1980-88
1. New York (1)	18,120	+3.3%
2. Los Angeles (2)	13,770	+19.8%
3. Chicago (3)	8,181	+3.1%
4. San Francisco (5)	6,042	+12.6%
5. Philadelphia (4)	5,963	+5.0%
6. Detroit (6)	4,620	-2.8%
7. Boston (7)	4,110	+3.5%
8. Dallas (10)	3,766	+28.5%
9. Washington (8)	3,734	+14.9%
10. Houston (9)	3,642	+17.5%

Source: Census Bureau

Cities: look to mid-size. Middle-sized cities will grow faster than big cities in the 1990s—look to towns like Cincinnati, Columbus, Sacramento, and Orlando to find solid growth because of their diversified economies and subsequent insulation from interest rate volatility. *The Conference Board.*

As the U.S. entered the '90s, San Diego surpassed Detroit, and San Jose surpassed San Francisco to become the 6th and 12th largest cities, respectively. *Census Bureau.*

Suburbia is America. Now the dominant commuting pattern in the nation is suburb to suburb. The suburbs house more than 57 percent of the nation's office space, up from 46 percent just ten years ago, and rising. At the turn of the century, the burgeoning suburbs will have created a new kind of urban village—desirable, self-sustaining, strictly regulated. Megalopolis, the Boston to Washington sprawl, now contains 17 percent of the U.S. population, and one-quarter of all Americans who live in U.S. metropolitan areas. *Census Bureau.*

Penturbia, the next suburbia. Those who want the space, relaxation, and healthiness that the suburbs once promised are now moving out of the suburban fringes to create new developments in once-rural outskirts, the fifth great migration wave. As downtowns fight to retain their vitality, penturbian job centers, maybe 30 to 40 miles from downtown, are exploding. Once quiet little towns beyond the mall sprawl, these will be the boom towns of the 1990s. Detroit, for example is straining, while once-inconsequential Troy, NY, will see job growth of over 45 percent between 1988 and 1993. *Cognetics, Inc, as cited in the Wall Street Journal.*

Exurbia sees slower growth. The 1970s saw widespread gains in non-metropolitan populations (at the expense of urban locations); the 1980s saw small increases—4 percent between 1980 to 1988 (with cities growing faster). The fact that the growth of exurbia (non-metropolitan areas within a commutable radius of metropolitan areas) is continuing at all is significant, in the face of straining rural economies, and the fact that the 1970s gains marked the first increases in rural populations in half a century. *Kenneth Johnson, Loyola University of Chicago.* The rural renaissance of the 1970s continues in the Northeast, where rural counties continue to grow faster than metropolitan counties. *Census Bureau.*

Affluence

What is affluence? Hard question, with no easy answer. It can be approximated with annual household income breakdowns, which show the explosive 1980s growth of affluence continuing into the 1990s. The number of households earning $60,000+ more than doubled in the last five years. The number of millionaire households (net worth) has increased more than 50 percent in the latter 1980s, and is now well over a million and a quarter. In this short space, suffice to say that there are very few clouds on the affluence horizon, and that in numbers, importance, and clout, the affluent market will grow steadily, if more slowly than in the past decade.

The affluent are getting younger. Just over a third (37 percent) are age 50+; 22 percent are under age 34. The share of this under-34 age group increased 23 percent in just two years (1986-1988). *Mendelsohn Media Research.* The plurality of affluents are age 35 to 49. *Mediamark Research.* The average age of those with net worth of more than half a million dollars has dropped to 50, from 53 in 1981. *Payment Systems, Inc.*

Hype Alert: "The affluent are more educated."
It seems that they are not becoming more educated. Contradictions abound on this topic, depending on your definition of affluence. There are both more non-college educated affluent households, and more highly educated affluents. The overall increase in U.S. education levels, however, sustains the growth of affluence.

Immigration

Immigration growing as share of population growth. Immigration accounted for 16 percent of the U.S. population growth in the 1960s; 27 percent in the 1980s. Its share will be 33 percent by the year 2000, and 54 percent by 2020. Before the year 2030, the number of deaths in the U.S. will surpass the number of births, making immigration the sole source of population growth. By 2000, about 4 percent of the U.S. population will be composed of immigrants who have arrived since 1986. By the year 2030, these will have risen to 12 percent of the population, when there will be 32 million post-1986 immigrants. *Census Bureau.*

Immigration will continue as the U.S. retains the image of a better life. A recent survey in 42 Mexican towns found 22 percent of the residents saying they were likely to be living in America within a year—that's about 19 million new arrivals. Even if this is more an expression of wish than of reality, it indicates the undiminished urge Mexicans feel to come to America. *Los Angeles Times.*

Faster than projected growth rates. The Census Bureau provides "low" and "high" series estimates for population trends, along with the "middle" series projections that commonly are used in published estimates. The low and high ranges allow for changes that unpredictable variables might bring about. However, current immigration rates place the trends along the "high series" projections. This means that the scenerio for increasing immigrant presence (primarily Hispanic and Asian) may move faster than reported here and elsewhere. Changes in immigration laws and international political/economic trends could influence this, but it appears as of this printing that the current "middle series" will actually turn out to be the low estimate.

U.S. naturalizations by decade and region of birth				
	1951-1960	1961-1970	1971-1980	1981-1988
Asia	8%	13%	34%	49%
Europe	72%	62%	31%	16%
North America	18%	21%	28%	26%
South America	—	2%	5%	6%
Other	2%	2%	2%	3%

Source: Immigration and Naturalization Service

Minorities

The slowing population growth will make the higher childbirth rates among minorities even more dramatic. By the year 2000, one-third of U.S. children will be from minority groups (with more than 50 percent in California, Texas, New York, and Florida). By 2010, 38 percent of children will be from minority groups. *Census Bureau.*

New York City has no majority group, though whites are still a plurality. In 20 years, Hispanics will comprise 35 percent of the Big Apple's population, whites and blacks 25 percent each, Asians 11 percent. Twenty years after that, Hispanics will rise to 41 percent, whites will drop to 15 percent. *The Population and Labor Force of New York, Population Reference Bureau, Inc.*

Hispanics

As the U.S. Hispanic population passed the 20 million mark, they have continued to be concentrated in urban areas. Hispanics are:

- **increasing their numbers** at about five times the rate of the U.S. as a whole, up 34 percent from 1980 to 1988.

- **aging along with the rest of the nation** (average age now 25.5 years), although their households remain *younger than the average* U.S. household.

- **remaining less wealthy than average.** Median family income of $27,290 is 36 percent below the national average—26 percent of Hispanic families live below the poverty line, 2.5 times the non-Hispanic percentage.

- **becoming more educated**—10 percent of those age 25+ now have a college degree, twice the 1970 percentage.

- **slowly changing language patterns.** The percentage of Spanish-only speakers will have declined very slightly by the end of the decade, to about 19 percent of U.S. Hispanics. The use of English among Hispanics will increase steadily, but the bilingual Hispanic will remain in the plurality. Increases in U.S.-born (and thus probably English-speaking) Hispanics will be offset by increases in immigration (primarily Spanish speakers). *Hispanic Policy Development Center.*

Distribution of foreign-born and native-born Hispanics within national origin groups

	1960	1970	1980
Mexican			
Foreign-born	17%	18%	26%
Native-born	83%	82%	74%
Puerto Rican			
Foreign-born	68%	54%	51%
Native-born	32%	46%	49%
Cuban			
Foreign-born	65%	73%	77%
Native-born	36%	27%	23%
Central/South American			
Foreign-born	62%	69%	80%
Native-born	38%	31%	20%
Other Hispanic			
Foreign-born	18%	12%	17%
Native-born	82%	88%	83%

Source: Census Bureau

African-Americans

Projected percentage of African-Americans within total U.S. population

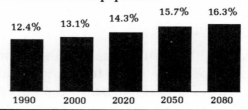

12.4%	13.1%	14.3%	15.7%	16.3%
1990	2000	2020	2050	2080

Source: Census Bureau

African-Americans now comprise 50 percent of the nation's minority population; 12 percent of the U.S. total. They are 25 percent less likely to be married; 48 percent more likely to be divorced. *Deloitte & Touche/Impact Resources.* The black birth rate will remain fairly constant for the next 50 years (at about 600,000 per year). Black poverty continues to increase slightly, as does the black middle class. The population can be roughly divided into income-group thirds: one-third in poverty, one-third lower-to middle-middle class, one-third middle class and above. *Census Bureau.*

Female-headed households increasing. By the year 2000, there will be equal 48 percent shares of black households headed by females and by married couples—currently they comprise 44 percent and 50 percent shares (in 1960 only 22 percent of black households were female-headed). More than half of black, female-headed families (54 percent) live in poverty. Only 32 percent of children in black, single-parent households do not live in poverty. *Census Bureau, National Urban League.* The high rate of single-parent households is not derived from dropout pregnant teens, as is generally surmised. The never-married woman in her 20s accounts for the bulk of these single-parent households; unmarried teen moms usually live with family (90 percent do). *Census Bureau.*

Blacks, children, and divorce. Blacks and whites are becoming more demographically alike in some ways. Childbirths to unmarried women are decreasing among blacks, increasing among whites. Expectations of childbearing, childlessness, and adult children living at home are converging. One big difference—black women wait nine years after divorce before remarrying; white women wait an average of two years. Black women have divorce rates twice that of any other group, and remarriage is dropping among blacks as it is increasing among whites. *Marketing to Women.*

Asian-Americans

Asian-American households
(Index of 100=U.S. average)

Household characteristics	U.S. Total	Asian-Am.	Index
Avg. # of persons	2.8	3.4	121
With persons <18 yrs.	34%	44%	130

Source: Deloitte & Touche/Impact Resources

Increasing their numbers at 14 times the U.S. population growth rate, Asian-Americans are the fastest-growing ethnic minority group. Their numbers will reach 10 million by the turn of the century, at which time they will surpass blacks as California's number-two minority group (Hispanics will remain number one). Asians constitute 46 percent of legal U.S. immigrants, and have more income per household than do Caucasian households—primarily because of the greater number of workers per household. *Census Bureau.*

U.S. ethnic Asian population, in thousands *(*projections)*			
	1980	**1990***	**2000***
Chinese	810	1,260	1,680
Filipino	780	1,400	2,080
Japanese	715	800	860
Indian	385	680	1,000
Korean	355	820	1,320
Vietnamese	245	860	1,530
Laotian	55	260	500
Cambodian	15	180	380
All Asian	3,465	6,550	9,850

Source: Pacific Bridges, *as cited in* The Economist

American-Indian populations are growing rapidly—with a 72-percent increase from '70 to '80. They are younger, less-affluent, and less-educated but more assimilated into the American mainstream than other ethnic groups. *Census Bureau.*

Youth

Expect to see fewer under-fives by 2000. According to the most probable scenarios from the Census Bureau (middle series projections), the under-five population will peak in 1990 at 18.4 million, fall to 16.9 million by the year 2000, and then remain below the 17 million mark for the next sixty years. The following tables from the Census Bureau track predictions in the changing youth population into the next millenium.

Population, by age: 1960 to 2080
(in thousands and percent of total population)

Year	Total		Under 5		5-13		14-17		18-24	
Estimates										
1960	180,671	100%	20,341	11.3%	32,965	18.2%	11,219	6.2%	16,128	8.9%
1965	194,303	100%	19,824	10,2%	35,754	18.4%	14,153	7.3%	20,293	10.4%
1970	205,052	100%	17,166	8.4%	36,672	17.9%	15,924	7.8%	24,712	12.1%
1975	215,973	100%	16,121	7.5%	33,919	15.7%	17,128	7.9%	28,005	13.0%
1980	227,757	100%	16,458	7.2%	31,095	13.7%	16,142	7.1%	30,350	13.3%
1985	239,279	100%	18,004	7.5%	30,110	12.6%	14,865	6.2%	28,749	12.0%
1987	243,915	100%	18,252	7.5%	30,823	12.6%	14,467	5.9%	27,336	11.2%
1990	250,410	100%	18,408	7.4%	32,393	12.9%	13,237	5.3%	26,140	10.4%
1995	260,138	100%	17,799	6.8%	33,864	13.0%	14,510	5.6%	24,281	9.3%
2000	268,266	100%	16,898	6.3%	33,483	12.5%	15,332	5.7%	25,231	9.4%
2005	275,604	100%	16,611	6.0%	31,980	11.6%	15,491	5.6%	26,918	9.8%
2010	282,575	100%	16,899	6.0%	31,001	11.0%	14,746	5.2%	27,155	9.6%
2020	294,364	100%	17,095	5.8%	31,697	10.8%	14,074	4.8%	25,018	8.5%
2030	300,629	100%	16,305	5.4%	31,282	10.4%	14,574	4.8%	25,290	8.4%
2040	301,807	100%	16,217	5.4%	30,214	10.0%	14,036	4.7%	25,408	8.4%
2050	299,849	100%	15,900	5.3%	30,093	10.0%	13,771	4.6%	24,411	8.1%
2080	292,235	100%	14,971	5.1%	28,348	9.7%	13,089	4.5%	23,288	8.0%

Source: Census Bureau

Other Demographics

Homosexuals are a big-money market. Findings from a variety of studies suggest that the gay market is larger than the 10 percent of U.S. adults the Kinsey report found in 1948—those statistics still are used, and will continue to be used since Congress killed a plan for a new national sex survey. The gay population may be as large as 15 percent of the total U.S. population. A Simmons study of primary readers of eight publications that serve the gay community finds that gays earn more household income (72 percent above U.S. average), more individual income (triple the Census average), are more educated (over three times the U.S. percentage are college educated), and more employed (97 percent work, a rate 53 percent above the national average). *Simmons Proprietary Data.*

Education

Education rates continue to climb. Only a quarter of U.S. adults now have no high school diploma; in 1940, three-quarters of the nation did not. More than a third of the nation's adults have been to college (36 percent in 1986), up from 10 percent before the G.I. Bill (1944). You may question the quality of these accomplishments, but the fact is that the U.S. is far more educated than it has ever been before. *Census Bureau.*

Hype Alert: "Dropouts rates are increasing."
Truth: Dropout rates are really decreasing.The annual dropout rate (proportion of students who dropped out in a single year without completing high school) for all students in grades 10-12 has declined over the past ten years, from 6.6 percent in 1978 to 4.4 percent in 1988. In 1988, the dropout rate for whites was 4.2 percent, for blacks, 5.78 percent, and for Hispanics, 9.27 percent. In addition, the proportion of the nation's total nongraduate 16- to 24-year-old population has also gradually decreased over the past 20 years—from 16 percent in 1968 to 12 percent in 1988. *National Center for Education Statistics.*

Percentage of dropouts, ages 16-24, by race/ethnicity and year
(figures rounded)

	Hispanic	Black	White
1973	34%	22%	13%
1976	31%	20%	13%
1979	34%	21%	14%
1982	32%	18%	13%
1985	28%	16%	12%
1988	36%	15%	13%

Source: National Center for Education Statistics

Some quick education stats for the future:

- By 2000, elementary and secondary school populations will increase. Total enrollment in the nation's elementary and secondary schools is expected to reach 49.5 million by the fall of the year 2000, an increase of about four million students from 1989-90's school year. This constitutes a 9-percent increase in student population during the next 11 years, a change from the previous 11 years (1978-88—1989-90), when school enrollments declined by 4 percent. The rising enrollments reflect the increase in births that began in 1977 and continued in most subsequent years (the Baby Boomlet).

- By the year 2000, current expenditures per pupil in public elementary and secondary schools is projected to increase in real value by 18 percent over the current school year, now at about $4,800 per pupil.

- College and university enrollment will fluctuate within a narrow range in the 1990s, and is expected to increase by 4 percent by the year 2000 (from 12.8 million students in 1988 to 13.4 million in 2000).

- Women will continue to earn more associate's, bachelor's and master's degrees than men throughout the 1990s, as they have for the past several years.

- In 1990, women, for the first time, are expected to earn more doctorates than men, while men will continue to earn more first professional degrees in such fields as medicine and law. *Natinal Center for Education Statistics*

We predict that the number of days children spend in school a year will increase in the 1990s. Here's a current international comparison:

Country	days in school year
Japan	243
Italy	210-215
United Kingdom	196
Canada	191
France	185
Mexico	180
United States	180
Sweden	180
Federal Republic of Germany	160-170

Source: Congressional Research Service

4

Politics
Will It Be A Kinder, Gentler Nation?

Trends evolve slowly, over decades. A suddenly appearing major trend in the social or political arena tends to be hype. There are incremental changes, and the pendulum swings on party affiliation, attitudes on racism, abortion, gun control, and so forth. Women have gained political clout, but still hold a small minority of elective offices. Men say they want to be more involved with their children, but they still work more after the baby is born. We caution you to look for slow change in the 1990s, even at the souped-up pace of normal life.

One significant general trend we see appearing, in a number of studies, is that Americans are defining themselves more as individuals and less as members of institutions or organizations (be it religious, political, or business). Fewer people are members of an organized religion, but the overwhelming majority still believe in God. People are still working—women more than ever—but more and more workers are opting to work at home or to open businesses. Americans are feeling increasingly alienated from power structures in the U.S. Voter turnout has hit a record low.

Political

Hype Alert: "The 1980s created a generation of young conservatives."

Nope. "No such pattern has emerged. The Reagan generation (those 18-24 in 1986-1989) shows no clear sign of a conservative reaction on either race or gender issues; they are more liberal than their age group was in the 1970s or early 1980s, and they are as liberal or more liberal than any other age group in the late 1980s." *University of Chicago.*

Political leaning by income group. Among those earning more than $50,000, 55 percent identify themselves as Republicans, while only 39 percent say they are Democrats. On the other hand, among those earning less than $15,000, 53 percent are Democrats and 30 percent are with the GOP. *The New York Times.*

Patterns in party loyalty	Democrat or leaning Dem.	Republican or leaning Rep.
Household Income		
under $15,000	53%	30%
$15,000-$29,999	50%	40%
$30,000-$50,000	41%	47%
over $50,000	39%	55%

Source: The New York Times

The patterns for Democratic and Republican loyalty measured against income are almost perfectly reciprocal. The data imply, however, that more independents and alternate party loyalists earn under $50,000. *The New York Times.*

More women politicians. Though women still hold a small minority of elective offices—at no level of office (Congress, statewide elective executive offices, state legislatures, county governing boards, mayoralties, and municipal and township governing boards) do women hold more than 16.9 percent of the available seats— women have made gains.

- In 1989 more women served in Congress than ever before, holding 29 or 5.4 percent of all Congressional seats.

- Women hold 13.9 percent of the 330 statewide elective executive positions in 1989, up from 10 percent in 1975.

- Women accounted for 17 percent of the state legislatures in 1989, up from 8 percent in 1975.

Center for the American Woman and Politics

Percentages of women in elective offices
(numbers rounded)

Level of Office	1975	1977	1979	1981	1983	1985	1987	1989
U.S. Congress	4%	4%	3%	4%	4%	5%	5%	5%
Statewide elective[1]	10%	8%	11%	11%	13%	14%	15%	14% *
State legislatures	8%	9%	10%	12%	13%	15%	16%	17%
County governing boards[2]	3%	4%	5%	6%	8%	8%('84)	9%	9%('88)
Mayors & municipal/township governing boards	4%	8%	10%	10%	NA[4]	14% [3]	NA[4]	NA

Although there has been an increase in the number of women serving, the percentage decrease between 1987 and 1989 reflects a change in the base used to calculate this percentage.
1. These numbers do not include: officials appointed to state cabinet-level positions; officials elected to executive posts by the legislature; members of the judicial branch; or elected members of university boards of trustees or boards of education.
2. The three states without county governing boards are CT, RI, and VT.
3. Includes data from Washington, D C. States for which data was incomplete and therefore not included are: IL, IN, KY, MO, PA, WI.
4. CAWP currently updates municipal figures every four years.
Source: Center for the American Woman and Politics

Voter turnout hits record low. The Census Bureau took its first turnout count in 1964 and found 69 percent of eligible voters voting. They estimate that turnout in 1988 dropped to 50 percent (actual counts were 57 percent, but are believed by the Census Bureau to be too high). *Census Bureau.*

Hype Alert: "The focus on ethics is making a difference."
More than 1,000 reports of ethical misconduct by 47 different members of Congress appeared in the national media in 1989. Sexual improprieties made up the most frequently reported type of misconduct. Overall, Democrats got better press than Republicans on TV news, with 54 percent to 27 percent positive evaluations. *Media Monitor.*

Newsweek asked, "Would any of the following disclosures prompt you personally to vote against a public official regardless of other factors?"

The Candidate:	
Accepted money from special interest groups pressuring him to vote a certain way	77%
Once failed to pay his income taxes	64%
Had a drinking problem	63%
Was a homosexual	45%
Had extramarital affairs	36%

Source: Newsweek/The Gallup Organization

Hype Alert: "We are becoming a kinder, gentler nation".
"'Wilding' will take on new meaning. It will come to describe the new moral-less behavior of industry and government leaders. Wilding will become a new spectator sport for those of us lacking the power and money of those at the top of their professions. In the grand American tradition, others will only respond by looking for their own piece of the action." *The American Forecaster Almanac 1990, Running Press.*

Social welfare in the U.S. is the lowest ever recorded. The annual Index of Social Welfare, and the Index of Children's Welfare (both combine a wide variety of indicators of well-being into a single index number) posted lowest-ever recorded figures. Eight of the 17 indicators used in the Social Welfare Index dropped to record lows, and the Children's Index has declined 49 percent since 1973. *Fordham Institute for Innovation in Social Policy.*

Americans are feeling powerless and alienated. Feelings of powerlessness and alienation from the mainstream are troubling 58 percent of the American public according to a recent Harris poll. The Harris Alienation Index is made up of basic questions that have not been changed since the index was founded 23 years ago. The latest trends:

- "The rich get richer and the poor get poorer" is now believed by 79 percent of the American people, up 7 points just in the past year. The all-time high on the measure was reached in 1986 at 81 percent.

- "Most people with power try to take advantage of people like yourself" has gone up in the past year from 62 percent to 66 percent of the public. This year's total is the second highest ever recorded.

- "What you think doesn't count very much anymore" is believed by 61 percent of the people, up from 53 percent just last year.

- "The people running the country don't really care what happens to you" is something 44 percent of the public feels from time to time, up from 39 percent last year.

A number of groups feel a sense of powerlessness far above the national norm:
—71 percent of those earning $7,500 or less annually
—68 percent of blacks feel alienated
—63 percent of Hispanics feel alienated
—61 percent of women feel alienated
Source: The Harris Poll, October 29, 1989, Louis Harris and Associates, Inc.

Religion

Membership in organized religions is down. A Gallup survey finds that in 1988 only 65 percent of Americans said they were members of a church or synagogue, the lowest point in the history of the study (the high point was 1947, when 76 percent of Americans were members). In 1986, 68 percent were members and in 1985, 71 percent were. Weekly attendance at church or synagogue services, however, has held steady at 42 percent since 1969. *The Gallup Poll.*

People are turning inward to find God. Declining membership in organized religion doesn't mean people are turning away from God. The majority of Americans believe in God or a universal spirit (94 percent); say religion is a very important part of their lives (53 percent); believe in the divinity of Christ (84 percent, up from 78 percent in 1978); agree prayer is an important part of daily life (76 percent); and think a person can be a good Christian or Jew even if he doesn't attend religious services (76 percent, up from 67 percent who agreed in 1964). *The Gallup Poll.*

In the past decade there has been little change in Americans' preferences for various denominations.

Percent who say the following is their religious preference:					
	Protestant	Catholic	Jewish	Other	None
1988	56%	28%	2%	4%	10%
1986	58%	27%	2%	4%	9%
1984	57%	28%	2%	4%	9%
1982	57%	29%	2%	4%	8%
1980	61%	28%	2%	2%	7%

Source: The Gallup Poll

Here are some of the things Americans believe in:

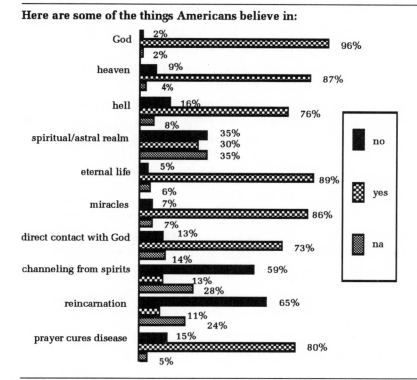

Source: Better Homes and Gardens

Hispanic Catholics. The predominantly Catholic Hispanic population is growing at three times the rate of the non-Hispanic population, a result of increased immigration and higher than average birth rates. By 2000, it's projected that Hispanics will account for about half of all Catholics in the U.S. *FutureScope, Joe Cappo.*

Social

Hype Alert: "Dramatic movements on social issues."
Public opinion changes slowly over time. There have been some, very slow changes in public opinion on a variety of social issues in the last two decades.

Racism

Much-publicized incidents of racism in New York and elsewhere have created a false impression of increasing racism in the U.S. Though there has been an increase in the number of bias crimes—acts of violence inspired by racism or other prejudice—reported throughout the country, it's not certain if there has been an actual increase in the number of crimes perpetrated or simply in the reporting of them. Headlines to the contrary, there has been virtually no dramatic change in the painfully slow, but steady decline in racism.

- In 1970, 59 percent of white Americans with school-age children said they would object to sending their children to a school where more than half the children were black. In 1988, 47 percent of white Americans with school-age children said they would object.

- In 1972, 38 percent of whites agreed that they have a right to keep blacks out of their neighborhoods if they want. In 1988, 24 percent of whites agreed. *Trends in Public Opinion—A Compendium of Survey Data.*

On the other hand, there is a general impression that racial segregation is getting better; it's not. Segregation patterns are close to what they were two decades ago. And the hoped-for integration in the suburbs isn't happening—urban segregation patterns are being recreated there.

Abortion

Despite front-page attention and spasmodic fluctuations in response to events, there has been little change in public opinion on abortion. Politicians may scramble, and the influence equation among the electorate may shift, but the same slight majority is pro-choice. In 1989, only 15 percent of Americans said abortion should not be permitted at all. *New York Times/CBS News Survey in the New York Times.* In 1975, 22 percent of Americans thought abortion should be illegal in all circumstances. *Trends in Public Opinion—A Compendium of Survey Data.*

Gun Control

Support for gun control grows, but slowly. In 1971, 72 percent of Americans were in favor of gun control laws. Today, 74 percent of American are in favor of them. *Trends in Public Opinion—A Compendium of Survey Data.*

Hype Alert: "The end of 'me-ism,' the beginning of 'we-ism,' a.k.a. Post-Materialist America."

Are Americans rejecting greed-is-goodism and personal gain for sharing, cooperation, and volunteerism? Yes and no. Yes, that is the direction in which the nation has turned. No, this isn't going to find important expression until well into the 1990s. And no, we aren't going to be post-materialistic, Americans love their stuff. The facts evidence no indication of decreasing desire for owning goods, and in fact, image-consciousness is alive and well, and going global.

Hype Alert: "Status goods are passe."

Au contraire. There will be fewer people in their Yuppie years (25-35), 10 percent fewer than a decade ago. And imported goods will be more expensive. However, the impact of demographics will be offset by the greater demand and reward of highly paid, upscale, younger workers and dual-income households. The symbols of affluence, paid for by cash or credit, will attract the same types of purchasers and number of purchases they always have. Flaunting accumulated and spent wealth will be frowned upon, but Americans will buy luxuries for their own quiet enjoyment. They want their rewards—material or experiential.

Hype Alert: "Volunteerism is growing in America."

Yes and No. A Gallup Poll shows that although volunteerism has been increasing steadily in the past decade, volunteerism has not been significantly rising in the last two years. While the number of Americans who were involved in social service work increased from 27 percent in 1977 to 39 percent in 1987, there was only a two percentage point increase in the number involved in 1989 (41 percent).

Hype Alert: "Yuppies are dead."

There will be a shifting of direction. However, the media overblew the factually-based Y-word image of selfish acquisitivism. Yuppies weren't that extreme, and they aren't going to become MTs (Mother Teresas) in the 1990s. The 1980's explosion of affluence is subsiding. Those who gained in the '80s will seek to maintain in the '90s; those who worked hard just to maintain, will be doing what they've always done—working hard. Affluents feel uncertain about the foundations of their affluence. That uncertainty will foster caution in the 1990s. The cautious affluence of the 1990s will find new heros.

Hype Alert: "The post-permissive society."

Maybe, but let's see some hard evidence. There has been some drop in promiscuity (mostly AIDS-fear driven), but most people still believe premarital sex is fine. In 1972, 35 percent of Americans thought premarital sex was always wrong; in 1983, 27 percent felt this way, and in 1988, 26 percent did. *Trends in Public Opinion—A Compendium of Survey Data.* A lot of informed thinkers, however, feel that "the trend toward a stricter morality is still in force, and it is being led by the older Baby Boomers who have settled down." *Florence Skelly, Vice Chairman of DYG, Inc. Group, Adweek's Marketing Week.* "Values show a movement away from the permissive individualism of the 1970s and back toward the more pluralistic conformity of the 1950s . . . The spending orientation of today's consumer reflects a more sober outlook characterized by a willingness to defer purchases, a psychology of saving, and a desire (without much success) to reduce credit spending." *DYG, Inc.,1988 Environmental Scanning Program as cited in Adweek's Marketing Week.*

Men

Hype Alert: "The new American male.

Hogwash. He is helping out more, but not sharing the household chores equally (see chapter 7—Home). He *is* more aware of issues of communication. Other than that, generally status quo. When you see headlines about the Sensitive New-Age Male, the Post-Feminist Pal, the New Macho, the Nice Guy '90s, please reread this paragraph and think of the men you know.

Hype Alert: "The new American father."

Fathers, though they express interest in spending more time with their kids, aren't doing it. There have been no substantial changes in fatherhood in recent or not-so recent years. *Fathers of young children work more paid overtime than any other workers*, and fathers aged 30 to 49 work the most paid overtime of all. New father spend about 2.75 hours per weekday at home while the baby is awake, most of it *not* with the child—fathers average under 15 hours a week of childcare. Two-thirds of men *claim* they would reduce work hours to spend more time with the kids, but only a third of the wives believe their husbands would do this. *Reassessing Fatherhood, Sage Publications.*

The emergence of do-dads. Traditional fathers will always be around, and will always be in the majority. However, because women are working more than ever before, and will continue into the future, we predict the emergence of a new kind of active, upscale dad—"do-dads." These fathers, though a minority, will become a sizeable market in the '90s. Do-dads *will* participate actively in child-rearing responsibilities. There's already a new magazine out for them. The papa-targeted journal *Dad* made its debut in February 1990, and according to Wendie Blanchard, its publisher, the magazine "speaks to a broad spectrum of issues . . . such as job- and family-related issues." *Industry Week.*

Women
Hype Alert: "The superwoman is dead."

Well, yes, in part. The superwoman myth is as much a media exaggeration as the Yuppie. All women ever wanted was a choice. More than three-fourths of the women in a *Good Housekeeping* poll work, either full- or part-time, and they do so in order to have money to survive or to have money to help provide for a better lifestyle. Survival/lifestyle income is not easily given up. Yes, some women feel nostalgic about staying home and raising the kids. The reality is that women work and men work, and providing a middle-class standard of living now requires two incomes.

Hype Alert: "Women want to go back home."

Not quite. *Some* women do want to return home, and some women have never left. What's really happening is that being home-oriented has become an acceptable option again. A *Time*/CNN poll conducted by Yankelovich, Clancy, Shulman, finds that almost equal percentages of American women feel that both successful business women and homemakers are "in -touch" with the American woman (70 percent and 69 percent, respectively).

Baby Boomers
Hype Alert: "Boomers are a homogeneous market."

There are really two distinct groups contained within the 26- to 44-year-old Boomer market, which accounts for 80 million Americans and spend $985 billion a year. The older Boomers, aged 36-44, number 35 million, and are the Boomers that marketers typically target. These more established Boomers are entering their big money years, but many have already made the majority of their big-ticket purchases (houses, cars, and so on) Consequently, in the '90s, older Boomers will be a prime market for non-durables, such as 1960s nostalgia goods and luxury items.

The 45 million younger Boomers, aged 26-35, however, are still struggling. They have had a harder time buying houses (mostly because of the downpayment hurdle) and getting jobs. They are more anxious about status symbols. They can't relate to '60s idealism or hippie images the way older Boomers do. Smart marketers will recognize the differences between the groups, and target older and younger Boomers separately. *Adweek's Marketing Week.*

Hype Alert: "Boomers are Yuppies."

Actually, there are eight times as many yuffies (young urban failures) as yuppies. *Baby Boomers, W.W. Norton.* Boomers tend toward yuppie-type expectations, but there are only four million "yuppies" within the 75-million-person Boomer population—only 5 percent. Most Boomers live within moderate means, most making less than $30,000 a year. Boomers face stagnant wages, high education costs for children, high housing costs, a Social Security system they distrust, and worry about retirement income. Real wages of aging Boomers haven't climbed as rapidly as their parents' did. The extent of future pay increases for all workers will make much more of a difference to consumer spending than any kick from the maturing of the Boom. *Wall Street Journal.*

Money
A Decade of Cents and Sensibility

The boom is over. Americans may never again see the kind of growth in affluence they saw in the mid-to-late 1980s. The U.S. Economy has slowed, and the '90s will bring a recession, possibly a serious one. Wage growth will be slow, barely keeping pace with inflation, if not falling behind. Averaged over the whole decade, however, both the economy and wages will grow, though slowly. Savings are up from 1987's low, but not to the levels reached in decades past. This decade will see continually larger percentages of income go into savings. The rate of borrowing is expected to slow, as consumers become more cautious about the economy, and middle-aging brings with it less necessity-borrowing. Perhaps most significant to business in the 1990s will be the overall slowing in the rate of increase in consumer expenditures. People are still purchasing, but they are shifting from durables to non-durables. Dual-income households, now the norm, have kept many families in the middle class. Many others, particularly DINK (dual-income, no kids) households, have risen into the ranks of the newly affluent.

The Economy

The economy will grow more slowly in the coming years, but grow it will
(Consensus forecasts of 55 business economists)

Indicator	1989	1990
Gross national product	2.5%	2.0%
Consumer price index	4.6%	4.2%
Unemployment rate	5.3%	5.5%
Housing starts (millions)	1.40	1.45
Car, truck sales (millions)	15.10	14.70
3-month T-bills	8.1%	7.1%
30-year T-bills	8.4%	7.8%

Source: National Association of Business Economists

We continue to spend money. Annual household expenditures rose 6 percent from 1987 to 1988. The greatest increase was in vehicle purchases, up 17 percent, from $2,022 in '87 to $2,361 in '88.

Annual expenditures of all consumer units and percent changes, Consumer Expenditure (CE) Survey, 1987 to 1988

	1987	1988	% change in CE
Number of consumer units (households)	94,150	94,862	.8%
Item			
income before taxes	$27,326	$28,540	4.4%
income after taxes	$24,871	$26,149	5.1%
average number of persons in consumer unit	2.6	2.6	
average age of reference person	47	47	
Average number in consumer unit:			
earners	1.4	1.4	
vehicles	2	2	
children under 18	.7	.7	
persons 65+	.3	.3	

Average annual expenditures	1987 $24,414	1988 $25,892	% change in CE 6.1%
Food	3,664	3,748	2.3%
Food at home	2,099	2,136	1.8%
cereal and bakery products	299	312	4.3%
meat, poultry, fish, and eggs	572	551	-3.7%
dairy products	274	274	0
fruits and vegetables	356	373	4.8%
other food prepared at home	598	625	4.5%
food on trips	31	30	-3.2%
Food away from home	1,565	1,612	3%
Alcoholic beverages	289	269	-6.9%
Housing	7,569	8,079	6.7%
shelter	4,154	4,493	8.2%
utilities, fuels, and public services	1,671	1,747	4.5%
household operations	371	394	6.2%
housekeeping supplies	341	361	5.9%
house furnishings and equipment	1,032	1,083	4.9%
Apparel and services	1,446	1,489	3%
Transportation	4,600	5,093	10.7%
vehicle purchases	2,022	2,361	16.8%
gasoline and motor oil	888	932	5%
other vehicle expenses	1,417	1,521	7.3%
public transportation	273	279	2.2%
Health care	1,135	1,298	14.4%
Entertainment	1,193	1,329	11.4%
Personal care products and services	330	334	1.2%
Reading	142	150	5.6%
Education	337	342	1.5%
Tobacco products and smoking supplies	232	242	4.3%
Miscellaneous	562	578	2.8%
Cash contributions	741	693	-6.5%
Personal insurance and pensions	2,175	2,249	3.4%
life and other personal insurance	294	314	6.8%
retirement, pensions, Social Security	1,881	1,935	2.9%

Source: Consumer Expenditure Survey 1988, *Bureau of Labor Statistics*

Consumer optimism will keep spending going. If the economy continues to grow from 1988 to 1993 (and according to some experts it will, though moderately), there will be above-average constant-dollar sales volumes over the next five years in the following retail stores: hardware, home improvement, auto and home supply centers, furniture, consumer electronics, sporting goods, hobbies/toys/games, women's ready-to-wear, child and infant's wear, family clothing, and optical goods. (The national average of the absolute level of retail spending per person is $8,921.) *Economic Perspectives.*

Long-term constant dollar growth rates for selected consumer expenditure categories 1988-1993

	1989	1990	1991	1992	1993
Total personal consumption expenditures	3.1%	2.2%	3.7%	3.8%	2.8%
Total durable goods	4.4%	2.8%	7.1%	6.2%	3.7%
motor vehicles/parts	4.7%	2.2%	8.1%	6.3%	3.3%
furniture/mattresses	2.2%	2.3%	4.7%	5.3%	3.2%
kitchen/household appliances	2.5%	1.9%	4.4%	5.0%	3.4%
china/glass/tableware	2.5%	2.0%	3.6%	4.8%	2.6%
radio/TV/records/music inst.	7.4%	6.2%	11.2%	8.1%	5.4%
jewelry	4.1%	1.8%	4.9%	5.4%	2.8%
wheel goods/toys/sports equip.	3.8%	2.8%	5.1%	6.2%	4.4%
Total nondurable goods	2.3%	1.7%	2.8%	2.8%	1.8%
food/beverages at home	1.2%	1.6%	1.8%	2.0%	1.3%
food/beverages in restaurants	3.3%	1.9%	3.5%	3.8%	2.9%
shoes/footware	4.4%	2.6%	3.7%	4.3%	2.8%
women's clothing	4.9%	2.9%	4.8%	4.3%	3.1%
drugs/sundries	2.3%	2.0%	1.8%	1.6%	0.7%
non dur. toys/sports sundries	3.9%	3.1%	5.2%	5.7%	3.5%
Total service expenditures	3.3%	2.4%	3.3%	3.8%	3.1%
medical care services	3.8%	3.4%	4.0%	4.6%	3.9%
personal business services	5.2%	3.3%	5.0%	5.8%	4.7%
recreational services	4.5%	3.7%	4.6%	5.3%	4.7%

Source: Economic Perspectives

Spending shifts from durables to non-durables. As interest rates rise, purchases will shift from big-ticket durable goods to non-durables in the early '90s. *Economic Perspectives.* A reason for big-ticket purchases declining is that Americans went on a spending spree in the early '80s—buying 70 million new cars, 7 million new houses and $83 billion dollars' worth of yuppie play toys such as car stereos and VCRs. Americans have slaked their thirst for many durable products. *U.S. News & World Report.*

Income Distribution Polarization

Hype Alert: "Everyone prospered during the Reagan years."
Nope. The polarization of income distribution continues. More and more we are becoming a country of haves and have nots. The lowest fifth of U.S. households now earns less than 5 percent of the nation's income (the lowest percentage since the '50s), while the top fifth now takes in 44 percent of the nation's wealth (the highest percentage ever recorded). *Census Bureau.*

Share of total income by fifths of households, selected years: 1980, 1982, 1984, 1986
(based on 1986 dollars)

	1986	1984	1982	1980
number of households (in 000s)	89,479	85,407	82,368	80,776
income before taxes				
lowest fifth of households	3.7%	4.0%	4.0%	4.1%
second fifth	9.7%	9.8%	9.9%	10.2%
third fifth	16.2%	16.4%	16.5%	16.8%
fourth fifth	24.3%	24.6%	24.6%	24.8%
highest fifth	46.1%	45.3%	45.0%	44.2%
income after taxes				
lowest fifth	4.4%	4.7%	4.7%	4.9%
second fifth	10.8%	11.0%	11.3%	11.6%
third fifth	17.2%	17.2%	17.5%	17.9%
fourth fifth	24.8%	24.8%	24.8%	25.1%
highest fifth	42.6%	42.3%	41.8%	40.6%

Source: Fairchild Publications

Household income distribution: 1986

	before all gov't. programs	after taxes and before gov't. programs	after taxes and gov't. programs
Share to richest 20% of households	52.4%	50.3%	45.7%
Share to middle 60% of households	46.7%	48.6%	49.6%
Share to poorest 20% of households	1.0%	1.1%	4.7%
Percentage of people in poverty	19.9%	21.2%	11.6%

Source: Fairchild Publications

Income

Household Income Distribution, 1990 and 1994 (projected)

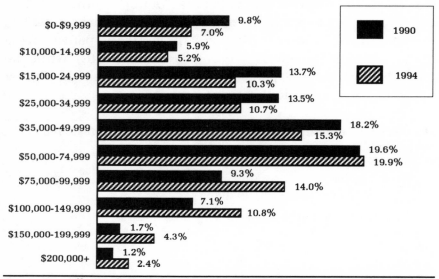

Source: Donnelley Marketing Information Services, 1990, A Dun & Bradstreet Company

Income continues to grow in America. Real per capita income reached an all-time high in the U.S. in 1988, up 1.7 percent, to $13,123 from $12,904 in 1987. Simultaneously, median household income and median family income remained unchanged at $27,230 and $32,190, respectively. *Census Bureau.* Both statements are correct, but they seem contradictory until we look at the population trends influencing the findings. Per capita income is calculated to include the income of all persons, whereas family income includes only the income of related persons living in households. Two trends that are affecting family income are: decreasing family size (the American household is the smallest it has ever been), and increasing numbers of non-family households (unrelated persons living together).

Comparison of income summary measures between 1988 and 1987, by selected characteristics

Characteristic	1988 median income	1987 median income	% change in real income
Households			
All households	$27,225	$27,139	0.3%
Families:			
All families	32,191	32,251	-0.2%
Type of family			
All races:			
Married-couple families	36,389	36,322	0.2%
Female householder,			
no husband present	15,346	15,290	0.4%
White			
Married-couple families	36,840	36,900	-0.2%
Female householder,			
no husband present	17,672	17,717	-0.3%
Black			
Married-couple families	30,385	28,441	6.8%
Female householder,			
no husband present	10,657	10,251	4.0%
Hispanic*			
Married-couple families	25,667	25,394	1.1%
Female householder,			
no husband present	10,687	10,101	5.8%
Per Capita:			
All races	13,123	12,904	1.7%
White	13,896	13,687	1.5%
Black	8,271	7,961	3.9%
Hispanic*	7,956	7,970	-0.2%

Hispanic persons may be any of race.

Source: Census Bureau

Black/white income gap widens. Black America is three economic nations: roughly one-third prospering, firmly established in the middle class or above ($25,000+ household income); a lower-middle-class third, suffering the same squeeze that the entire U.S. middle class is experiencing; and an underclass third, economically struggling, and losing ground. Black median family income fell from 1986 to 1987, and the black/white earnings gap continues to widen—black families now earn $561 for every white $1,000—in 1970, the gap was $613 to $1,000. *Census Bureau.*

Percentage of black and white families with income in selected ranges

	1987		1986		1978		1970	
	Black	White	Black	White	Black	White	Black	White
Under $5,000	13.5%	3.2%	13.4%	3.3%	8.4%	2.4%	9.0%	2.9%
Under $10,000	30.0%	9.3%	29.3%	9.8%	26.6%	8.5%	25.7%	9.6%
$10,000-$34,999	47.7%	45.1%	48.2%	45.7%	51.7%	47.7%	56.6%	51.8%
$35,000+	22.3%	45.7%	22.5%	44.5%	21.7%	43.8%	17.7%	38.6%
$50,000+	9.5%	24.4%	9.5%	23.7%	8.5%	21.1%	5.7%	16.4%

Source: Census Bureau

Hispanic /white income gap also widens. In 1979, Hispanic family income, as a percentage of white income, was 69 percent, sinking to 64 percent by 1988. *National Council of La Raza.*

Hype Alert: "It takes two incomes to make it."
For many, it takes more than two incomes. Second jobs are becoming more popular—among more than 40 percent of U.S. couples at least one of the partners has a second job, and in almost half of this group (43 percent) the extra income is important to the family budget. In an economic downturn, many second jobs would disappear (they are one of the first things to go during a recession), leaving 18 percent of working households failing to meet financial obligations. *Krannert Graduate School of Management, Purdue University.*

Nonfamily household income grows four times as fast. The fastest-growing segment of household formations is the non-traditional household, growing at twice the rate of the traditional household. Though nonfamily households (29 percent of all U.S. households) earn only half the income of family households ($16,148 median 1988 income vs. $32,491), their earnings are increasing significantly faster than that of family households. Nonfamilies increased their earnings 4.4 percent from 1987 to 1988, while families decreased their earnings by almost 1 percent. The real median income for families had risen in the past five years until this year's slowdown, supporting many economists' concerns that there will be a wage pinch upcoming. *Census Bureau.*

Number of households, 1988 median income, and percentage change from 1987 real median income (based on a new processing procedure), by selected household characteristic

	Number (in 000s)	1988 median income	% change in income '87-'88
All households	92,830	$27,225	+.3%
Family households	65,837	32,491	-.2%
Married couple families	52,100	36,436	+.1%
Male householder, no wife present	2,847	28,642	+3%
Female householder, no husband present	10,890	16,051	-.4%
Non-family households	26,994	16,148	+4.4%
Male householder	11,874	20,999	+1.2%
Living alone	9,193	18,284	+3.3%
Female householder	15,120	12,877	+5.0%
Living alone	13,515	11,622	+4.1%

Source: Census Bureau

Bankruptcy is rising. Not since 1979—after the 1978 amendments to the bankruptcy laws lowered the cost of declaring bankruptcy and lawyers began to advertise the availability of bankruptcy—have there been so many filings. After leveling off in the early 1980s, *the number of personal bankruptcy filings increased more than 50 percent from 1984 to 1988.* Last year saw no signs of a slowdown; personal bankruptcy filings totaled 616,753, a 12-percent increase over 1988.

Some areas are particularly hard hit. Accounting disproportionately for one quarter of all filings nationwide in the 1980s were the western states (Arizona, California, Idaho, Montana, Nevada, Oregon, and Washington, as well as Arkansas, Hawaii, and some other island territories). The number of filings in these states increased 34 percent in 1986. States experiencing economic downturns (such as Texas) also have crowded bankruptcy courts. Through 1988, the northeastern and midwestern regions were less fertile grounds for bankruptcy, with the exception of Maine, Massachusetts, Rhode Island and Puerto Rico, which together saw filing increases of 27 percent in 1986, 15 percent in 1987, 27 percent in 1988, and 47 percent in 1989, a reflection of the slumping New England economy. Also now in trouble are Connecticut, Vermont, and New York, together reporting a 27-percent rise in filings from 1988 to 1989. *American Financial Services Association.*

Discretionary Income

The affluent control the nation's discretionary income. Only one-third of U.S. households have discretionary income (money that's left after the bills and taxes are paid), with the average amount being $12,300. Not surprisingly, the rich have the most DI. Just over one-quarter (26.5 percent) of all U.S. households earn $40,000+ a year, but they account for two-thirds (68.8 percent) of those households in the DI group, and control almost 90 percent of the nation's DI. *Census Bureau/The Conference Board.*

Households with discretionary income

	Households		Spendable Discretionary Income		
	number (thous.)	proportion of HHs	after-tax avg. inc.	average	per capita
Total	25,869	28.9	$41,940	$12,332	$4,633
<$15,000	197	0.7	13,213	1,014	890
$15-$19,999	694	7.5	16,108	2,304	1,962
$20-$24,999	1,011	11.7	19,303	3,438	2,474
$25-$29,999	1,662	21.5	22,733	3,737	2,328
$30-$34,999	2,248	31.8	26,323	5,841	2,480
$40-$49,999	4,807	55.5	35,190	6,746	2,500
$50-$74,999	8,146	80.8	45,618	11,493	3,761
$75-$99,999	2,885	100.0	61,466	22,818	6,830
$100,000+	1,940	100.0	86,745	47,320	14,163

Source: Census Bureau/The Conference Board

Hype Alert: "Real income is rising faster than discretionary income."
Between 1983 and 1987, the amount of spendable income per family and aggregate spendable income for the country rose dramatically. More than two million (2.1) new discretionary income (DI) households appeared between '83 and '87, and the amount of DI these households received rose by 12 percent. Adding together the increase in the number of households with DI

and the mean amount received, there was a 22-percent rise in aggregate DI, from $262 billion to $319 billion. The people most likely to have DI are two-earner couples, aged 35-59, with some college education, working in professional or managerial jobs. *Census Bureau/the Conference Board.*

Savings

Saving is up since the '87 low, but considerably lower than in decades past. Saving is happening—but it's not why you think. (Boomers coming into their high-saving years is too simplistic a reason.) The personal saving rate jumped to 5.5 percent during the first six months of 1989; that's $100 million more annually than in 1987, but far below the 7-percent to 8-percent norm of previous decades. Reasons: large fluctuations in household wealth (which soared in the early '80s) and prices of big-ticket items (which became much less expensive in the early '80s) had discretionary cash flowing. Spending is now slowing because of the overall economic slowdown—which is depressing household wealth and slowing the appreciation of house values. Also, big-ticket items are more expensive now that income-tax deductions are being phased out. The Cold War defrost might improve the savings rate. Some speculate that with the Cold War over, optimism for the future may spur consumers to start saving again. *The Wall Street Journal.*

Consumer Debt

Consumer debt growth rate slowing. Even with some monthly fluctuations, the growth rate of consumer debt and of consumer spending is slowing. Over the past two years, the ratio of debt to income grew only 0.4 percent annually, compared to 9.7 percent annual growth in previous years. *Cahners Economics in Graphics Arts Monthly.*

Consumer borrowing will slow. Many experts predict that cautious consumers will cause borrowing to grow less quickly over the next year, a turnaround from the early days of the economic expansion when borrowing grew faster than income.

Credit Unions

About a third of Americans (32 percent) now use a credit union, and an additional 24 percent say they could belong to one but choose not to. These percentages have not changed significantly in the last couple of years. However, membership patterns are changing. The 35- to 44-year-old age group, which had the highest membership percentage (44 percent) as recently as 1987, has dropped to 38 percent now. The reasons for this drop are still not clear, but must be examined because the Baby Boom now dominates this formerly peak membership group, and will for most of the 1990s. The industry cannot afford to be under-represented in this huge chunk of the market. Another warning is sounded by the dropping membership of younger-than-Boomer adults. It is of concern because eligibility is reported as particularly high among younger adults, and they are just choosing not to join. Typically, younger people get involved with their credit unions by taking out a loan. The increase of loan options (like dealer financing for autos) may be reducing involvement rates. Two things that may bring them in: information (they are twice as likely as others to feel underinformed about credit unions), and good reasons to join (appealing loan products). *Credit Union National Association Economics and Research.*

Main reasons people joined a credit union:		Main reasons people left a credit union:	
Convenience	17%	New job/company	28%
Ties to company	15%	Moved	19%
Good rates	12%	Lost job	11%
Payroll deductions	11%	Bad rates/fees/	
Get a loan	10%	service	9%
To save	10%	Retired	8%
Family/friend		CU is inconvenient	6%
recommended	7%		

Source: Credit Union National Association Economics and Research

Credit Union membership among mature Americans is increasing, and the 55- to 64-year-old group now has the highest percentage of membership (40 percent). Two reasons seem to be contributing to this shift: 1) good rates have been attracting pre-retirees into retirement savings plans (Boomers will begin to experience this need in about 10 years.) 2) many credit unions have offered special retirement plans that have attracted pre-retirees. Involvement among pre-retirees bodes well for continued involvement by seniors, and those age 65+ are already showing significantly higher involvement rates—19 percent belonged in 1987; now 26 percent do. It is worth noting that almost a third of all seniors (65+) don't know if they are eligible or not, and the participation increases have been primarily from those who knew their eligibility and have only now chosen to get involved. *Credit Union National Association Economics and Research.*

More blacks (37 percent) and Hispanics (36 percent) are credit union members than whites (32 percent), even though these minorities are under-represented in the income groups ($30-40,000 and $40-80,000) that have the highest membership percentages. Minority populations will steadily increase their share of the U.S. population, and with continued attention, credit unions can continue to hold their strong participation. *Credit Union National Association Economics and Research.*

Money Worries

Hype Alert: "Only the middle class and poor are worried about money."

Actually, everybody is worried about money. Nearly two-fifths of people (39 percent) say that it's more difficult to pay the bills now and have something left over than a few years ago—and this year men found it more difficult than women, a reflection of women's career progress. Topping the list of Americans' money worries is paying the mortgage. Even the affluent are worried—their households' mortgage fears have tripled, while the rest of the nation's have only doubled. *International Association. for Financial Planning.* In general, all Americans feel a growing insecurity about the underpinnings of the national economy, and consequently, their personal financial security.

Biggest economic and financial concerns facing households over the rest of this year

(multiple response results, total higher income = $50,000+ annual household income)

	Total Public			Total Higher Income		
	1989	**1988**	**1987**	**1989**	**1988**	**1987**
House payments	19%	9%	11%	21%	6%	10%
Monthly expenses	11%	13%	11%	7%	8%	6%
Taxes	11%	11%	9%	11%	12%	14%
Kids' college tuition	11%	8%	10%	17%	12%	19%
Car	10%	6%	7%	9%	4%	5%
Medical bills	9%	9%	15%	4%	3%	7%
Renovating/ refurnishing home	7%	2%	3%	7%	2%	4%
Groceries/food	5%	5%	6%	1%	1%	3%
Insurance rates	4%	4%	4%	4%	1%	3%
Job security	3%	4%	3%	2%	3%	2%
No real concerns	6%	15%	11%	7%	23%	19%

Source: International Association for Financial Planning

Affluent America

Affluents will preserve their wealth in the 1990s. In the 1980s this country saw an affluence explosion—Mendolsohn Media Research finds that the number of $50,000+ households quintupled during the Reagan years. In the 1990s, as the nation's economy slows down, we will see the newly wealthy working to preserve their affluent status. They will be saving more and looking for value for their dollar. Exemplifying these new preservationist values, a new image of affluents will emerge—the Influentials who will be best symbolized by three groups: Old Money (traditional affluents with traditional values), Entrepreneurs (the key status symbol in the '80s and into the '90s is owning a business), and Asian-Americans (the fastest growing ethnic group in America, and the wealthiest ethnic-origin group in the U.S.). *Town & Country.*

Percentage of households with incomes of $50,000+			
	Whites	**Blacks**	**Hispanics**
1972	18.2%	6.5%	7.2%
1976	17.2%	6.1%	6.9%
1980	16.9%	6.3%	8.2%
1984	18.6%	7.3%	9.0%
1988	22.1%	9.9%	10.8%

Note: figures are calculated in 1988 dollars
Source: Census Bureau in U.S. News & World Report

Adding to the ranks. More than 20 multimillion-dollar lotteries now take place across the country each week, creating some 100 new millionaires each month, says Univ. of Southern California marketing professor Jagdish Sheth. This means that at least 120,000 more lottery millionaires will be added to the ranks of more than a million American millionaires by the end of the century. *Adweek's Marketing to the Year 2000.*

Banking

Satisfaction up with ATMs. Consumers like their banks more (69 percent rated them good/excellent in '87; 77 percent in '89), particularly the service they are getting. And the most service-satisfied (execs, affluents, the best-educated) are the biggest users of ATMs. ATM usage and availability are both rising. *The Public Pulse, the Roper Organization.*

Banking packages increase in popularity. Competition for Americans' dollars has banks scrambling to lure customers. Potential customers are being offered packages that include free checking, savings, deposit box, and so on, all in exchange for a CD or line of credit as an attempt to capture new depositors. Niche marketing hasn't escaped the banking industry, as these packages are now being segment-specific marketed. *The Wall Street Journal.*

Supermarket banking. In an effort to grab customers, banks (especially in the Midwest and the South) are now offering small, full-service branches in supermarkets. Supermarket banking is far more convenient for most people, and logical, considering consumer traffic in supermarkets (1.3 visits/week) is greater than in department stores or bank branch offices. *The Wall Street Journal.*

The most important factors in choosing a bank. The number-one thing that influences customers' bank choice is branch location (4.21, on a one-to-five scale, with one being the lowest score), followed by deposit interest rates (4.19), account fees (3.88), branch hours (3.81), automated teller machines (3.02), and premium gifts (1.59). *American Banker.*

What people look for in a bank
(mean scores on a scale of 1-5; five is highest)

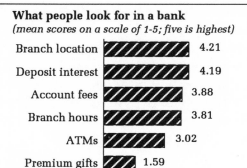

Branch location	4.21
Deposit interest	4.19
Account fees	3.88
Branch hours	3.81
ATMs	3.02
Premium gifts	1.59

Source: American Banker

Important factors in choosing a new bank

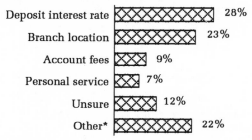

Deposit interest rate	28%
Branch location	23%
Account fees	9%
Personal service	7%
Unsure	12%
Other*	22%

Bank security and soundness, branch hours, ATMs.
Source: American Banker

In selecting the ideal bank, not necessarily the one you use, how important are the following: (mean score on 1 to 10 scale, 10=very important)

	White	Black	Hispanic	Asian/ Native Amer.
The rates you are paid on interest-bearing accounts	8.34	7.90	8.39	8.07
Local community ownership of bank or savings/loan	6.36	6.36	6.52	6.14
Fees you pay for the services	7.80	6.74	7.26	7.00
American ownership	8.59	8.10	8.52	6.80

Source: SRI/BAN Poll, The Gallup/BAN Poll

Poverty

Poverty is basically unabated. Although U.S. per capita income reached an all-time high of $13,120 in 1988 (up 1.7 percent since

1987) this did little to help the nation's poor. In 1988, the poverty rate was 13.1 percent, virtually unchanged from 1987's level, 13.4 percent. And although the number of poor and the poverty rate have declined since 1983's high of 15.2 percent, it is not near 1978's low of 11.4 percent. *Census Bureau.*

Hype Alert: "Children living in poverty are mainly welfare-dependent inner-city kids in large families."
Currently, one out of every four children under age six lives in poverty in the U.S., and more than half of them have at least one working parent (53 percent), live outside urban areas (28 percent in surburban and 26 percent in rural areas), and in small families (51 percent live in families with two children or fewer). Little more than a quarter (28 percent) of poor young children live in families that rely completely on public assistance. Children under six are more likely to be poor than any other age group in the U.S. *Columbia University, as reported in the Wall Street Journal.*

Currently one in five children under age 18 lives in poverty. About 15 percent of all white children lived in families below the poverty level in 1988, compared to 38 percent of children in Hispanic families, and 44 percent in black families. *Census Bureau.*

Philanthropy
Giving is at an all-time high. In 1988, philanthropic giving reached record levels, an estimated $104 billion. This is almost three-quarters the amount that Americans saved. Individuals account for the majority of contributors (83 percent). Giving even outpaced the inflation rate in '87-'88, increasing 6.7 percent, while inflation only grew 4.78 percent. *AAFRC Trust for Philanthropy. "Between 1985 and 1987, average giving declined by about 23 percent, but only a portion of this decrease was caused by the increase in the implicit price of giving that was legislated in the 1986 tax reform." National Bureau of Economic Research.*

Hype Alert: "Those who have more give more."
Actually, those with less give more. Households with income levels below $10,000 (the poverty level is $11,611 for a family of four) give 2.8 percent of their earnings to charitable organizations (primarily churches), while households with income from $50,000 to $75,000 give only 1.5 percent. Of course, upscalers give more in total dollars. *Independent Sector.*

Women

Wives' wages increase faster than husbands. The average earnings of working wives grew twice as fast as their husbands' from 1981 to 1987. Wives' earnings grew 23 percent, from $10,740 in '81 to $13,250 in '87 (inflation adjusted), whereas their spouses' earnings grew only 12 percent, from $26,080 to $29,150. Despite this increase, working wives still average less than half their husbands' earnings, though wives who work full-time fare better, making 57 percent of their full-time working husbands' earnings. Some reasons for the rise in wives' income: more wives are working full time, up from 44 percent in 1981 to 50 percent in 1987; wives in 1987 were more likely to be better educated, work in professional and managerial jobs, and have no children under 18. There has also been an increase in the number of wives who earn more than their husbands, up from 4.1 million in 1981 to 5.3 million in 1987. *Census Bureau.*

The wage gap decreases slowly. The male/female wage gap holds at 66¢ in 1989, reduced 10 percent since 1980. *Census Bureau.*

Percent of women age 18-49 who say, "I have a plan for my future financial security that I follow every month"	
Total women	22%
Homemakers	19%
Employed wives—children	23%
Employed wives—no children	32%
Unmarried under age 30	12%
Unmarried age 30-44	26%
Age 45 or over	32%
Two-job couples	22%
Dual career couples	31%

Source: Self

Women are gaining more financial clout. A *Ms.* magazine readers poll found that between 1977 (average age of respondent was 29) and 1988 (average age was 37), women had more home loans in their own name (up from 36 percent to 58 percent), and an increase in the amount of cash they carry (in 1977, 4 percent carried more than $50 with them; now 28 percent do).

Baby Boomers

Boomers are entering the big money years in the 1990s, increasing their spending power more than 90 percent. From the present until the turn of the century, almost 70 percent of the growth in the nation's income will be created by people aged 35 to 50, primarily Boomers. By the year 2000, 35 percent of households headed by 35- to 50-year-olds will be earning more than $50,000. *Town & Country.* Three basic keys to marketing to the Boomers: 1) they like change, get bored easily; 2) they are pragmatic, seek authenticity, hunger for information, and are hype-hip; 3) there is a huge gulf between the older Boomers and younger Boomers. The older have had a much easier economic ride, and are more expansive and relaxed with their money. The younger have grown into adulthood with economic limitations, and are more money-focused, often suffering from a feeling of financial scarcity. *American Marketing Association*

Aging Boomers are doing little about retirement planning. While 97 percent of Boomers say that ensuring a steady source of income at retirement is important, only half (53 percent) say they are doing very well or extremely well at retirement preparation. Currently, Boomers are too busy worrying about how to pay for their kids' education (37 percent), reducing credit burdens (36 percent), and making ends meet (35 percent). Nearly two-fifths (39 percent) of Boomers say they have no idea how much money they'll need for retirement, and 65 percent say they say they have not spent enough time planning for retirement. Less than a quarter of Boomers (23 percent) feel that they will be able to retire (preferably at age 60) without lowering their standard of living. *IDS Financial Services.*

Why people are not doing a lot of saving for retirement

	total	Boomers (age 25-44)	pre-retirees (age 45-64)
Plan to live on less than current income	36%	30%	41%
Not enough money left over to save after basic living expenses	29%	34%	24%
Relying primarily on a company pension	21%	23%	20%
Intimidated by how hard it is to set aside enough to retire on	19%	21%	17%
There's still plenty of time to save for retirement	18%	22%	15%
Plan to continue working well past age 65	18%	14%	21%
More concerned with saving/paying for children's education	17%	20%	14%

Source: IDS Financial Services

Mature Market

The big wave. The mature market has been the darling of the marketing world throughout the 1980s, as the realization of the power of the age wave washed over business America. However, the clout of the mature market has yet to hit anything like it is going to. Beginning at the end of the century, 76 million Baby Boomers turn mature. In 1990, 25.8 percent of the U.S. population will be 50+; in the year 2000, this will increase to 28.4 percent; in 2010, to 33.7 percent; and in 2020, the number will reach 37.2 percent. *The Mature Market by Probus Publishing.*

Senior income growing. Between 1990 and 1995, the median household income for households headed by 55- to 64-year-olds will increase from $26,100 to $27,020. During this same time, the number of households with incomes over $50,000 headed by 55- to 64-year-olds will rise 7 percent, while those with incomes of less than $10,000 will decrease 4.4 percent. *1990-1991 Almanac of Consumer Markets, American Demographics.*

More spending power. Mature Americans have $900 billion dollars combined annual income, with an estimated $160 billion in discretionary income. Nearly 80 percent of savings dollars in S&Ls and 68 percent of all money-market accounts are controlled by the 55+ group. The spending power of matures (age 55+) is five times that of people under 30. Mature Americans account for 75 percent of the U.S.'s assets, and half its discretionary spending power. The average annual household income of matures (50+) is almost 22 percent greater than that of households headed by 20- to 49-year-olds. *Senior Direct.*

Youth

It costs more to have a baby today. In real dollars (inflation adjusted), it cost almost $3,000 more to raise a baby for one year in 1990 than it did in 1958. According to *American Demographics* (January 1990), in 1990, the typical baby cost Mom and Dad almost $6,000 before its first birthday. In 1958, it cost only $800 (that's $2,892 in 1990 dollars).

Average costs of a baby in its first year		
(dollars not adjusted for inflation)		
	1958	1990
Bedding, bath supplies	$54	$223
Clothes	127	352
Day care	*	2,184
Diapers	38	570
Food, feeding equipment	216	855
Furniture	199	995
Medicine, vitamins and personal care	82 **	396
Toys	43	199
Total cost	$800	$5,774

*Not calculated; **includes formula
Source: Life Magazine *and* American Demographics, *as cited in the New York Times*

Children's money. There are 32 million children in American aged 4 to 12, and they have an annual income of $8.6 billion. Where are they getting all this dough? See the chart below.

Annual income of children aged 4 to 12	
source	earnings (in millions)
Allowances	$4,580
Household tasks	1,296
Parental gifts	1,296
Work outside the home	1,037
Gifts from others	432
Total	8,641

Source: James McNeal, Texas A&M University, as cited in The Marketer

Increasing teen population with money to spend. The Census Bureau says there are a little more than 13 million 14- to 17-year-olds in the U.S. By the year 2000, their population is expected to increase to more than 15 million. Currently, teens 12-19 receive a mean amount of $64.20 a week. *Teenage Research Unlimited.*

Mean amount of money received per week by age group	
age group	amount of money
12-15	$24.00
16-17	61.70
18-19	134.80
Average	**$64.20**

How teens get their money	male	female
Full-time job	13.2%	11.9%
Part-time job	33.3%	30.0%
Odd jobs	37.9%	38.6%
Regular allowance	27.8%	27.3%
Obtain money from parents when needed	37.5%	48.4%

Source: Teenage Research Unlimited

6

The Sophisticated Shopper

"Consumers will be more isolated, more regionalized, more fragmented, more individualistic, more demanding, more informed, more stressed, more discriminating. In a nutshell, harder to get."
—*Adweek Marketing to the Year 2000*

Is shopping leisure, or is it a chore? For some it is still the great American pastime; for others it is a drag to be sped through. Just as leisure and work have splintered into dozens of different expressions, so shopping has fragmented, driven by differing demands and attitudes. Consequently, there are more ways to shop than ever before, many of which do not require leaving the house—phone shopping, TV shopping networks, online shopping, catalogs, direct mail. The store is no longer the only site of sales, and retail is changing dramatically. And brand names? "Brillo" may have more impact as an art work than as an inducement to buy a particular steel wool pad.

A word of caution: In the '90s, marketers had better be careful about how and to whom they are selling their products. Americans aren't taking kindly to marketers who are making a buck at the expense of their customers' health or the environment. Consumer activism is rising, and extremely vocal Americans are scrutinizing products and companies like never before. Boycotts have become chic. The Seattle based newsletter, *National Boycott News*, "has logged more than 200 protests coming from both the political left and right and aimed at American and foreign companies." *The New York Times.* Some examples of the new consumer activism:

- In New York City, anti-smoking activist Joe Cherner attempts to stop tobacco companies from distributing cigarette samples—samples that he documents are ending up in minors hands.

- The whitewashing of inner-city billboards that promote cigarettes and tobacco to minorities. Grass-roots activists, who were previously protesting R.J. Reynold's targeting of blacks with its Uptown cigarette, are now attacking advertising of all products that are injurious to minorities' health.

- Tuna boycotts by consumers who are disturbed that dolphins are being inadvertently killed by tuna fisherman has led the three major distributors of tuna in the U.S. to institute a policy of purchasing tuna that is caught only by means that do not injure dolphins—before such policies became mandated.

Brand Loyalty

Everyone agrees there are too many brands. The clutter-confronted consumer is becoming more perceptive in distinguishing between and among brands, and he/she likes having many high-quality brands to choose from (particularly affluent consumers). However, marketers are not succeeding in presenting the salient attributes of their products amid the clutter, and consumers are not seeing new products as new. Consumers like the price competition, but have become numb to newness for the sake of newness. Consumers seem most aware of brand clutter in the food aisles—over half (52 percent) feel there are already too many choices in the cereal aisle, and only 4 percent would like to have more cereal options. *The Public Pulse, the Roper Organization.*

Recognition of differences among some brand categories

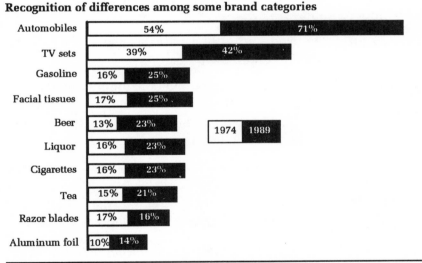

Source: Roper Reports, as cited in Adweek's Marketing Week

Upholding brand image. To uphold a brand image on the retail level, the meaning to be conveyed must be consistent. For example, additions to a merchandise line must be consistent with what the consumer thinks is the manufacturer's area of expertise. Overall, those who care about brands tend to be disproportionately younger, affluent, and black. Retailers and manufacturers must prevent competing brands from becoming so indistinct that "the brand is vulnerable to being evaluated, like a commodity, primarily on the basis of price." *Management Horizons.*

Pumping up brand image. To give fading brands a second chance, firms must capitalize on consumers' fond memories. Rejuvenating aging brands is cheaper and less chancy than trying to create brands from scratch. Marketing consultants estimate that though consumer-product companies today spend at least $20 million to introduce a new brand, over 70 percent of new brands will flop. *The New York Times.*

Americans' shopping habits have changed.

- Today's savvy consumer puts bargain prices, nutritional and environmental concerns, and other priorities ahead of old-fashioned brand loyalty.

- Of 25 products used, more than half the users of 17 of the products say they're brand switchers.

- Brand loyalty is stronger among older consumers. Nearly one-fourth of participants age 60 and older claim brand loyalty for more than 10 of the 25 products in the survey; only 9 percent of those age 18-29 have such strong allegiance.

- Higher-income people also tend to be more brand loyal these days. The bottom end of the market is becoming less loyal— they're buying whatever is cheaper. The wild card is the Baby Boom generation. They have shown less allegiance so far.

- Consumers believe all brands are about the same in a number of categories, particularly credit cards, paper towels, dry soups, and snack chips. *Wall Street Journal Centennial Survey.*

Consumer trends: How brands function

- Time-scarce, dual-income households: Brand names function as time savers.

- Older and more educated consumers: Rely more on their own abilities to evaluate products than they do on brand cues. Well-known alone isn't enough.

- Secondary shoppers (like teens): Reach for well-known, familiar, advertised brands.

- Fragmentation of consumer markets: More specifically targeted brands, particularly in the case of private store brands being in tune with core customers.

- Growth in minority populations: Brand names function as a means of reducing risk (especially social risk), in particular among the less assimilated (e.g., Hispanics and new Asian arrivals).

- Income distribution polarization: Upper end wants brands to function as time-savers rather than risk-reducers. The lower end will expect brands to reduce financial risks. *Management Horizons.*

What motivates store brand purchases?

	Strong interest	Moderate interest	No interest
"Compare and save" signage	48%	33%	16%
Nutrition/ingredient equivalency signage	54%	30%	13%
Guarantee of satisfaction	53%	29%	17%

Source: The Lempert Report/Gallup Study for PLMA.

Brand parity running high internationally. Two-thirds of international consumers find that various brands, in diverse product categores, have no relevant differences because technological advances allow competitiors almost immediately to imitate a new product's performance, and the growth of global consumer parity has marketers developing similar products. *BBDO Worldwide.*

Retailing

The customer will be harder to get. The slowing of population growth, and smaller supply of young people (the Baby Bust, babies born between 1965 and 1976, is about half the size of the Baby

Boom generation—37 million Busters vs. 76 million Boomers—also the Baby Boomlet has peaked) will cause retailers to scramble for customers. Also, developers have over-stored many areas. There are twice as many stores as the American population needs, and more are being built every day. The 1990s should see a dramatic slowdown in new store construction. *Find/SVP.*

Types of growing retail stores. "The competitive trend toward incorporating all merchandise categories under one roof will probably continue over the 1990s. Distended forms—superstores, super warehouses, superspecialty stores, hypermarkets, and hypermalls—may completely supersede the mass merchandiser and department store sectors. In complement, focusing on a particular aspect of merchandise or a specific merchandising variable, will proliferate. Micro retailing doesn't mean small—just highly concentrated." *Find/SVP.*

Retail turns theater. Retailers, and not just upscale ones, are now discovering the power and value of spectacle, or the "theatricalization of the store environment"—aesthetic atmosphere, entertainment, increased services and amenities, and higher quality merchandise. Hypermalls are beginning to incorporate golf courses, swimming pools, theaters, sports areas, and other attractions to draw shoppers in. *Find/SVP.*

Department stores continue to lose customers to specialty shops. "Department store market share has decreased during the last decade primarily because of the emergence of specialty store retailers. More recently the causes are: 1) Consumers do not form store loyalties quickly in a high-growth market of a highly transient population. 2) Merchandisers may still be using a macromarketing approach instead of a micro-marketing one. 3) Too few department stores in a market limits consumer choice, or too many department stores offer too many options." *MarkeTrend, Impact Resources.*

Department store-within-store trend continues. Department stores will continue to add specialty departments and perpetuate the store-within-a-store trend. *Find/SVP.*

Department stores lose customers; discount stores gain them. The number of Americans that have visited a chain department store during a typical month has dropped from 65 percent in 1974 to 47 percent in 1990. During the same period, the number visiting discount stores has grown from 61 percent to 65 percent. Two reasons for decreasing patronage in department stores: less leisure time; middle-class income squeeze. *The Public Pulse, The Roper Organization.*

Hypermarkets aren't taking off. There are only five major hypermarket operators in the U.S., and their success has been moderate— as of January 1989, no U.S. hypermarket had yet made a profit. *Chain Store Age.*

Home shopping is growing by leaps and bounds. The largest growth in non-store retailing (companies selling directly to retail customers) has been in TV home shopping. It increased 360 percent from 1986 to 1988 to $1.6 billion. By 2000, it could reach $10 billion. The largest market in non-store retailing is direct retail marketing (mail order, door to door, and party plan sales) at $57.7 billion in 1988. *Find/SVP.*

TV home shopping is also growing. TV home shopping will be a $1.58 billion market by the end of 1989, and by 1991 it will grow to $2.02 billion. The industry is expected to experience annual growth of 12-13 percent over the next few years. *PK Services, as cited in Marketing News.*

Prodigy, the interactive computer shopping catalog by Sears, expects to have 10 million customers by the year 2000. Earlier, duller versions of interactive home shopping have not done well. Prodigy, on the other hand, presents itself as fun. User friendly, the system offers creative graphics and a greater variety of options— news, weather, sports updates, games, health tips, and so on. It is expected to succeed where videotext failed, and is far less expensive, with customized shopping features. *Find/SVP.*

Catalogs are multiplying like bunnies. There were 116 catalogs per U.S. household produced in 1987. In 1987, of the 88 million persons who used mail order, 56 percent were women. *Direct Marketing Association.*

Clothing is the most popular mail order purchase—93 percent of buyers purchase clothing, followed by non-food gifts (80 percent), gardening products (71 percent), home furnishings (70 percent), housewares (66 percent), food (62 percent), hardware (61 percent), and sporting goods (49 percent). *Direct Marketing Association.*

Uniqueness is valued in mail order purchases. Catalog buyers are generally married, college-educated, homeowners, 30 years or older. In some product categories (clothing, home furnishings) uniqueness is even more valued than price. *Direct Marketing Association.* Most (52 percent) mail order shoppers use the service to save time. Catalog shoppers are very or extremely satisfied with the goods they receive (77 percent). *Maritz Marketing Research.*

In the Supermarket

Who is doing the family shopping? The media has been reporting that everyone—men, teens, and children—does the family grocery shopping. This is partially true. Though men, and kids are helping out more with the family grocery shopping, and are influencing some purchases, you're still more likely to see Mom pushing a cart down the aisle. According to a Gallup survey on dining habits, nearly three-quarters of women say they do *most* of the shopping and cooking.

Teens

- Teens spend an estimated $40 billion on groceries and other family items. *Deloitte & Touche/Impact Resources.*

- The average age of primary teen grocery shoppers is 15.5. *Deloitte & Touche/Impact Resources.*

- Most primary teen grocery shoppers come from households with annual incomes below $10,000; almost a third come from minority homes. *Deloitte & Touche/Impact Resources.*

Teens in the grocery store		
(percent of teens)		
Shop for food	**1987**	**1988**
yes	70%	73%
no	30%	27%
Of yes how often		
More than once a week	14%	18%
Once a week	22%	26%
Once every two weeks	17%	16%
Average amount spent per visit		
<$10	11%	18%
$10-$19.99	14%	16%
$20-$29.99	12%	11%
$30-$49.99	15%	15%
$50 or more	46%	39%

Source: Food & Beverage Marketing

- **Specific brand names are not important to teens.** Though grocery shopping teens purchase national brands 77 percent of the time, only 12 percent rate specific brand names as an important factor in their product selection (down from 16 percent in 1987). *Scholastic, Inc.*

- **Fewer teens are making up their own shopping lists.** Only 45 percent of food shopping teens developed their own grocery lists in 1988, compared to 62 percent in 1987. With teens making more purchase decisions in-store, the importance of teen targeted point-of-purchase campaigns is obvious. *Scholastic, Inc.*

Young Women
Hype Alert: "Young women are doing all the family grocery shopping now that moms are working."

A *Seventeen* study of young women 13- to 21-years-old finds they are definitely helping out with the grocery shopping, but the majority are not responsible for the major family food shopping. While 69 percent of young women have gone grocery shopping at least once during the past month, only 29 percent of these shoppers did major food shopping. The majority (63 percent) did fill-in shopping. The average amount spent per week by these young women is $46, or 44 percent of their families' total food expenditure for groceries ($101.20). Two-thirds of young women (69 percent) say they did grocery shopping in the last two weeks. Here's what they filled their carts with:

The 12 most popular grocery items bought by young women 13-21 when grocery shopping in the last two weeks
(of those who have grocery shopped in the last two weeks)

milk	67.0%	ice cream-regular	35.3%
bread	58.2%	beef/veal/lamb/pork	33.6%
gum	47.6%	soaps	32.8%
potato chips	39.8%	diet cola	32.1%
regular cola	38.9%	margarine	32.1%
cold cuts	37.9%	pre-sweetened cold cereal	31.6%

Source: Seventeen *magazine*

Children

Time-pressed parents are relying on their children to do some of the family shopping chores.

- Sixteen percent of parents with children 7 to 17 years old say their kids help with the family grocery shopping, and 8 percent say their kids do the grocery shopping. Children play a significant role in grocery shopping in 25 percent of all households that have kids 7 to 17 years old.

- Over a quarter (27 percent) of child-shopper households furnish Junior with a list of things to be bought. However, 18 percent of these households let the children choose the products. In the majority of child-shopper households kids are given a list, but can make adjustments as long as they buy the essentials. *The Public Pulse, The Roper Organization.*

Children influence brand purchases. A third or more of children aged 7 to 17 have an influence on the specific brands of food that the family purchases. *USA Today/Roper Organization in the Public Pulse, 2/90.*

Hype Alert: "Men are sharing the food shopping responsibility."

Men *are not* sharing food shopping responsibility equally, and *are not* likely to do most of the picking and choosing when they go food shopping.

- Less than half (43 percent) of men who are married to or living with a woman either help their partner do the grocery shopping or do most of the shopping themselves. Of those who share shopping responsibilities, 41 percent say that the woman does most of the shopping, while 35 percent say that the male and female shop together.

- With regard to brand decisions, 56 percent say that the female decides on most of the purchases, but 37 percent say that the male and female decide together. Men also tend to buy products based on brand: 63 percent choose the brand of soft drink; 61 percent, snack food; 53 percent, soup; 48 percent, over-the-counter drugs.

- More than 50 million adult men shop for their household's groceries at least part of the time, spending about $98.8 billion a year at the supermarket. Men who are more educated, earning more than $25,000 a year, in relationships, and in dual-earner households are the most likely to voice their opinions to their partners-in-shopping, even though women are most likely to have the final say. *Men's Health.*

Influential factors on brand decision-making, (percent very/somewhat influential)

men ■ ▨ women

56% 58%	60% 61%	72% 75%	81% 84%
brand you grew up with	brand name	price	experience using the product

Source: Men's Health

Since the 1980s, groceries can be found everywhere—in pharmacies, gas stations, convenience stores, department stores, even hardware stores. Groceries are the second largest U.S. retail industry, accounting for 20 percent of all retail spending (autos are largest, with 22 percent). Yet, even in the face of omnipresent competition, grocery stores took in 5.3 percent more in 1988 sales than in 1987. This small but sustained growth was a bit ahead of inflation, a bit behind overall retail growth.

The watchwords in grocery buying are not new, but continue to be strong—convenient and fresh. Service delis increased sales 21 percent during 1988, in-store bakeries rose 29 percent (a 15-percent increase in one year in share of grocery store sales), and all the fresh food departments saw increases (though meat and produce saw their *share* of sales decrease because of more dynamic growth in other departments). *Supermarket Business magazine.*

The average U.S. household weekly spending in grocery stores, 1988 and 1987, and percentage change

	1988	1987	% change
Perishables	**$30.21**	**$28.78**	**+4.9%**
Baked goods	$2.55	$2.27	+12.3%
Dairy	$4.44	$4.19	+5.9%
Frozen foods	$3.18	$3.05	+4.2%
Fresh meat/provisions	$10.96	$8.61	+27.2%
Fresh fish	$.73	$.77	-5.4%
Fresh poultry	$1.74	$1.63	+6.7%
Produce	$5.67	$5.57	+1.8%
In-store bakery	$1.29	$1.01	+27.7%
In-store deli	$2.02	$1.68	+20.2%
Dry grocery (food)	**$18.39**	**$18.07**	**+1.7%**
Beer	$2.98	$3.03	-1.6%
Wine, liquor, coolers	$.63	$.66	-4.7%
Baby food	$.45	$.41	+9.7%
Breakfast foods	$1.43	$1.29	+.8%
Candy/chewing gum	$.73	$.73	—

Canned foods			
Fruits	$.36	$.34	+5.8%
Juices/drinks	$.83	$.76	+9.2%
Meat/poultry	$.31	$.31	—
Milk	$.07	$.08	-4.3%
Seafood/fish	$.42	$.39	+7.6%
Soups	$.38	$.46	-1.0%
Vegetables	$.65	$.64	+1.5%
Prepared drinks	$1.56	$1.62	-3.8%
Dried foods	$.61	$.57	+7.0%
Jams/jellies/preserves	$.42	$.42	—
Pasta	$.24	$.23	+4.3%
Desserts	$.12	$.12	—
Soft drinks	$2.10	$2.02	+3.9%
Sugar	$.30	$.30	—
Miscellaneous	$3.80	$3.69	+3.0%
Dry grocery (nonfood)	**$8.53**	**$8.32**	**+2.5%**
Paper goods	$2.30	$2.08	+.5%
Soaps/detergents	$1.17	$1.15	+1.7%
Other household supplies	$.88	$1.13	-22.0%
Pet foods	$1.24	$1.19	+4.2%
Tobacco products	$2.94	$2.77	+6.1%
General merchandise	**$5.25**	**$5.02**	**+4.6%**
Health/beauty aids	$2.60	$2.44	+6.5%
Prescriptions	$.45	$.43	+4.6%
Housewares	$.25	$.24	+4.1%
All other general merch.	$1.95	$1.91	+2.1%
All other sales	***$2.54***	***$2.35***	***+8.0%***
Grand total	**$65.68**	**$62.54**	**+5.0%**

Source: Supermarket Business *magazine*

Characteristics of grocery buyers according to place of purchase.

Traditional grocery store—Consumers who shop in traditional grocery stores are 21 percent more likely than the average population to be homemakers. They are also older than the average population and use coupons regularly.

Super Warehouses—Super warehouse shoppers are likely to be from dual-income households, and they are 16 percent more likely than the average person to shop at convenience stores regularly. Shopping at super warehouses is popular among minorities, especially blacks and Hispanics.

Hypermarkets—Hypermarket consumers are more likely to be married than the average consumer. These consumers, although shopping less often, spend 16 percent more per trip on groceries than the average population does.

Membership warehouse clubs—The consumers who shop at these clubs have a higher average income and greater number of dual-income households compared to the average population. They spend an average of $79 per trip on groceries, or 43 percent more than the average population. *Deloitte & Touche/Impact Resources.*

Frequent users' clubs grow in popularity. To win back consumer brand loyalty, some merchandisers are awarding free merchandise to consumers who clip UPC codes from certain brand name packages. Consumers save their clippings to accumulate points, which are then presented in return for free merchandise via participating frequent users clubs. *Adweek's Marketing Week.*

Generic labels disappearing. Consumers' fears about inflation (creating the generic boom in the late '70s), have decreased, prompting the generic slide. Other reasons include 1) chains found that carrying generics was no longer a forceful selling point; by 1982, nearly all major supermarket chains were offering these products, so promotion decreased. 2) major advertisers, nervous about slackening sales for higher-priced brand goods, countered with heavy coupon promotion. Consumers ate it up, especially when major chains offered to double the cents-off value, thereby giving shoppers brand name goods for nearly generic prices. *SAMI.*

Product introductions are down, while line extensions are growing more popular. The annual rate of new products introduced was down 11 percent in 1989 from the prior year. *The Lempert Report.* The majority of food company execs say that in the last five years, over half of the new products introduced were extensions of existing lines, and 90 percent say that this trend will continue into the next five years. *Group EFO Limited, as cited in the Lempert Report.*

Product Quality

Americans rate the quality of American products slightly ahead of Japanese products. More than half (56 percent) of Americans feel that the "Made in U.S.A." label means they are buying a quality product most of the time. Only 45 percent of Americans say this about products that have "Made in Japan" labels. The country foremost in Americans' minds as a producer of high-quality goods is the U.S.—44 percent of people think of the U.S. first, followed by Japan (38 percent) and West Germany (8 percent). Interestingly, of those Americans who purchased a product of exceptionally poor quality, a plurality also say the product was made in the U.S.A. (43 percent), followed by Japan (14 percent), and Taiwan (8 percent). Product categories in which American-made goods are perceived as poorer quality than other countries' goods are televisions (56 percent of Americans feel other countries produce better-quality TVs) and automobiles (52 percent). Product areas in which American-made products are seen as being of better quality than other countries' are major appliances (88 percent), clothing (82 percent), and telephones (71 percent). *Time/CNN/Yankelovich Clancy Shulman.*

Car Buying

Car sales are expected to grow more slowly until the year 2000, prompting car dealers to be more attentive to customers. *Adweek Marketing to the Year 2000.* Passenger car sales in the U.S. are expected to grow less than 1 percent per year over the next decade, from 10.1 million in 1990 to 10.9 million in 2000. Light truck sales will also grow slowly, but faster than passenger car sales. *Leasing cars is expected to boom,* climbing from 15 percent of new-car sales today to 27 percent in 2000. The average total lifespan of cars is also expected to climb to 12 years by 2000, from 11 years in 1990. *David Cole, University of Michigan.*

People are keeping cars longer. Only 8 percent of Americans plan to keep a new car for two years or less; 14 percent say three years, 16 percent say four, 26 percent say five, and 15 percent a decade or more. Median ownership is 5.3 years for domestics and 5.6 for imports. *Motor Vehicles Manufacturers Association.*

There is growing parity in consumer's view of cars—satisfaction with the best (Asian) cars improved in 1989, and the worst (domestic) improved even more. For the first time since the Customer Satisfaction Index was introduced, domestics pulled ahead of European cars, but Asian cars still lead. *J.D. Power & Assoc.*

The role of the salesperson grows in importance. As consumers' view of auto quality approaches parity, sales performance is becoming the key ingredient in overall customer satisfaction in the first year of ownership. U.S. nameplates lead the others in this category, mostly because older consumers buy more U.S. cars, and are more satisfied with all sales experiences. *J.D. Power & Assoc.*

Car burglar alarms. In the past six years the number of households owning car burglar alarms has increased 69 percent. Currently, 5.6 million households (6.1 percent of the population) own them. *Mediamark Research, as cited in Adweek's Marketing Week.*

Hype Alert: "Hispanics love and buy American-made cars."
Partially true. They still love them; they just can't afford them. It's a tradition—Hispanics overwhelmingly prefer American cars (82 percent vs. 45 percent of the U.S. public). *Market Development Inc.* But now Hispanics are buying imported cars at a greater rate than non-Hispanics, and purchasing domestics less frequently. The decision is money-motivated—Hispanics are younger than non-Hispanic car buyers, with larger families and lighter paychecks. They cannot afford higher-priced, though preferred, domestic makes. *R.L. Polk.*

Hispanic and non-Hispanic car purchases

	Hispanics
Full-size	8% / 16%
Intermediate	15% / 19%
Compact	19% / 19%
Subcompact	12% / 13%
Economy import	27% / 17%
Other import	18% / 16%

Hispanics
Non-Hispanics

Source: R.L. Polk

Hype Alert: "Car sellers should continue to pitch to men."

Big mistake. Women are influencing the majority (80 percent) of today's new car purchases. They bought 36 percent of new cars in the U.S. in 1980, are buying 47 percent currently, and will buy 50 percent in 1995—possibly 65 percent in 2000. They also are more likely than men to take their cars in for servicing (3.8 times/year vs. 3.3 times/year, respectively). Though both sexes have similar service attitudes, women place more importance on convenience and trustworthiness when deciding to return to a dealership for service after the first year. *Family Circle.* In general, however, women do not like car ads obviously targeted at them; they say they want to be spoken to as if they were any car purchaser, not a female car purchaser.

Reasons for selecting a dealership or non-dealership as usual service facility after first year of ownership

	Dealership		Non-dealership	
	Male	Female	Male	Female
Good quality work	24%	16%	14%	21%
Convenient location	16%	20%	19%	31%
Know me/know my car	14%	16%	7%	8%
Competent mechanics	15%	15%	10%	8%
Fast service	6%	7%	18%	16%
Friendly/polite	6%	10%	9%	12%
Good parts availability	6%	4%	-	-
Trustworthy/reliable	5%	10%	14%	22%
Reasonable/inexpensive	4%	4%	39%	43%
Convenient service hours	1%	1%	7%	6%

Source: Family Circle

Women buy less expensive cars. Women car buyers are relatively young with lower incomes. Women buy 55 percent of all sub-compacts, 44 percent of all mid-sized cars, but only 28 percent of more expensive cars. *Ford Motor Co.* Women purchased over half (52 percent) of all imported cars bought in the U.S. in 1988. *Reuters.* Women account for 61 percent of all new car buyers under 25 years, and 49 percent of car buyers aged 25 to 45. Men buy 72 percent of all cars sold to those 45 years old and up. *Motor Vehicles Manufacturers Association.*

Hype Alert: "All pickup buyers are good ol' boys."
The truth is that pickup buyers have become more upscale. The profile of the average pickup buyer is a 38-year-old (who feels 30), metropolitan, college-educated, married male, with a household income of $59,000/year. The profile of the pickup buyer has upscaled as the sales proportions of the two primary types of pickups have shifted. In 1986 there were twice as many compact pickups as compact sports utility trucks sold, now they are almost even. Compact sports utilities cost 52 percent more (median total 1989 price $17,500 vs. $11,500 for compact pickups), and attract that Yuppie-image buyer. The compact pickup buyer is still that younger, less-affluent, less-metropolitan young man. *Newsweek.*

Share of compact truck market	Total Compact Trucks	Share of total Compact Pickup	Compact Sport Utility
Household income			
Less than $30,000	23%	76%	24%
$30,000-$49,999	32%	59%	41%
$50,000-$74,999	24%	45%	55%
$75,000+	21%	27%	73%
Male	81%	57%	43%
Female	19%	34%	66%
Under age 25	12%	69%	31%
25-44 years	56%	45%	55%
45+	32%	56%	44%
High school or less	39%	67%	33%
Some college	30%	51%	49%
College grad +	30%	35%	65%
Professional/manager	53%	40%	60%

Blue collar	29%	71%	29%
Spouse employed	73%	46%	54%
Spouse not employed	27%	59%	41%
East	20%	31%	69%
North Central	20%	57%	43%
South	35%	59%	41%
West	24%	58%	42%
Counties with population of 150,000+	64%	48%	52%
Counties of less than 150,000 pop.	36%	62%	38%

Source: Newsweek

Women shoppers

Women's buying considerations have changed in the past three years. Now women:	
Compare prices more	77%
Shop more carefully	75%
Use coupons more	74%
Look for more sales	72%
Read labels more	65%
Buy more items	37%
Buy fewer items	36%
Buy more expensive foods	16%

Source: Conde Nast

Women are mall shoppers. The plurality of general items shopped for by women are bought in malls (46 percent), neighborhood stores (28 percent), and downtown stores (17 percent). Women will purchase 43 percent of the items they shop for in the first store they visit. *Newspaper Advertising Bureau.*

Women are unhappy with clothes offerings. Most women like clothes shopping (71 percent), but the majority (59 percent) are buying fewer pieces, and the plurality (40 percent) say they have less money to spend. *Newsweek.* Over half the women from 20 to 44 feel the clothing industry doesn't give a darn about what they want (56 percent). Most women can't find clothes with a good fit (51 percent), or clothes that flatter them (56 percent). Women want to wear their clothes for at least three seasons. *Glamour.*

Percent of women 18-49 who say "I frequently buy things on impulse; I see something in a store and I decide I want it"	
Total women	24%
Homemakers	18%
Employed wives	21%
Single	37%
Formerly married	22%
Two-job couples	20%
Dual-career couples	21%

Source: Self

Men Shoppers

Married vs. single men. Married men are more than three times as likely as single men to own a home, and more likely to be in the market for home appliances. Single men are less likely to have a preference for a men's clothing store, but if they do, their choice of store is more strongly motivated by selection as compared to price, quality, or service. Married men are more likely to clip coupons, and single men are more likely to shop in convenience stores. *MarkeTrend, Impact Resources.*

Young Shoppers

Children
Children are exerting greater influence in family decisions than in the past. Compared to when they were children, the majority of today's parents (68 percent) say that their children are more involved in making family decisions. Today's families, however, while increasing children's say in family matters, are operating on two different decision-making styles. Control families (49 percent of families with children 7-17) are "those in which authority for deciding about family matters rests (as it has traditionally) with the parents, who make these choices with little or no imput from children." Consensus familes (48 percent) "operate according to a higher-involvement, more egalitarian mode, in which decisions are made in consultation with the children rather than by parental decree." *The Public Pulse, the Roper Organization.*

In which of these shopping situations, if any, are your children present and involved in the decision about what to buy?

	All parents	Consensus families	Control families
Clothing	82%	89%	74%
Fast food	81%	83%	78%
Grocery shopping	61%	65%	57%
records, tapes, and CDs	47%	60%	36%
Sporting equipment	39%	50%	30%
Home computers and software	10%	14%	7%
Car buying	8%	10%	6%
Household electronics	8%	13%	4%
Household furnishings	7%	12%	3%
Home appliances	5%	6%	3%
None of these	5%	2%	7%

Source: The Public Pulse, *The Roper Organization*

Teens

- In 1989, teens ages 12-19 spent $71 billion—$30 billion came from their own funds (jobs, allowance) and $41 billion came from their parents. The average teen spends more than $50 per week. *Teenage Research Unlimited.*

Average teen spending per week by sex

	Male	Female
Amount of own money spent	$22.12	$21.07
Amount of family money spent	$26.68	$34.43
Total spending	$48.80	$55.50

Average teen spending per week by age group

	12-15	16-17	18-19
Amount of own money spent	$12.94	$23.39	$34.69
Amount of family money spent	$22.26	$30.51	$44.11
Total spending	$35.20	$53.90	$78.80

Source: Teenage Research Unlimited

Teens not only purchase products themselves; they *exert strong influence on family purchases.* And logically, teens tend to have greater influence on the products they are most likely to use and enjoy. For example, teens are more influential in the purchase of video games than of video cameras. *Teenage Research Unlimited.*

Male and female teen dominated purchase influence

Male dominated Product	Percent who "strongly influence" purchase	
	Male	Female
Home video game system	70%	42%
Sports/recreational equipment	65%	42%
Personal computer software	59%	35%
Motorcycle/dirt motorcycle/ motorscooter	50%	16%
Personal computer	49%	33%
Stereo TV	30%	20%
Car/truck/van	22%	17%

Female dominated Product	Percent who "strongly influence" purchase	
	Female	Male
Vacations/travel	48%	40%
Telephone answering machine	31%	23%
Typewriter	29%	13%
Camera	27%	13%
Luggage	22%	14%
Microwave oven	20%	11%

Source: Teenage Research Unlimited

Teen shopping patterns compared to the total population

Category	Total population	Teen consumers	Index
Shop convenience stores	14.0%	21.4%	153
Use coupons	35.1%	18.3%	52
Shop by catalog/direct mail	9.7%	7.1%	73
Buy from TV shopping shows	1.9%	4.1%	216

Source: Deloitte & Touche/Impact Resources

- Teens, on the whole, show less store loyalty than older consumers. *MarkeTrend, Impact Resources.*

- **Selection is the choice for teens.** The most important factors to teens when choosing a retail outlet are selection (18 percent of teens say that this is their prime motivation), followed by price (17 percent), quality (15 percent), location (12 percent), and service (9 percent). *Deloitte & Touche/Impact Resources.*

College Students

There are 13 million college students, who spend an estimated $20-50 billion a year. *Youth Markets Alert estimate.*

- College students have an average personal buying power projected at $6,240 a year, and their discretionary spending is $155 a month. *CollegeTrack.*

- College students are living on their own for the first time, making purchase decisions for items that their parents traditionally bought (*e.g.,* cleaning supplies, some food purchases, household items). They are in experimental years, taking some of their families' brand loyalty, rejecting some of it, and developing their own. *CollegeTrack.*

Baby Boomer Shoppers

Boomers have higher levels of education than the average consumer. Their average household income is $34,030 (almost $4,000 higher than the average consumer), and their incomes are projected to rise in the next 10 to 15 years. *Boomers show a strong loyalty to stores they shop in.* Once you get 'em, you keep 'em. The thing they want most in a retailer is good price (26 percent, vs. 22 percent for the average consumer), followed by selection (22 percent), and quality (19 percent). *Boomers are department store shoppers.* They are more likely than the average consumer to shop in a department store, buy by direct mail or catalogs, and pay with a major credit card. *MarkeTrend, Impact Resources.*

Mature Shoppers

- Mature shoppers consider their big ticket purchases necessities, whereas younger adults consider them luxuries. *The Mature Market, Probus Publishing.*

- Compared to younger consumers, mature consumers place more importance on the fact that the brand they buy is one they have heard of or is nationally advertised. *The Mature Market, Probus Publishing.*

- The majority of matures (age 50+) would rather spend more for one quality product than for several cheaper versions. *Senior Direct.*

- A third of matures have stopped buying certain products and services because of ads that stereotyped them by age. In addition, a third have bought products because they liked the ads. *Senior Direct.*

- Almost half (46 percent) of matures say the number-one shopping barrier is poor service before and after the sale of a product or service. *Senior Direct.*

- When mentioning age, older consumers prefer the terms "mature" (28 percent) and "senior" (24 percent) instead of "old" and "elderly." *Senior Direct.*

Minority Shoppers

Asian-Americans

Adult Asian-American consumers (18+) are more educated and have higher household incomes than black, white, or Hispanic consumers. They are also relatively young (average age 35.7, compared to 43.7 for white adult consumers and 37 for blacks). Sixty percent of adult Asian consumers are male, while white, black, and Hispanic consumers are pretty much 50/50 male female. *MarkeTrend, Impact Resources. Minority Markets Alert* estimates Asians' spending power to be $35 billion annually.

- **Quality** is number-one in importance to Asian consumers. Asian-Americans are traditional and conservative consumers who want to buy the best without concern for the higher costs. *American Management Association.*

- Asians have *high brand loyalty, limited brand awareness.* They are very loyal to many premium brands that they use. Unfortunately, they have relatively low levels of brand identity. High-ticket items such as cars, major appliances, and so on, score over 50 percent in brand-name importance. *American Management Association.*

- Asian consumers are the *least interested in coupons and catalog shopping* when compared to white, Hispanic, and black consumers. *MarkeTrend, Deloitte & Touche/Impact Resources.*

African-Americans

Black shoppers are younger than the average U.S. shopper. Family income is $56 for every $100 the average white family has, and price is a major issue. *Impact Resources. Minority Markets Alert* estimates this group's spending power to be $220 billion annually. Black grocery shoppers are more price sensitive than Asians or whites. Blacks also grocery shop less frequently than do whites (only half shop once a week vs. 70 percent for whites), but blacks spend 12 percent more per trip ($58.70 for blacks vs. $52.30 for whites). Blacks are 12 percent less likely than whites to have a primary shopper for the household. Price—rather than location—is the chief reason for blacks' grocery store preference. *Deloitte & Touche/Impact Resources.*

Black vs. white consumer shopping habits *(Index of 100=black equals white)*			
	White	**Black**	**Index**
Shop department stores	41.1%	34.7%	84 *
Use coupons	38.4%	28.6%	74
Shop convenience stores	13.3%	16.8%	126
Shop by catalog/direct mail	10.0%	9.2%	92
Buy from TV shopping shows	1.4%	4.0%	285

*Read as: blacks are 16 percent less likely than whites to shop department stores
Source: Deloitte & Touche/Impact Resources

Black shoppers, more than whites, want the amenities that stores have to offer, and are willing to pay a higher price to have them. *Warwick Baker & Fiore.*

Price/value relationship of extras: percentage who want extra and agree that it's worth paying higher prices, by race
(black equals white means index=100)

	Black	White	Index
Information booth	65%	35%	186*
Money refunded at any time	63%	40%	158
Places to sit down	62%	32%	194
Open 24 hours	58%	35%	166
Free delivery	58%	40%	145
Restrooms	53%	46%	115
Ability to shop by phone	50%	33%	152
Coffee shop	47%	26%	181
Everyday low prices instead of periodic sales	47%	26%	181
Ability to use credit cards	45%	34%	132
Free coffee/tea	36%	30%	120
Babysitting	36%	30%	120
Contests	32%	13%	246
Playground and/or rides and games	32%	19%	168
People greeting you at the door	31%	13%	238
Salespersons who know who you are	31%	18%	172
Valet parking	30%	10%	300
In-store entertainment	25%	5%	500
Personal shopper	28%	16%	175
Coat check	15%	9%	167

Read as blacks are 86 percent more likely than whites to want an information booth
Source: Warwick Baker & Fiore

Hispanics

Hispanics are currently 8 percent of the total U.S. population, but their numbers are increasing at four times the national rate. Hispanic families are larger than the average U.S. family (3.5 persons to 2.62) and generally younger (median age is 24 vs. U.S. median age of 33). *Census Bureau, Strategy Research, Research Response. Minority Markets Alert* estimates their spending power to be $145 billion/year.

• Hispanic consumers spend more than other minorities (blacks, Asians) on groceries, and are more price sensitive than whites or Asians in terms of grocery shopping. *MarkeTrend, Impact Resources.*

- Seventy-two percent say they stick to a brand once they've tried and liked it; only 30 percent of blacks and 28 percent of whites see themselves as brand loyal. *Bevmark.*

- Seventy-seven percent say they are not persuadable in purchase decisions, and 72 percent label themselves non-experimenters. *Bevmark.*

Affluent Shoppers

Affluents turn to quality and preservation of the gains they made. Cautious about quick money gains in the '80s and looking to preserve their wealthy status in the '90s, affluent values will turn traditional and enduring in the future. Whereas the explosive new affluence of the 1980s "Trumped" up new and visible consumption, the coming traditionalist-affluents will shop for quality, but will also consider value, enjoying their ability to discern quality. Quality and value will become leading social and consumer values for all consumers in the 1990s. Cautious due to uncertain economic futures, affluent attitudes will change from "conspicuous consumption" to "enlightened consumption." *Town & Country.*

Quality is key to the upper affluent. The upper affluent look for quality first, status second—for many, foreign products have very high appeal. They're in the market for products they can count on. Affluents are willing to pay more for quality, caring more about quality than uniqueness. *Yankelovich Clancy Shulman.*

Affluents set the tone for the nation. Following the lead of the affluent, the mass market will turn toward smart values, quality at a fair price, especially brand names. Legacy items and home improvement products will be in synch with the preservation theme the affluents set. *Town & Country.*

Trickle-down marketing will grow. You will see once-mass-market-type products targeting new product launches at the affluent. Affluents are more experimental (largely because the financial risk of innovation is less of a hurdle for them); they are variety-seekers. If they accept a new product, the mass market will flock to it, to acquire some of the sparkle that affluent-sanctioned products acquire. The affluent is likely to move on to other products (they bore easily), but the mass will stay with that product for a long time. *Affluent Markets Alert.*

CHAPTER

7

Home
Managing the American Dream

Homeowning, a major part of the American dream, is no longer simple to realize for young, hard-working couples. During the '80s, the home-ownership rate declined to 64 percent. The unprecedented housing demands of the older Baby Boomers caused home prices to soar and left many people—especially younger Boomers—unable to overcome the down payment hurdle to buy into that first home. In the '90s, however, the homeownership rate will begin increasing. The smaller Baby Bust population will enter homebuying years, bringing with them commensurately smaller housing demands, causing housing prices to fall. Also, younger Boomers will get a chance in the '90s to buy the homes they couldn't afford in the '80s, as the high housing prices caused by older Boomer demand decline. And as prices ease up a bit from their record highs, those older Boomers will be buying up to fancier homes, as well as fixing up existing homes, fueling the second and vacation home market.

Americans are continuing to do-it-themselves when it comes to home improvement, and by 2000 the do-it-yourself market (for repair and remodeling) will be as large or larger than the home-building segment. Home care still rests heavily on women's shoulders, though men are helping out more. Women aren't the housekeepers their moms were, but remain the primary home carers, and they realize something has got to give when they juggle work, family and home care.

Homeowning

Hype Alert: "In the decade of affluence, the 1980s, homeownership edged up, particularly among young people."

In spite of economic growth, homeownership rates have declined by some two million households since 1980 with 64 percent of U.S. families currently owning homes, down from 66 percent in 1980. Homeownership for families under age 35 has declined even faster—to 50 percent in 1988, down from 59 percent in 1980. *Census Bureau and National Association of Realtors.*

Homeownership among the relatively young declined. In 1973, 23 percent of 25-year-olds owned a home; in 1988, the rate was 15.5 percent. Among other groups of the relatively young, the situation was similar. For the 30- to 34-year-old group, 60 percent owned homes in 1973, dropping to 53 percent in 1988. In the 35 to 39 bracket, the rate fell from 69 percent in 1973 to 63 percent in 1988. *Joint Economic Committee of Congress.*

Income and housing costs, selected categories
(in 1988 dollars)

	1967	1974	1981	1988
Income				
Owners	$26,731	$29,179	$28,655	$32,300
Renters	$17,277	$17,553	$14,985	$15,900
Young renters*	$26,079	$27,127	$23,266	$24,300
Owner costs				
House price	$53,885	$58,545	$71,999	$65,949
Mortgage rate	6.40%	8.78%	14.51%	9.01%
Mortgage payment	$3,501	$4,684	$8,650	$5,376
Tax savings	$306	$428	$1,200	$196
After-tax cash	$5,801	$7,066	$10,347	$7,980
Equity buildup	$1,588	$4,429	$6,229	$1,086
Total cost	$4,777	$3,638	$6,308	$8,015
Renter costs				
Contract rent	$311	$300	$290	$338
Other costs	$40	$41	$55	$54
Cost as a percent of income				
First-time buyers				
Total burden	18.3%	13.4%	27.1%	33.0%
All renters				
Gross rent burden	24.4%	23.3%	27.6%	29.6%

* Married couples age 25 to 29
Sources: American Housing Survey, Bureau of Labor Statistics, as reported in
The State of the Nation's Housing 1989, *Joint Center For Housing Studies at
Harvard University*

Mortgage blues. First-time home buyers are in a tight bind to qualify for mortgages. First-time buyers have an average of 77 percent of the income needed to qualify for a starter home mortgage. Those who already have a home have an average of 112 percent of the income needed to qualify for a median-priced home. *National Association of Realtors.*

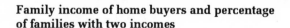

Family income of home buyers and percentage of families with two incomes

<$30,000	65%
$30-$40,000	76%
$41-$50,000	78%
$50-$60,000	80%
$61,000+	82%

Source: Chicago Title & Trust Co., as cited in USA Today

Empty houses. More houses are going begging as potential first-time buyers struggle to move up. The average first home costs $79,000, but would-be buyers have a median income of $22,388 — too little to qualify for financing, even with a 10-percent down payment. *Lomas Mortgage USA.*

Fewer but fancier homes. Builders are constructing fewer houses for first-time buyers, instead building fancier houses that only families who have made money on their first homes can afford, with bigger master bedrooms, separate showers, higher ceilings, and bigger and better-appointed kitchens. *Wall Street Journal.*

Hype Alert: "Glamour features are the main components of the American Dream House."

Whatever images of Tara may lurk in people's fantasies, closets and storage space are top priorities to 97 percent of the women polled in the *Family Circle* Consumer Panel. Other key desired features include: two extra multi-functional rooms designed for hobbies, crafts, a home office, or even more storage space. Both rooms should have sleeper sofas. The women also wanted expanded living space—combined kitchen and family room, including a built-in entertainment center with TV, stereo, and computer—and state-of-the-art appliances for cooking, cleaning, entertainment and communications. Mud room, keyless entry system, and walk-in pantry are all also highly desired.

Renters and mortgagers. Couples with children are much more likely to be paying a mortgage than paying rent—three out of four couples with children under thirteen own their own homes, compared to only half of childless couples aged 18 to 34. The median income for both groups is comparable. *Standard Rate and Data Service/National Demographics and Lifestyles*

Homeownership and income of couples without and with children
Index of 100=U.S. average)

	Married, 18-34 no child at home		Married, children under 13 years old	
	% of households	*Index*	*% of households*	*Index*
Homeownership				
Owner	50.5%	77	74.2%	114
Renter	49.5%	143	25.8%	74
Household Income:				
<$20,000	18.3%	49	16.5%	44
$20-$29,999	17.5%	101	17.2%	99
$30-$39,999	21.9%	151	21.4%	148
$40-$49,999	17.2%	168	16.3%	160
$50-$74,999	19.0%	142	20.1%	150
$75,000+	6.1%	84	8.6%	118
Median Income	$36,491		$37,626	

Source: SRDS/NDL

The typical apartment tenant. In modern, market-rate apartments, renters are overwhelmingly female (76 percent) and single (55 percent). Seventy percent are between 18 and 34 years old, with income between $10,000 and $39,999; 41 percent have lived in the apartment between one and three years. The majority (74 percent) are childless, 28 percent work in professional jobs, 25 percent in service jobs, and 23 percent in clerical. *Apartment Resources Newsletter.*

Over the last decade, residential building has become the largest market for new construction activity. *Cahners.*

Estimated spending for types of new construction in 1990		
	$(billions)	% of total
*single-unit residential**	*$128.4*	*34%*
retail	$29.9	8%
highways and streets	$28.1	8%
utilities and misc. buildings	$26.6	7%
office	$25.7	7%
apartment buildings/condominiums	*$24.1*	*6%*
government buildings/facilities	$16.3	4%
industrial	$17.6	5%
educational	$17.5	5%
sewer and water	$13.7	4%
telecommunication	$8.6	2%

hospital/health	$9.5	3%
hotel	$8.0	2%
misc. public works	$5.2	1%
misc. institutional	$4.5	1%
conservation and development	$5.1	1%
military	$3.5	1%
religious	$2.9	1%
Total	**$375.2**	**100%**

Italics added

Source: Cahners Advertising Research Report

Minority Homes

Black homeowning percentages. Only 44 percent of blacks own homes, as opposed to 64 percent of the nation. *Census Bureau.*

Income/housing selected categories			
	Blacks	**Hispanics**	**Total**
Homeownership rate	44%	40%	64%
Buildings with 5+ units	25%	28%	16%
Female household, 2+ persons	31%	21%	13%
Public/subsidized housing	16%	12%	5%
No savings/investments	52%	45%	24%
Income below poverty level	34%	26%	14%
No cars, trucks, or vans	32%	23%	12%

Source: Census Bureau

Blacks are more than twice as likely as whites to have home loan applications rejected by savings and loan institutions.

1988 mortgage loan applications			
	Granted	**Rejected**	**Withdrawn**
Black	66%	26%	8%
Hispanic	76%	16%	8%
Asian/Pacific Islander	80%	11%	8%
American Indian/Alaskan native	79%	17%	5%
Whites	83%	9%	8%

Source: Atlanta Journal-Constitution

Nine-tenths of U.S. Hispanic householders live in metro areas, and over one-half live in central cities. Half live in single-unit homes, and almost half live in multi-unit buildings. Median monthly housing costs are $357, almost exactly the U.S. average, but Hispanics spend 26 percent of their income on housing (the U.S. average is 21 percent). Both blacks (27 percent) and Hispanics (26 percent) spend a larger share of income on housing than does the nation as a whole (21 percent). *Census Bureau.*

Remodeling

The do-it-yourselfer is taking on more responsibility, and professional remodelers are raking in the business as the trend toward upscaling the home (rather than buying a new one) continues. The bathroom is the number-one spot to start remodeling and redecorating.

Moving couches. Almost two-thirds of Americans rearrange their furniture annually—20 percent move their furniture once a month. One-third redecorate their homes at least once a year, and a majority of people choose to replace a few pieces of furniture/decorations when refurbishing. *Spiegel Inc./R.H. Bruskin.*

Hype Alert: "Repair and remodeling are nice but unimportant hobbies."
By 2000, the do-it-yourself market (for repair and remodeling) will be as large or larger than the homebuilding segment. *Louisiana Pacific.*

Spending on repair and remodeling. Last year, homeowners spent an estimated $101 billion on professional remodeling and do-it-yourself improvements, more than double the $45 billion spent in 1982. The average existing home is 23 years old. *Staying Relevant (Lintas:USA).*

Hype Alert: "When Americans hire a contractor, they get out of the way."

More than half of homeowners who plan to hire a contractor to remodel their homes next year plan on doing part of the job themselves. Here are the percentage who say they will do the following chores: painting (82 percent), general cleanup (77 percent), wallpapering (40 percent), laying carpet (20 percent), demolition (20 percent), electrical (15 percent), building walls (14 percent), laying ceramic tile (11 percent), plumbing (10 percent), concrete (3 percent), and masonry (3 percent). *Professional Builder.*

Remodeling after relocation. Homeowners make almost 70 percent of their improvements within three years after purchase. *Repair and remodeling is the fastest-growing segment of the housing business, expanding faster than new construction.* Renovation spending has risen an average of 10.3 percent annually since 1980 (though the rate of growth has slowed). Repair expenses are still rising. New construction spending has been flat, while sales of existing homes set a nine-year record in 1988. *Wall Street Journal.*

The bathroom is the room to do. More people (5.6 million) remodeled bathrooms in 1988 than ever before. The average age of someone redoing the bathroom is 41; people in two-income households are most likely to remodel the bath. *Kitchen and Bath Business.*

What gets replaced? More than 18 million Americans bought new bathroom or kitchen faucets in the past 12 months. Second most-purchased items are wallpaper/wall covering, purchased by 16.2 million in the past year, followed by other bathroom or kitchen plumbing fixtures (9.8 million), interior light fixtures (7.9 million), vinyl flooring (6.6 million), exterior (5.3 million), kitchen counter tops (2.9 million), insulated or thermal windows (5.1 million), outdoor lighting fixtures (2.8 million), concrete or masonry work (2.7 million). Typically, married suburbanites in above-average income brackets are most likely to channel efforts and expenditures into these home improvements. *Mediamark Research Inc. (MRI)*

Home innovators—consumers who are the most receptive to new home products (19 percent of all U.S. adults as identified by MRI) are improving their homes rather than trading up to better ones. They buy 78 percent of solar hot water heaters, 69 percent of burglar alarms, 69 percent of water filters, 59 percent of wood/coal stoves, and 54 percent of hot tubs. *Mediamark Research, Inc.*

Backyard, U.S. style. The American backyard: 63 percent measure under one-quarter of an acre, 97 percent have grass, 81 percent nonflowering trees, 68 percent have a fence, 65 percent a patio, and 59 percent a picnic table. Half of American yards have an outdoor lighting system. This is the yard addition of greatest interest to the unlit half—three-quarters of those without outdoor lighting are interested in getting lit. *Good Housekeeping Consumer Panel.*

Consumer Electronics

Americans love gadgets. Now, however, consumers are technologically sophisticated and are not as likely to pay for a new electronic product that doesn't offer real ease, real value, and substantial quality. Added features are going to become less attractive than ease of use.

Hype Alert: "Consumer electronics—sales going forever upward."

The rate of sales growth of consumer electronics is slowing. Most observers say the industry will continue to expand to record proportions, but the rate of growth will slow. Factory sales of consumer electronics more than tripled over the course of the 1980s to $34 billion. *Electronics Industries Association.*

Hype Alert: "New technology means higher quality."

Quality is no longer immediately associated with new technology. Consumers aren't as ready as they were a few years ago to associate new technologies with product quality. In one year (1988 to 1989), there has been a 5-point drop (to 53 percent) in those who say new technology enhances product quality. This group has shrunk by 10 points over the past three years. In that time, the shift has been almost entirely to the view (now held by 27 percent) that the relationship between new technology and quality varies from product to product. *Cambridge Reports' Trends & Forecasts.*

Stereo TV—not enough value for the price. The Electronics Industries Association reports that about 28 percent of television sets sold to dealers now have stereo capacity. As consumers replace old sets, stereo is perceived as only a marginal advantage.

The trading-up trend. Upscale products are now the trend in home entertainment products—trading up from affordable to high quality. *Business Trend Analysts.*

Hype Alert: " Singles and Yuppies are the live wires of the home electronics market."

Households with kids are much more likely to be chock-full of high-tech electronics than are singles' households. Homes with children have almost twice as many VCRs (78 percent vs. 40 percent of singles), boom boxes (63 percent vs. 33 percent), and audio systems (47 percent vs. 25 percent); three times as many home computers (24 percent vs. 8 percent), and a third more CD players (15 percent vs. 10 percent). *Electronics Industries Association.*

Percent of Asian consumers compared of to average U.S. consumers who own various home communications equipment

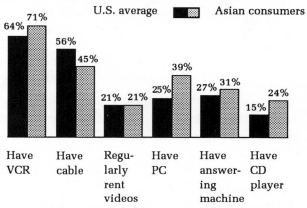

Source: Deloitte & Touche/Impact Resources

Home security. Self-installed home security systems have seen dramatic sales gains recently. The do-it-yourself segment of the home security market rose 25 percent between '82 and '87. Industry experts project sales to rise to $650 million by 1992, approaching $1 billion by 1997. *Good Housekeeping Institute Newsletter.* By 1992, 13.5 million homes will be secured by either do-it-yourself or professionally installed electronic home security systems (14 percent of households); by 1997, more than 20 percent of all U.S. homes. *Find/SVP.*

HypeAlert: "The cellular phone user is an affluent, middle-aged male."

More than two million Americans are now tuned into cellular systems, a 68-percent increase in the last year. Five years ago, the typical user was male, over 55 years of age, and earned over $60,000 a year. Today, one-quarter of subscribers are women; ages range from 35-55, and income is often as low as $35,000. By 1995, the ranks of mobile-phone users could top 20 million. *U.S. News & World Report.*

New features on phones: call back, call trace, priority call, return call, repeat call, caller ID. About 20 states, including much of the East Coast and the South, already have these services in some cities, and most of the U.S. will be able to sign up for them over the next 18 months or so.

Time on the phone. From 1980 to 1987, the time Americans spent on the telephone increased 24 percent, from 3.02 trillion minutes to 3.75 trillion minutes, while the population grew only 7 percent. Answering machines are now owned by 28 percent of American households. *The New York Times.*

Computers are in affluent homes with kids. Upper Deck households (top ten percent of households ranked by income) with children are 36 percent more likely to own a computer and 38 percent more likely to own software than are Upper Deck households in general. Upper Deck households with teenagers (age 12-17) are 46 percent more likely to own a computer and 47 percent more likely to own software than the average Upper Deck household. *Mediamark Research, Inc.*

Housewares

The home fashions market—upscaling and softening. Consumers are planning to buy less this year, but the best. They will also stick to basics. Color is the most important variable in the buying decision—solid colors are particularly popular. Expectations of the cost of items generally exceeds the actual cost of the goods. In general, the higher the income, the higher the predisposition to buy, with one exception: those in the $50,000 to $60,000 range were least likely of all income groups to plan purchases of most products this year. *HomeMarket Trends.*

Hype Alert: "Homes in the '90s will be futuristic,
or very designer-y."
On the contrary—think design-friendly. The design of the decade will be: classic, comfy, country, with an international flair. *House Beautiful.*

Heightened health and environmental concerns (particularly regarding radon gas) will promote a 12-percent annual growth for air cleaners until 1992. Trash compactors will also enjoy renewed growth, while microwave ovens and refrigerators will experience slowed growth; the growing popularity of central air conditioning will hinder sales of room air conditioners. *The Freedonia Group.*

Hype Alert: *"Microwave ownership has hit saturation."*
No way. Four-fifths of households own a microwave oven. By 2000, 92 percent of homes will have microwaves in them. *New markets for non-food microwave products are being created*, as microwaves become multipurpose—consumers are already using microwaves for drying wet newspapers, wet underwear, heating body lotion, and so on *Adweek's Marketing Week.* You will see microwave units installed in college dorm rooms, as well as in cars.

Men are interested in high-end cookware. "Although the market for cookware and bakeware remains predominantly female, more men are interested in high-end cookware—they are gadget-oriented, brand-conscious and want to know what product is considered best—heavy gauge aluminum cookware appeals to this upscale masculine market." *Incentive.*

Home Care
Hype Alert: *"The New American Male is sharing home care tasks equally."*
Not quite. Men are doing a bit more than they have in the past — married men now do about 30 percent of the housework; two decades ago they did 20 percent. *Time. There is still little home and family care equality in dual income families.* A study of dual-income families finds that women are working 13 months a year to the man's 12. When adding together the time it takes to work a paid job, clean the house, and care for the kids, *women work on average 15 hours a week longer than men do* . Over the course of a year, this translates to women working one extra month of 24-

hour days. Although some dual-income couples make an effort at sharing domestic responsibilities, the bottom line is that for all the couples studied, only 20 percent of the husbands shared household tasks equally. *The Second Shift, Viking Penguin.*

Home care is still work for women. Only one-third of mothers are happy about the way their home is kept, mainly because they say their standards are not as high as they were in the home where they grew up. Only one-quarter of mothers feel that everyone in the household contributes a fair share. *Good Housekeeping.*

Time spent (hours:minutes) on chores and leisure activities on the weekend, by sex, age, and presence of children

	Men	Women	18-24	25-34	35-49	50-64	65+	with kids	w/out kids
Cleaning	1:35	2:57	2:14	2:49	2:37	2:04	1:33	3:05	1:51
Doing laundry	:46	1:48	1:25	1:31	1:38	1:09	:35	1:40	1:06
Paying bills	:35	:33	:35	:38	:41	:27	:25	:42	:30
Working at job	3:07	2:42	4:51	3:14	3:04	1:49	1:22	3:23	2:37
Running errands	1:35	1:51	1:57	1:59	1:51	1:44	:54	1:57	1:35
Household repairs	1:51	:37	1:28	1:20	1:27	1:00	:40	1:28	1:03
Grocery shopping	:51	1:08	:40	1:00	1:06	1:06	1:06	1:04	:57
Visiting friends	3:12	2:38	5:06	3:21	2:08	2:06	1:56	2:43	3:01
Interests/ hobbies	4:09	3:19	4:57	3:47	3:49	3:16	2:36	3:32	3:49
Attending entertainment	1:52	1:31	2:47	1:55	1:45	1:04	:49	1:50	1:36
Visiting relatives	1:45	2:30	2:30	2:33	1:48	1:37	2:21	2:03	2:12
Exercising	1:58	1:00	2:13	1:40	1:10	1:11	1:05	1:20	1:32
Dining out	1:50	1:39	1:52	1:49	1:46	1:42	1:30	1:39	1:47
Playing with kids	2:21	3:08	2:05	4:54	3:28	1:28	:58	5:35	1:13
Gardening	:55	:52	:15	:40	:55	1:34	:56	:53	:53
Reading	2:03	1:58	1:55	1:40	2:00	2:07	2:27	1:38	2:13

Source: The Hilton Survey on Weekend Leisure Time

A Message for the Media

Television still dominates household media—sets are in nearly every home. They are on seven hours a day, serving as entertainment, "infotainment," baby sitter, and background to many activities. To many media planners, network and cable are becoming a single entity, but TV, though it does reach the masses, does not exert as much influence as it once did. There are so many more outlets from which consumers may choose information and entertainment. The audience is getting harder to define, harder to find, and choosier.

Television

Hype Alert: "Mass media isn't massive anymore."

The truth is, mass vehicles still control a dominant share of leisure time among most American consumers. Renewed commitment to mass media was demonstrated during the 1989 upfront negotiations with the broadcast networks—advertisers purchased a record $4.3 billion in primetime commercial time, a 30-percent increase over 1988. Nearly all homes with a TV set tune into network each week, and almost 95 percent view network during primetime alone. Though network's share of primetime audience is declining (last year it reached an all-time low), network programming still accounts for the majority of primetime viewing—the average share of audience viewing network affiliates during primetime was 68 percent last year. Cable now captures a 20-percent share in primetime. The average American only views eight of the average 25 cable channels available to him/her during a week's time. *Nielsen and J. Walter Thompson.*

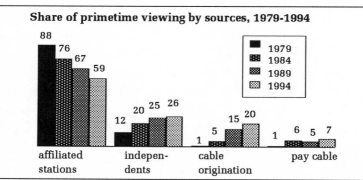

Share of primetime viewing by sources, 1979-1994

Legend: 1979, 1984, 1989, 1994

affiliated stations: 88, 76, 67, 59
independents: 12, 20, 25, 26
cable origination: 1, 5, 15, 20
pay cable: 1, 6, 5, 7

Source: Nielsen in the BBDO Media Update *April 2,1990*

Hype Alert: "Americans are zapping through commercials."

Zapping does occur, but commercial audiences are only 6 percent smaller than program audiences. *J. Walter Thompson.*

Hype Alert: "New Puritanism grips America."

Not quite; it's more like a New Centrism, pulling back from extremes; extremes in social and sexual mores, as well as in politics. Public opposition to sexual and violent themes in TV and movies is strengthening. Network and consumer product managers are ripe for manipulation by audience pressure. One result of the current morality trend may be new programming targeting the self-defined "moral" audience segment, but this will be barely noticeable amidst the existing channel pickings. *American Forecaster Almanac 1990, Running Press.* Trash or not trash, outspoken critics and sensitive advertisers won't kill "reality" TV shows— they have an audience with a seemingly unlimited appetite for news and sensationalized reality programs. No wonder the media celebrates the "New Puritans"—they generate publicity without major programming consequences—"Married . . . With Children" became Fox's biggest hit.

Future TV. By 1995, a walking TV will be a reality. This contraption will have two legs, follow you around the house, and will probably dance to TV music. Price: $5,000. *Future Stuff, Penguin Books.*

Demographics: who watches, how long. Women 55 and over watch more TV (41 hours: 01 minutes) per week than any other group. Men 55 and over follow with 37:32. Sunday night draws the largest audience, with more than 106 million viewers. Households that watch the most TV tend to contain three or more people, have children, and subscribe to pay cable. Lowest viewing group: single-member households. Female teens watch 21:26 per week. Male teens watch 22:18 per week. *Nielsen.*

Number of TV households. The January 1, 1990 estimate of U.S. television households is 92.1 million, including Alaska and Hawaii. *Nielsen.*

How many channels can we get?	
number of channels	percentage of TV households
1-14	36%
15-29	19%
30 or more	45%

Most popular programming
(average network viewership during an
average minute between 7-11 pm, in millions)

Sitcoms	23.75
Feature films	20.92
Drama	20.00
Suspense	17.95
Adventure	15.90

Source: Nielsen

Background viewing is growing. Nearly two-fifths of viewers (39 percent) say they frequently leave their TV set on in the background, even when not watching it—up sharply from 25 percent a decade ago. Nearly half of 18- to 29-year-olds, and 44 percent of parents with young children typically have the TV on in the background. Boomers are much more likely to be reflexive viewers (about half turn on the TV before deciding what to watch) than those aged 45-59 (41 percent). Only 28 percent of people 60+ are reflexive viewers. *The Public Pulse, The Roper Organization.*

Hours of TV usage per week, by household characteristics
(Mon.-Sun., 24 hours)

Household Income	hours:minutes
<$30,000	52:43
$30,000+	49:22
$40,000+	48:44
$50,000+	48:26
$60,000+	47:49
Household size	
1 person	39:36
2 persons	47:13
3+ persons	59:45
Any children present	58:43
No children present	46:17

Source: Nielsen, 1990

Hype Alert: "In info-crazed America, news is number one."
News-watching on TV continues its decline. During the 1980s, network news has seen a slow, steady attrition in its ratings, reflecting the impact of increasingly sophisticated off-network/ independent stations and pay cable. In 1979, 29 percent of adults

watched one or more late network newscasts on a typical weekday; by 1988, viewership had dropped to 26 percent. The greatest decrease since 1979, for both early and late newscasts, has been in the 35-44 age group. *Media Dynamics.*

Hype Alert: "Women don't watch sports."

Since 1983, women 18+ have increased their percentage of the total audience for seven sports events. The largest gainers were the NBA, multi-sports series, and college football. In 1988, women constituted a key adult viewing audience of horse racing (52 percent), bowling (51 percent), tennis (49 percent), multi-sports series (45 percent), and golf (42 percent). Sports events ranked by total audience size: 1. NFL, 2. baseball, 3. NBA basketball, 4, college football. *BBDO Worldwide.*

Male sports viewing by income. Men with incomes under $30,000 constitute the largest male audience share for all sports viewing; affluent men constitute the second largest male audience share for every sport category. Below is a chart of television sports audiences (male) broken down by income and sport—in descending order of preference by affluent men. *Bozell, Jacobs, Kenyon & Eckhardt.*

Male income percent composition of network sports (regular season)
(Rows add to 100%)

	$50K+	$40-50K	$30-40K	<$30K
Total U.S. population	*28%*	*13%*	*17%*	*42%*
Tennis	33%*	9%	16%	42%
NFL Football	28%	14%	19%	39%
College Basketball	27%	12%	16%	45%
Golf	26%	12%	17%	45%
College Football	25%	12%	18%	45%
NBA Basketball	24%	11%	17%	48%
Anthology	23%	12%	17%	48%
Baseball	21%	13%	15%	51%
Auto Racing	21%	9%	19%	51%
Bowling	17%	10%	22%	51%

A third (33%) of male television tennis audiences have household incomes of $50,000 or more.
Source: Bozell, Jacobs, Kenyon & Eckhardt

Teen TV viewing. Thirteen- to 18-year-olds average 3.1 hours of TV viewing each weekday, and 5.9 hours on the weekend; young teens (13-15) watch significantly more TV than older teens (16-18). *Management Horizons.* By the time a young person turns 18, he or she will have spent almost two years of his/her life in front of the tube. By age 18, he/she has spent: 17,000 hours watching TV; 11,000 hours at school; 1,160 hours at the movies. *Premiere.*

Hype Alert: "Senior citizens turn to reading."
Simmons Market Research Bureau finds that older people are avid TV viewers. About 32 percent of 65+ers and 24 percent of 55- to 64-year-olds are heavy TV watchers, compared to 15 percent of people 18 to 49. While persons 55+ represent only a third of all adults, they account for 45 percent of early morning viewers, 44 percent of mid-morning viewers, and 40 percent of those who watch in the afternoon. *The Mature Market, Probus Publishing.*

Minority households and TV. In 1988, blacks accounted for 12 percent of the total population, 11 percent of TV households, and approximately 15 percent of all hours spent watching TV. Hispanics accounted for 6 percent of TV households, but only 3 percent of the total hours spent watching TV. On average, then, Hispanic households are undelivered by primetime network television by about 26 percent. *BBDO Worldwide.*

Blacks watch more television throughout the programming day than others do. The primetime difference is substantial, with hours watched 14 percent higher in black households than in others, but even that is much less significant than during other parts of the day. Blacks watch 30 percent more on weekend afternoons, 55 percent more during daytime Monday-Friday, and 95 percent more during late night. *Bozell.*

Black and non-black household ratings by parts of day
(Nov. 1988 -Jan. 1989)

	Black	Non-black	Percent difference
Early morning	5.5	3.3	+66%
Daytime	9.7	5.0	+94%
Early eve. news	12.9	11.5	+12%
Prime time	18.1	14.0	+29%
Late fringe (after prime time)	6.6	3.9	+69%
Sat. morn. kids	6.9	3.9	+77%
Weekend sports	10.2	7.2	+42%

Source: Bozell

Prime time program types, black and non-black household ratings
(Nov. 1988 - Jan. 1989)

	Black	Non-black	Percent difference
Situation comedy	22.0	16.4	+34%
Police/detective	18.9	12.2	+55%
General drama	18.0	13.4	+34%
Feature films	17.2	14.2	+21%
Adventure	14.2	9.7	+46%
Documentary/news	12.5	13.2	-7%

Source: Bozell

Minority children and TV. Eight out of ten black fourth graders watch 3+ hours of TV per day, while five in ten watch 6+ hours daily. And although white and Hispanic levels also run high at this grade level, their TV time drops off in greater percentages as their grade level increases. By 11th grade, only 39 percent of whites and 45 percent of Hispanics are watching three hours or more daily, compared to more than 60 percent of blacks. *U.S. Department of Education.*

TV viewing by minority groups (age 14+)

	U.S.	Blacks	Hispanics	Asian-Amers.
Watch TV for leisure	69%	69%	64%	69%
Have cable TV	53%	54%	54%	45%
Watch cable regularly	38%	45%	43%	32%
Watch regularly:				
CNN	9%	11%	11%	9%
ESPN	10%	15%	13%	8%
MTV	8%	5%	12%	9%
HBO	15%	24%	22%	12%
The Movie Channel	7%	11%	9%	5%
Cinemax	7%	12%	10%	6%
The Disney Channel	4%	5%	6%	3%
ABC	43%	48%	42%	43%
CBS	39%	43%	34%	35%
NBC	44%	47%	40%	42%
PBS	19%	17%	17%	18%
Fox	16%	23%	17%	15%
Independents	23%	32%	28%	23%
Type of programming viewed regularly:				
Movies	64%	64%	64%	58%
Local TV News	64%	65%	60%	58%
Documentaries/News	50%	42%	44%	50%
Sitcoms	47%	44%	41%	40%
Sports	39%	44%	39%	40%
Police shows	36%	45%	35%	32%
Talk shows	34%	42%	32%	26%
Game shows	31%	35%	26%	24%
Variety shows	28%	31%	31%	24%
Daytime soaps	22%	29%	22%	15%
Cartoons	17%	28%	22%	22%
Night-time soaps	16%	24%	16%	12%
Religious shows	8%	16%	8%	5%

Source: Deloitte & Touche/Impact Resources

Hispanics prefer Spanish television. A majority (57 percent) of Hispanics watch Spanish television exclusively, 7 percent watch English-language TV only, and 46 percent watch varying amounts of each. Hispanic tastes are very close to national tastes—seven of the Hispanic top ten programs are among the most popular with all TV viewers. The preferences also affirm that Hispanics are drawn to family-oriented programming, especially sitcoms. *BBDO Worldwide.*

Hype Alert: "Viewers graze because there are so many juicy programs."

On the contrary, people are grazing out of boredom. About 30 percent of the adult TV viewing population could be defined as serious grazers, and there may be more of them in the future. After all, remote control makes grazing easy and *75 percent of viewers have remote control.* Also, options continue to multiply—54 percent of viewers now have basic cable service, and 46 percent have both cable and remote. *Currently, 67 percent of remote users graze frequently.* People's number-one reason for grazing is boredom, followed by hoping to find something better, and to avoid commercials. "Almost two-thirds of the channel-changing during programs is a result of insufficient viewer interest in what they're watching—that is to say boredom." *Grazers enjoy TV less than non-grazers.* By a three-to-one margin, viewers who use their remote control enjoy TV less (rather than more or about the same) than when they stay with one program. *Channels magazine.*

Major reasons for changing channels during programs, by sex and age group

(based on those who change channels during programs, figures rounded, don't know/no answer figures omitted)

	total	Sex		Age				
	total	male	female	18-24	25-34	35-49	50-64	65+
Get bored with the program watched	29%	26%	33%	22%	20%	26%	55%	40%
Want to make sure they're not missing a better program	28%	29%	28%	38%	34%	28%	10%	25%
To avoid commercials	23%	24%	22%	32%	22%	19%	23%	15%
Keeping track of more than one program at one time	11%	14%	8%	5%	14%	13%	10%	10%
Want all information they can get	4%	4%	4%	3%	7%	4%	3%	0%
Other	3%	3%	2%	0%	3%	4%	0%	5%

Source: Channels *magazine*

The way people select a TV show

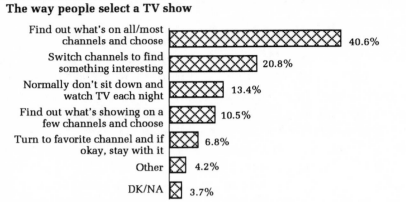

Find out what's on all/most channels and choose — 40.6%
Switch channels to find something interesting — 20.8%
Normally don't sit down and watch TV each night — 13.4%
Find out what's showing on a few channels and choose — 10.5%
Turn to favorite channel and if okay, stay with it — 6.8%
Other — 4.2%
DK/NA — 3.7%

Source: Channels *magazine*

Cable

Hype Alert: "People prefer cable programming to network."

Between 1988 and 1989, there has been a noticeable decline in customer satisfaction with cable networks and system operators. Just under half of current subscribers say basic cable programming is better than network TV (a significant decline since 1988). Self-reported viewership of broadcast TV is holding steady, and *researchers find that the longer a person subscribes to cable TV, the better network programming looks to him or her.* Also, as big movie hits are released on cassette faster and the selection of tapes get larger, *increasing numbers of cable viewers see the VCR as a valuable alternative to pay cable.* Seven in 10 cable households own a VCR, and most of these households do not subscribe to premium pay-TV channels. *Bruskin Associates.*

Rate your feelings about the following:

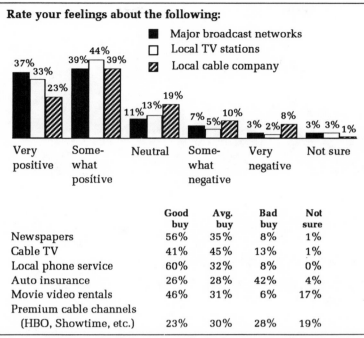

- ■ Major broadcast networks
- □ Local TV stations
- ▨ Local cable company

	Good buy	Avg. buy	Bad buy	Not sure
Newspapers	56%	35%	8%	1%
Cable TV	41%	45%	13%	1%
Local phone service	60%	32%	8%	0%
Auto insurance	26%	28%	42%	4%
Movie video rentals	46%	31%	6%	17%
Premium cable channels (HBO, Showtime, etc.)	23%	30%	28%	19%

*Source: NBC News/*Wall Street Journal *telephone survey of 1003 registered voters, March 10-13, 1990*

Cable penetration continues to grow. As of November 1989, 57 percent of all U.S. TV households had cable, an 8-percent increase over November 1988. According to Nielsen, cable penetration has been growing by an average of 327,250 homes per month and at an annual rate in excess of 8 percent for the past six quarters. *Cable Advertising Bureau.* Over two-fifths (42 percent) of the total cable universe have two or more cable hookups installed. *Marketing & Media Decisions.* Cable growth will virtually end in 1992, when all potential markets will be cable-ready. *American Forecaster Almanac 1990, Running Press.* Cable will be in 70 percent of households by 1994. *BBDO.*

Cable penetration rates 1979-1994

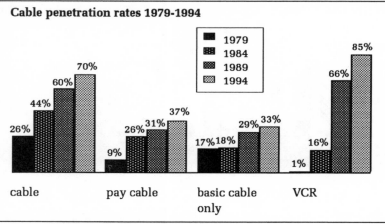

Source: Nielsen in the BBDO Media Update *April 2, 1990*

Basic cable vs. other options during primetime:

1. In cable households during primetime, basic cable's average audience share increased from 22 percent to 25 percent.

2. Basic's rating grew to 15.3 from 13.6, or by 13 percent. However, basic networks' ratings in total TV households increased by 20 percent, to 8.9 from 7.4, and share increased to 15 from 13 as a result of increased cable penetration.

3. Meanwhile, broadcast network affiliates saw their share in cable households drop to 58 percent from 60 percent. *Cable Advertising Bureau.*

Top four designated market areas ranked by total TV households
(May 1989)

rank	DMA	Total TV Households	% cable penetration	cable TV Households
1	New York	6,921,240	49.8%	3,449,530
2	Los Angeles	4,800,200	49.1%	2,356,900
3	Chicago	3,106,690	43.4%	1,347,600
4	Philadelphia	2,610,400	62.7%	1,636,720

Source: Nielsen

Pay cable. In May 1989, pay cable penetration reached 29 percent. *Nielsen.* Eighty-seven percent of pay cable subscribers say they subscribe for variety, followed by getting better reception (60 percent), and to avoid commercials (55 percent). Most frequently recorded from pay cable are movies (67 percent), followed by soap operas (20 percent), specials (18 percent), adventure programs (16 percent), sports (15 percent), sitcoms and concerts (13 percent each). *The Cable Guide.* Pay-per-view cable television systems will grow from less than 1 percent now to 7 percent of cable revenues by 1992. *Frost & Sullivan.*

Video Cassette Recorders

VCR penetration. As the U.S. enters the 1990s, 68 percent of American households own a VCR. *Arbitron.* Households with VCRs tend to be larger, younger, and more upscale: 66 percent live on the West Coast; 64 percent live in the largest metropolitan areas; 76 percent have 4+ persons in home; 74 percent have kids aged 6-17; 84 percent have income over $40,000. *Nielsen.*

VCR market reaching saturation. VCRs, a mature product, will move from 50 percent penetration in 1987 to 70 percent in 1992. Rapid growth has passed for three reasons: high penetration levels; those who have yet to buy a VCR are less affluent than those who already have one; and competition from cable and pay-per-view. Sales and rentals of prerecorded video cassettes are also forecast to moderate. *Frost & Sullivan.* By 1994-95, VCRs are expected to be in 85 percent of households. *BBDO.*

Opportunities for limited growth exist, particularly among lower-income consumers, Southerners, and those ready to trade up to more advanced machines. The middle class loves VCRs—72 percent of households that earn $20,000 to $40,000 own a VCR. Brand names seemed to be of overriding importance in buying decisions, followed by price, value, and technological features. *Discount Store News.*

African-American TV households show a slightly lower VCR ownership rate and a substantially lower cable saturation rate. However, in households that do have cable, blacks are more likely than whites to sign up for pay cable. *Newspaper Advertising Bureau.*

Recording on videocassette. Half (52 percent) of all VCR recording is done while the TV is off. Two-thirds of all recordings made in VCR households were of programs telecast by network-affiliated stations. *Nielsen.*

What do VCR households record?

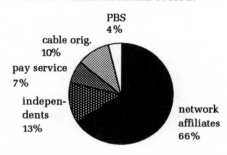

PBS 4%
cable orig. 10%
pay service 7%
independents 13%
network affiliates 66%

Source: Nielsen

Videotape rentals. Americans will spend $13 billion in 1990 on videos ($9.9 billion on rentals, $3.1 billion on sales), a 24-percent increase since 1989. *USA Weekend as cited in NEA Today.* About one out of four videotape renters (23 percent) account for a high proportion of rentals—24 or more tapes in the past six months. These videophiles are concentrated among: households with children aged 6 to 11 and households with teenagers; adults aged 35 to 44; those who attended college; those employed in executive, admin./managerial positions; and those living in the suburbs. People with household incomes of less than $14,000 (35 percent) and more than $50,000 (23 percent) are the most likely of all income groups to rent videos. *Deloitte & Touche/Impact Resources.*

Hype Alert: "Only adults rent videotapes."
Children account for more than one-third (38 percent) of all movie and/or program rentals. *Bohbot and Cohn.* Unit sales of kids' videocassettes are expected to grow to 60 million by 1991, a 135-

percent increase in four years; that's 21.3 percent of all unit sales and 14 percent of all dollar sales. *Knowledge Industry Publications, Inc.*

Hype Alert. "Adults handle the household VCR."
Kids use VCRs more than adults do. AGB Television Research shows that in households with VCRs, children under 18 use the machine an average of 3.4 hours a week, as opposed to 2.3 hours for adults. Eighty-seven percent of all videos viewed by kids are prerecorded; only 78 percent of Mom's and Dad's videos are. *American Demographics, March 1989.*

Magazines

Slower circulation growth and continued specialized targeting. According to the Magazine Publishers Association, 94 percent of U.S. adults read an average of 9.6 issues of different magazines during the average month of 1988. The number of consumer magazine titles has grown by 404 over the past five years and by 660 over the last decade. However, unfavorable demographic trends and anticipated increases in magazine prices will probably limit circulation growth in the next five years. *Veronis, Suhler & Associates, Inc.* At least 200 new lifestyle and niche magazines will be introduced each year for the next 10 years. Paradoxically, a similar number of lifestyle/niche magazines will probably fail from lack of reader and advertiser attention. *Advertising Age.*

Specialized titles: *Modern Maturity*, which projected 22.7 million single-copy sales by its February 1990 issue, is the largest-circulation publication in the U.S. *Adweek Marketing to the Year 2000.* New Age/alternative titles such as *New Age, East/West, Utne Reader*—covering spiritualism, health, alternative lifestyles, human potential—will continue to strengthen. *Publishing News.* Mature women's magazines like *First, Mirabella, Victoria, Lear's,* and *Moxie* have found an audience (no surprise, with the first Boomers turning 40), while the seven sisters magazines' circulation and ad pages have declined over the past decade. Most striking is the audience loss among women 18-34 with some college education—the group assumed to have the greatest buying power. *Media Industry Newsletter.*

Magazines reach the affluent and the more educated. Magazines and newspapers offer greater media exposure among college-educated Americans, as well as those earning more than $50,000 a year. Magazine readers are more active and are bigger spenders than heavy TV watchers. *Simmons Market Research Bureau.*

Blacks and print media. A "black media" has evolved to serve the 11 percent of U.S. readers who are black. While remaining loyal to black publications such as *Essence, Jet,* and *Ebony,* (black readership of 90 percent, 90 percent, and 86 percent, respectively), African-Americans are buying certain general market magazines at rates higher than non-blacks. The general market periodicals with the highest black total audience numbers are *Parade* (36 percent), and *TV Guide* (26 percent), however, their percentages of black readers are roughly equal to those of the non-black audience. By contrast, the percentage of black readers of *GQ* is more than twice as great as the percentage of non-black readers. For the *Washington Post Magazine,* the percentage of black readers is 93 percent higher than the percentage of non-black readers; *Working Mother* has a 65-percent higher black readership. *BBDO Worldwide.*

Teenagers regularly reading various magazines				
Magazine type	Males *13-15*	Males *16-18*	Females *13-15*	Females *16-18*
Auto	34%	38%	3%	5%
Sports/hobby	66%	55%	12%	20%
News	17%	23%	12%	15%
Teen/lifestyle	11%	8%	80%	74%
Fashion	5%	7%	41%	45%

Source: Management Horizons

Children's magazines will continue to proliferate. There are now about 160 children's magazines, up from 85 in 1986. Combined circulation is 40 million. College magazines are expanding again after a period of little growth. *American Forecaster Almanac 1990, Running Press.*

Newspapers

Circulation stats: daily and weekly. Almost 63 million people buy a newspaper every day, then spend an average of 45 minutes reading it. Daily circulation changed little in the '80s. Circulation of weeklies, meanwhile, has grown by 50 percent, and now equals that of dailies. Most (61 percent) adult newspaper readers say they usually look at every page in their daily paper. *Newspaper Advertising Bureau.*

Newspaper reader demographics. The reader of the daily newspaper is more likely to be male (index=107 compared to the U.S. average adult, 100); 45 to 64 years old (index=116), college-educated (index =123); married (index=106). He's a professional (index =124) or executive/manager (index=128), with a household income of $60,000+ (index=138). However, within the 45- to 64 year-old age group, women, particularly those between the ages of 55 and 64, are more likely to be readers than are men. *Newspaper Advertising Bureau.*

A more mature audience. The highest proportion of heavy newspaper readers is among 55- to 64- year-olds. Nearly 74 percent of adults 55 to 64 read a daily paper, and 72 percent read a weekend paper. About 69 percent of people 65+ read a daily paper, and 62 percent read a Sunday newspaper. *The Mature Market, Probus Publishing.*

Hype Alert: "Teens don't read newspapers."
Most teens (64 percent) *do* read the local daily paper; six out of ten teens report reading the Sunday paper, with young female teens (13-15) the least likely to read the Sunday edition. *Management Horizons.*

Minorities and media. A majority of affluent Hispanic women (household income $50,000+) are regular readers of their newspaper's lifestyle section; blacks spend more time each week with TV/cable (16.6 hours) than with radio (8.2 hours) and newspapers (3.3 hours) combined. *Deloitte & Touche/Impact Resources.*

Book Buying

Book buying is on the increase. An increase in the number of heavy book readers, the increase in the general population, and Baby Boomers' unprecedented receptivity to books are fueling an increase in consumer book buying—in 1972 the average consumer spent $20.96 for 11 books; in 1987, he/she spent $21.63 for 14 books. *Book Industry Study Group.*

Sales of juvenile books are through the roof. Juvenile book sales increased 68 percent between 1980 and 1986, reaching $386.2 million. Predictions for continued annual growth run as high as 21 percent for hardcover and 16 percent for softcover—significantly higher than the forecasted across-the-industry annual growth rate of 10 percent. Moms account for 80 percent of children's book purchases. *Knowledge Industry Publications. Further evidence of the incredible growth in children's book buying:* the brand-new, twice-yearly, 176-page magazine-format book guide entitled *The Horn Book Guide to Children's and Young Adult Books.*

Professional books are the fastest growing segment in the book industry. Between 1972 and 1984, professional-scholarly publishers' sales growth outpaced both consumer and textbook publishers' sales growth. This trend is due to the increase of working professionals, and the information demands of an increasingly high-tech society. *Book Industry Study Group.*

Hype Alert: "A more-educated America is reading more sophisticated literature."
Over half (56 percent) of adult Americans say they read fiction, drama, or poetry in 1988. But it seems that only 10 percent to 25 percent of what these adults read were "works of merit," and only 7 percent to 12 percent read "worthwhile" contemporary literature. And though reading literature is increasing among older

Americans, it is decreasing among young adults. *National Endowment for the Arts.*

Radio

Ubiquitous radio. Ninety-nine percent of all households have a radio; the average is 5.6 radios in each house. Sixty-one percent have a radio at work (more women have them at work, 63 percent, than do men, 59 percent). *Radio Advertising Bureau.*

Share of radio audience by location *(Mon. to Sun., 24 hours)*	at home	in cars	other places
teens (12-17)	68%	17%	15%
men (18+)	36%	31%	33%
women (18+)	56%	20%	25%

Source: *Radio Advertising Bureau*

AM isn't happening. Less than 25 percent of all radio listeners will tune into AM stations in 1990. *American Forecaster Almanac 1990, Running Press.*

Radio's reach. Data from the Spring 1989 RADAR report shows that 96 percent of the U.S. population over 12 years old listens to the radio every week. During the morning drive-time, 53 percent of the radio audience is at home, 23 percent in cars, and 24 percent elsewhere. *Media Industry Newsletter.*

Talk radio. Adults 55+ account for 47 percent of the listening audience for news/talk stations, 42 percent for all-news stations, and 29 percent of the audience for other contemporary stations. *The Mature Market, Probus Publishing.*

Radio promos/contests. Nearly two-thirds say they don't participate in radio promo contests. The same number agree that there are too many contests, sweepstakes, or other promos used to sell products. Those who do participate—more likely blacks, and 35- to 44-year-olds—take part in about four in three months. *RadioTrends.*

Teens and radio. Teens average 3.7 hours of radio listening on weekdays and 6.4 hours on weekends. As they mature, time devoted to radio listening increases as TV viewing time decreases. Older teens (16-18) listen to more radio than do younger teens (13-15)—4.0 vs. 3.3 hours weekdays; 3.6 vs. 2.9 hours per day on the weekend. *Management Horizons.*

Radio reach by day part: percent of all teens (ages 12-17), black teens, and Hispanic teens who are reached by radio

Mon-Fri.	all teens	black teens	Hispanic teens
6am-10am	79%	83%	79%
10am-3pm	48%	41%	42%
3pm-7pm	78%	77%	84%
7pm-midnight	77%	80%	84%
Weekend			
6am-midnight	82%	88%	87%

Source: Radio Advertising Bureau

Percentage of teens (14-17) who engage in various media activities

	all teens	rent video	watch TV for leisure	movies 3+ times a month
Male	50%	49%	47%	50%
Female	50%	51%	53%	50%
Black	17%	12%	17%	17%
Hispanic	5%	4%	4%	5%
White	69%	75%	70%	69%
Native American	2%	2%	2%	2%

Source: Deloitte & Touche/Impact Resources

Leisure
The Active Currency of the '90s

The most valuable currency of the 1990s will be discretionary time. It will be collected through convenience-buying and services, and it will be spent along with substantial amounts of cash. Consumers use their valuable free time—to enjoy home and family, to increase health and fitness, and still, very often, just to cozy up with Cosby, a good book, or a videotape with the kids. Researchers are not even sure whether we have more or less leisure time. The confusion results from 1) a shifting definition of leisure, and 2) the fact that many Baby Boomers have less leisure, while other age groups seem to have about the same or more. Because most women are working, those who are also wives and mothers tend to have the least leisure time (not to mention sleep time), particularly since home and child care are still preponderantly women's work. Leisure time is stress relief time. [Note: Since a great deal of free time is spent with the media, please see Chapter 8 (Media) for more television and music listening information.]

Finding Time

Hype Alert: "There's no more leisure."

Leisure is just changing definition, becoming more active. Work hours have increased for Boomers, but very little, if at all, for the rest of the population. Boomers' active-leisure-in-condensed-time creates an impression that leisure is gone (because of the Boomer impact on the social fabric), but leisure is alive (even if it is harried) and spending its way into the 1990s. *John Robinson, American Demographics, July 1989.* Convenience will continue to overpower most other considerations. However you want to slice it, there are 168 hours in a week, and whether people are really short of leisure time or not, they feel they are. People always have, and always will, trade money for time. If they do have enough time, they want more. Smart advertisers will continue to position products for a stressful lifestyle. Smart marketers will explore convenience shopping—via personal computer services, mail-order catalogs, television shopping shows, and even fax machines. Smart product planners will provide convenience.

Different views on leisure

- The amount of leisure time the average American possesses has shrunk 37 percent since 1973. *Louis Harris and Associates.*

- Since 1965, sleeping and eating time have remained stable. Free time (everything excluding work, sleep, eating, shopping, housework, and childcare) is up about 10 percent, to 5.5 hours a day; two-fifths of that is spent watching television. *Newsweek.*

- Actual time spent at jobs is dropping. Since 1965, men's weekly hours have decreased from 49 to 42; women's from 39 to 31. *Newsweek.*

- The majority (55 percent) of Americans under age 50 report having insufficient leisure time (56 percent of those employed full time). Overall, 45 percent of the public report not enough free time. *Yankelovich Clancy Shulman.*

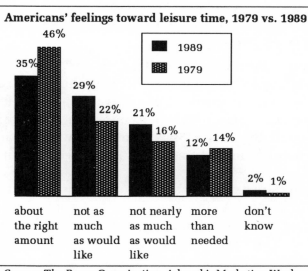

Americans' feelings toward leisure time, 1979 vs. 1989

Source: The Roper Organization, Adweek's Marketing Week

Whether one feels he/she has more or less, no one wastes free time. A plurality (42 percent) of Americans say they waste hardly any free time, and 27 percent waste only a little. A minority think "most people spend too much time enjoying themselves," and 61 percent feel that people have a right to as much free time as they need. *Facts on File.*

Two-income families lack leisure time. Most (62 percent) two-income families complain of scarce leisure time—73 percent of women and 51 percent of men. Compared to five years ago, four in ten Americans report having less leisure, and nearly half (49 percent) of two-income couples say so—60 percent of the women, and 42 percent of the men. *Yankelovich Clancy Shulman.*

Chores take up weekend time. The average person spends a full weekend day (13 hours) taking care of chores, including cleaning, groceries, cooking, household repairs, bill paying, and take-home work. Parents spend 66 percent more time cleaning, cooking, and doing laundry than those without kids. *Psychology Today.*

We have more leisure time than our parents did. Fifty-four percent say they have more leisure time than their parents did; 23 percent think less. *Yankelovich Clancy Shulman.*

Leisure Purpose

Hype Alert: "Leisure means doing nothing."
Actually, for Americans, leisure is often goal-oriented. Sixty-one percent of Americans think leisure is best spent if it is focused on achieving certain goals, and the most important goals are spending more time with the family (79 percent), followed by companionship (68 percent), and relaxation (67 percent). *Facts on File.*

Home is the center of many leisure activities. A plurality of consumers (40 percent) say the home is the focus of their leisure, and solid percentages are watching more TV and reading more than they used to. They are doing less eating out, visiting friends, and going to places of entertainment. *Adweek's Marketing Week.*

Hype Alert: "The electronic hearth is the heart of America."
Yes, we have all that equipment, and log a lot of hours in front of the TV. However, the kitchen remains as much the heart of the home as the den. The average American spends 2.1 hours a day in the kitchen doing such things as listening to the radio (48 percent), entertaining (47 percent), doing paperwork/paying bills (40 percent), and so on. Half of America's dinners are eaten in the kitchen. *G.E. Spacemaker/R.H. Bruskin.* Americans spend less time cooking, but probably spend more time communicating in the kitchen than ever before.

Reading

Hype Alert: "Americans aren't reading."
We still curl up with books. Eighty-five percent of people claim to read at least one book per year, 46 percent read ten or more books a year, and an additional 20 percent read four to nine. There is a resistant 16 percent of men who never read a book; 12 percent of women. *Maritz Marketing Research.*

Both extreme high- and low- brow reading segments will prosper.
For the immediate future at least, the trend of increasing popularity for serious books is expected to continue. Especially hot in the next year: science, nature, environment, mythology, and history. *New York Newsday. Sales of comic books have more than doubled in three years, from $125 million in 1986 to $275 million in 1989.* And it ain't just kids—most comic book readers are said to be between the ages of 18 and 24, and most are college-educated professionals. *Adweek's Marketing Week.* Due to sluggish hardcover sales, the next year will see fewer hardback titles, with more new lines of paperbacks, such as travel, mystery, and classic fiction. Look for children's books and sports books to be everywhere in the coming year. *American Forecaster Almanac 1990, Running Press.*

Music

The ways and places Americans have access to music have grown tremendously over the past decade—99 percent of homes have radios and stereo systems, as do cars, grocery stores, elevators, and so on. Music is reflecting the tastes of the me-generation market—an affectation of cross-cultural consciousness ("worldbeat"), and ersatz spirituality ("new age" music is now mainstream).

Musical instruments, sheet music, and accessories increased sales by 8 percent in 1987. Electric pianos saw a 29-percent sales increase, and synthesizer sales were up 9 percent. *American Music Conference.*

Pop is top. On record, tape, and CD, pop is consumers' top choice, followed by classical, jazz, country, black, hard rock, new age, folk, heavy metal, and rap. *Soundata.*

Cable TV: an audio sleeper. Here comes a new music service offered by cable TV systems: sending digital audio signals to a special decoder connected to a user's stereo system. On one system, 88 percent of the 450 customers who have tried it say it has met or exceeded expectations, and 68 percent say it is the most used stereo music source in the house. *USA Today.*

Sports

Swimming is the most popular participatory sport. Swimmers tend to participate in other sports as well—46 percent riding bicycles, 34 percent walking, and 33 percent camping. Among those who walk for exercise, 27 percent are age 55+; 31 percent of all persons 55+ers are walkers (their top participatory sport). Women are more likely than men to walk for exercise. Bicycling is the third most popular sporting activity, with 25 percent of the population participating, averaging 57 days of riding per year. Sales of all bicycles peaked in 1987 at 12.6 million units, falling to 9.9 million units in 1988, and are expected to have risen to only 10.2 million units in 1989. *National Sporting Goods Association.*

Walking favored for fitness. It has one of the highest participation rates of any fitness activity, and 25 percent of walkers say the activity is their favorite—the highest percentage for any fitness exercise. Low impact aerobic exercise is outpacing high impact—4.4 million new participants, vs. 3.9 million. *American Sports Data Inc.*

Most (62 percent) execs "do" sports. A solid majority (77 percent) of execs play sports with business associates or clients, and 39 percent use sports to generate business. Golf is the most popular, played by 82 percent of the executives. *Epyx Inc.*

Sport hunting less popular. The number of hunting licenses has decreased steadily since 1984. *Department of the Interior.*

Spectator sports still popular. Thirty-six percent of households and 28 percent of individuals attend sports events; 17 percent of households and 15 percent of people go to only one type of sport (vs. 4.8 percent of households and 2.5 percent of individuals who attended four or more types of sports events). *Harrison Owen Co.*

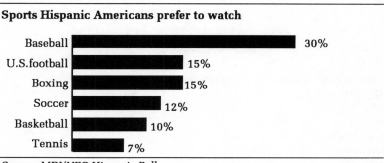

Sports Hispanic Americans prefer to watch

Baseball	30%
U.S.football	15%
Boxing	15%
Soccer	12%
Basketball	10%
Tennis	7%

Source: MDI/NFO Hispanic Poll

Movies

Hype Alert: "The main movie audience is teenagers."
The audience is maturing—admissions for persons under age 30 have declined 15 percent from 1985 to 1988, while those for 30- to 39-year-olds and 40+ers have increased 21 percent and 14 percent, respectively, since 1987. Admissions have experienced an 11-percent decline among teenagers, from 22 percent in 1985 to 19 percent in 1988. Cinema admissions overall increased, up 7 percent from 1987 to 1988, with the average moviegoer watching more films—7.6 a year in 1987, 8.2 in 1988. *Motion Picture Association of America.*

Americans' views on movies
Nationally representative movie poll May 5-13, 1989 (figures rounded)

	all	female	male	white	black	Hispanic	other
When was the last time you went out to see a movie?							
past week	10%	9%	10%	9%	12%	15%	12%
past month	19%	18%	20%	19%	18%	25%	34%
past 3 months	17%	18%	16%	17%	20%	19%	17%
longer than that	54%	54%	53%	54%	50%	41%	32%
Of those who have been to a movie, about how many times did you go to the movies in the past 12 months?							
none	35%	35%	34%	36%	26%	27%	27%
1-4	38%	39%	38%	38%	43%	50%	24%
5-10	14%	14%	14%	14%	15%	12%	20%
11-20	8%	7%	8%	7%	10%	-	24%
21-30	3%	3%	2%	2%	5%	4%	-
How likely are you to go see a movie that has scenes of . . . ?							
Violence							
more likely	3%	2%	5%	3%	6%	-	13%
less likely	60%	77%	41%	61%	54%	64%	46%
doesn't matter	35%	20%	53%	35%	39%	32%	41%
Profanity							
more likely	2% *	1% *	3% *	2% *	4% *	-	7% *
less likely	57%	69%	44%	57%	50%	69%	46%
doesn't matter	40%	29%	52%	40%	46%	32%	47%
Nudity							
more likely	4%	1%	6%	3%	5%	-	7%
less likely	57%	72%	42%	58%	51%	64%	58%
doesn't matter	38%	26%	51%	37%	43%	36%	36%
These days do movies contain too much . . . ?							
Violence							
yes	82%	91%	73%	82%	89%	83%	82%
no	14%	6%	22%	14%	7%	13%	19%
Profanity							
yes	80%	89%	70%	80%	86%	83%	80%
no	16%	8%	25%	17%	11%	17%	20%
Nudity							
yes	72%	83%	60%	71%	78%	84%	70%
no	22%	13%	32%	22%	18%	16%	30%
The quality of movies is getting . . .							
better	17%	12%	23%	17%	16%	15%	42%
worse	56%	64%	48%	56%	55%	70%	41%
not much change	24%	22%	26%	24%	25%	15%	12%

Source: Media General /Associated Press poll "The Movies"

Games and Hobbies

Beyond personal stereos: personal flight simulators. With the success of amusement park "rides," which generate thrills by use of imaging devices based on flight simulators for pilot training, look for helmets with miniature high-resolution video screens and stereo sound. *American Forecaster Almanac 1990, Running Press.*

If I had a hammer. Home woodworking is now practiced by 10 million Americans, and most learn from magazines. Furniture and cabinetmaking are the most popular pursuits, and more than half of these enthusiasts aspire to advanced levels. *Better Homes & Gardens' Wood Magazine.*

Gardening will grow as the population ages. Currently, 36 percent of U.S. households garden, with those having household heads 55 to 64 years old and 65+ digging in 29 percent and 22 percent more than the average, respectively. *Standard Rate and Data Service/ National Demographics and Lifestyles.*

Photo opportunities. Nearly one-quarter (23 percent) of homes have photo buffs, particularly households headed by 18- to 24-year-olds (21 percent above average) and 25- to 34 -year-olds (25 percent). Single men are more likely than single women to be interested in the hobby. *Standard Rate and Data Service/National Demographics and Lifestyles.*

Upscale products are now the trend in home entertainment items. The emphasis is on trading up from affordable products to high-quality ones. Camcorders, introduced in 1983, and HDTV are projected to have growth potential for the 1990s. *Business Trend Analysts.* However, there may be limited potential for camcorder growth because of high prices and consumer confusion over multiple formats. *Frost & Sullivan.*

Projected demand for services over the next 15 years.

Live theater	+98%	Entertaining at home	-10%
HMOs	+32%	Health clubs	-13%
Sailing	+19%	First mortgages	-22%
Vitamins	+10%	Bowling	-38%
Psychiatric care	+8%	Camping	-48%

Source: National Decision Systems

Travel

Flying for fun. 1988 was the sixth consecutive record year for the total number of airline passengers on U.S. carriers—455 million in 1988, projected to be 480 million in 1989, and more than 500 million in 1990. Two-thirds of those who flew last year took pleasure trips only. In 1988, 57 percent of pleasure trips were to visit friends, down from 63 percent in 1987. In '88, the share of pleasure travel spent on tourism reached a new high, 32 percent (20 percent in '77). *Air Transport Association.*

Shorter trips, smaller hotels. The number of trips taken for entertainment and outdoor recreation rose 9.6 percent, and vacation trips as a whole rose 8.4 percent in 1988 over 1987. All trips (except weekend travel) tended to average four nights. The number of short cruises (3 to 5 days) has grown by more than 200 percent in this decade, while the week-long cruise has grown 100 percent. *U.S. Travel Data Center.* Leisure travelers are most likely to stay at smaller hotels (fewer than 150 rooms)—comprising 78 percent of those hotels' guests. *Laventhol & Horwath.*

Affluents account for larger proportion of all trips taken. Affluent travelers (household income $40K+) accounted for 37 percent of all trips taken in the U.S. in 1988 (243 million of the 656 million total). This is up from 1984, when they accounted for only 28 percent, and '86, when they accounted for 31 percent. And affluents, like the rest of Americans, are taking shorter trips—the average stay is down to 4.0 nights from 5.1 nights in 1984. *U.S. Travel Data Center.*

Other Pursuits

Shopping sprees. The majority (71 percent) of women enjoy clothes shopping either somewhat (37 percent) or a great deal (34 percent), with under-age-30s more likely than over-30s to like it a great deal (52 percent vs. 28 percent). Still, 59 percent of women are buying fewer clothing pieces. *Newsweek/Gallup Poll.*

The "Experience Industry" is growing. As our desire for material possessions wanes in middle age, the desire for new experiences grows. The experience industry—travel, amusement parks, theme parks, concerts, theater—is growing rapidly, and greater demand is still ahead. *More people are going to amusement parks.* In 1988, the nation's amusement and theme parks hosted record numbers of more than 250 million visitors a year. That is an average of one visit for every man, woman and child in the U.S. Ditto for sports attendance, which has been growing steadily. *Attendance at professional sports events is increasing.* In the past 20 years, attendance at professional football games has increased by 154 percent, at baseball by 89 percent, and at professional basketball by 214 percent—increases that are much higher than the population growth for the same period of time. Sports participation is growing even more rapidly than sports attendance. In the desire to explore mysterious and exciting terrain, Americans are also turning inward in droves, with the help of psychotherapy and quasi-religions, such as est, group therapy, and evangelical religions, which can also be considered to be related aspects of the experience industry. *Future Scope: Success Strategies for the 1990s & Beyond, Joe Cappo.*

Culture—Americans are spending more. In 1970, U.S. spending for sports events was twice that of cultural events, but by 1986 cultural spending was 10 percent greater than for sports. *National Endowment for the Humanities.*

Gambling. Slots are up. Slot machines have overtaken table games to become the single largest gaming attraction in casinos in Nevada and Atlantic City. In 1978, 35 percent of the dollar volume of legal gambling in Nevada went through slot machines. Last year the figure was nearly 60 percent. *The New York Times.* In 1988, Americans gambled $253 billion—more than half on gaming; about $56 billion on sports, a third of that legal. *Christiansen/ Cummings Associates*

Percentage of consumers who rate these forms of entertainment as the best values for the money *(up to 3 choices)*	
A nice dinner/restaurant	55%
Rent a movie for home viewing	36%
A paperback book	22%
Tickets to a sports event	17%
Subscription to basic cable	16%
Subscription to pay cable	12%
A hardcover book	12%
A live theater performance	10%

Source: The Wall Street Journal *Centennial Survey*

The six most "fun things to do" for boys and girls ages 6-7 and 8-10

	Ages 6-7			Ages 8-10	
	boys	*girls*		*boys*	*girls*
Play with friends	74.6%	79%	Outdoor sports	81.5%	61.9%
Outdoor sports	70.6%	53.2%	Play with friends	67.7%	58.7%
Watch TV	63.5%	50.8%	Ride a bike	62.9%	46.8%
Ride a bike	61.1%	50.0%	Watch TV	54.8%	46.8%
Play videogames	55.6%	*	Play videogames	46.8%	*
Read a book or magazine	42.9%	60.5%	Read a book or magazine	35.5%	65.1%
Draw or art	*	43.5%	Draw or art	*	35.7%

* Was not one of the top six picks for that age group
Source: American Library Association

10

Health and Fitness
The High Cost of Living

As people age they work out less strenuously, but good health and a youthful appearance are priorities, nonetheless. The fitness craze is getting less crazy, aerobics are already getting softer, running is slowing to walking and there aren't as many fitness zealots as the media would have us think. There is much that Americans are dissatisfied with in terms of their own health and the U.S. health care system, although we spend more money on it than any other country in the world.

Health

Overall health-promoting activities improve. The Prevention Index, a measure of 21 health-promoting activities, has reached an all-time high, 65.4, since 1984. Americans' two biggest areas of improvement in the past year have been in limiting consumption of high-cholesterol foods, from 42 percent of people in '87 to 48 percent in '88, and in not drinking and driving, from 74 percent to 78 percent. *Prevention.*

Consumers are increasingly interested in self-care. Now, more than ever, Americans are reading food and drug labels and are, in general, better informed about personal health care. This trend is shown in the increased usage of over-the-counter (OTC) drugs, now accounting for 32 percent of the drug market. Their usage is expected to triple by 1995. *Health Foods Business.* In the early 1990s, a large number of prescription drugs will become OTC.

Americans are dissatisfied with their health. Only 28 percent of Americans are satisfied with their health overall. Higher income groups (earning $25,000+year) tend to be more satisfied with their overall health than lower income groups are—32 percent vs. 23 percent. And Americans are even less satisfied with their eating habits (23 percent for higher income groups and 22 percent for lower), and overall fitness (18 percent for higher, 13 percent for lower). Despite their dissatisfaction, three out of five Americans think they eat a well-balanced diet. *Parade.*

Americans' health-promoting activities by cluster.
Prevention groups Americans into clusters according to their health practices:

The Healthy and the Wealthy (25 percent of the population) rate tops in overall health behavior, have a desire to improve their health even more, and are most willing to spend extra money on healthy products.

The Safe and Satisfied (7 percent) are generally satisfied with their state of health, with little interest in improving it.

The Sedentary but Striving (8 percent) are a little above average in health behavior, but want to improve even more.

The Young and the Restless (39 percent) are relatively young (49 percent are under 35 vs. the 39 percent U.S. average), with slightly higher educations and household income levels. They are aware of healthful practices, but are not willing to implement them. Though they're more likely that the average American to undertake frequent strenuous exercise (8 percentage points above the national average of 36 percent), they are below average in their nutritional behaviors, especially in limiting fat consumption. They say they want to spend on healthy foods, but they don't.

The Fat and the Frustrated (7 percent) want to be healthy but have limited resources and knowledge to do so.

The Confused and the Indifferent (5 percent) are the poorest of the groups in terms of health behavior. *Prevention.*

Skin cancer to increase in the '90s. While the government champions go-slow policies regarding ozone depletion, the sunburning public may begin to prod for more speed. The rate of deaths from melanoma, a serious form of skin cancer, is increasing at least four percent per year—currently, 6,300 Americans die from melanoma each year. *American Cancer Society.*

Stress

Stress is rising in America. There has been a steady rise in the past few years of the number of Americans who feel they are under a great deal of stress, (55 percent in 1983, 63 percent currently). Women are more likely than men to feel under frequent stress—36 percent to 30 percent. College-educated people report high stress levels, as do people in the lowest and highest household income brackets. *Prevention.* Half of all adults in the U.S. feel more stress today than they did five years ago. Only 31 percent say they feel less stressed. While men and women feel similar increases in stress (women slightly more), young adults are feeling much more frazzled—70 percent of today's 18 to 24-year-olds feel more stressed than their counterparts did five years ago. Only 28 percent of senior citizens feel more stressed. Work is the number-one cause of stress (particularly for affluents); money the second greatest cause. *The Mitchum Report on Stress in the 1990s.*

Trends in stress over the past few years				
Frequency of stress	1983	1985	1987	1988
Almost every day	16%	14%	17%	18%
Several days a week	12%	13%	15%	15%
Once or twice a week	27%	33%	30%	30%
Less often than once a week	29%	30%	27%	27%
Never	16%	10%	10%	9%

Source: Prevention

Smoking

Smoking is down. The percentage of Americans who smoke has fallen from 40 percent in 1965 to 29 percent in 1987. Almost half (45 percent) of all Americans who ever smoked have quit. But while the smoking rate has declined substantially among certain male groups, it has fallen only slightly among women.

Percentages of adults who smoke
(figures rounded)

	1965	1976	1983	1987	% change per year 1965-85
Total adults	40%	36%	32%	29%	-.50
Male	50%	42%	36%	32%	-.84
Female	32%	31%	29%	27%	-.21
Whites	40%	36%	31%	29%	-.50
Blacks	43%	41%	37%	34%	-.39
Less than HS grad	37%	36%	35%	36%	-.06
HS grad	41%	38%	36%	33%	-.32
Some college	43%	35%	30%	26%	-.70
College grad	34%	26%	20%	16%	-.76

Source: The Surgeon General's Report

No smoking in public. A majority of Americans favor restricting smoking in public places, prohibiting cigarette sales to minors, increasing cigarette taxes to funnel money to Medicare, and banning cigarette advertising. Smoking is responsible for one in six deaths in the U.S., and garners the number-one spot for preventable disease. *The Surgeon General's Report.* The anti-smoking juggernaut will roll through the 1990s. You will see severe restrictions on advertising in print media and on billboards, limitations on promotions, and further restrictions on public smoking as the health reports on secondary smoking add up.

High school seniors are not cutting down on smoking. There was virtually no reduction in cigarette smoking among high school seniors during the 1980s—29 percent of the class of 1989 were current smokers, the same proportion as in 1981. *University of Michigan, Institute for Social Research.*

Stopping children from starting. The tobacco industry will continue to be under many watchful eyes in the '90s. The Federal Trade Commission, fearful that marketers targeting 18-year-olds are reaching younger children, plans to scrutinize marketing practices of tobacco companies that may encourage consumption by minors. Also, in another example of the "activist consumer/ citizen," anti-smoking activists in New York City are now working to stop distribution of free cigarette samples on city streets (samples they say children can obtain easily) and to make vending machine purchases more difficult for minors.

Plastic Surgery

Plastic surgery is increasing. More than a million Americans had facial plastic surgery in the U.S. in 1988, a growth of 17 percent since 1986. The most popular procedure is rhinoplasty (nose job), followed by eyelid surgery and facelifts. The fastest-growing procedure is chin augmentation or reduction (often performed with rhinoplasty), up 26 percent since 1986. Ear surgery is also on the rise, increasing by 19 percent overall in 1986. *American Academy of Facial Plastic and Reconstructive Surgery.*

Teens are snipping and tucking too. According to the American Society of Plastic and Reconstructive Surgeons, of the 73,250 nose jobs done in 1988, 16 percent were performed on people under 18, and some doctors estimate that plastic surgery on teens has grown by as much as 300 percent over the past few years. A new publication from the American Academy of Facial Plastic and Reconstructive Surgery called "Facial Plastic Surgery for Teens: A Parent's Guide," provides information in a question-and- answer format for parents wrestling with the issue of permanent makeovers for their teens.

Exercise

Soft exercise continues to replace strenuous exercise. Participation in sports such as running, swimming, aerobics, racquetball, calisthenics, and tennis has declined since 1984, while participation in walking, bicycling, and golf has grown from '84 to '87. *National Sporting Goods Association in the Lempert Report.* Exercise walking drew the most new participants among 44 sports in 1988 (7.6 million), for a total of 62.3 million total participants, making it the second most popular sport in the country. First is swimming, with 71.1 million participants. Women compose the majority (66 percent) of exercise walking participants. *National Sporting Goods Association.* We also see the change in exercise focus reflected in the types of exercise apparel and equipment being purchased.

What Americans spend on exercise clothes

	1988 sales	Change since 1987
Sweatshirt/pants	$2 billion	+9%
Walking shoes	$752 million	+47%
Warm-up suits	$461 million	-4%
Running shoes	$460 million	-3%
Aerobic shoes	$327 million	-19%
Leotards/bodysuits	$88 million	-33%

What Americans spend on exercise equipment

	1988 sales	Change since 1987
Exercise bicycles	$451	+22%
Treadmills	$283	+139%
Multipurpose home gyms	$184	-3%
Cross country ski machines	$159	-10% *
Rowing machines	$121	-18%

*estimate

Source: *National Sporting Goods Association*

Percent of adults (age 18+) who exercise/play sports regularly
(figures rounded)

	Total	18-29	30-44	45-64	65+
		Age groups			
White men	43%	58%	43%	31%	32%
Black men	45%	67%	41%	27%	22%
Hispanic men	41%	56%	33%	23%	39%
White women	39%	49%	41%	33%	28%
Black women	32%	40%	34%	24%	19%
Hispanic women	31%	39%	32%	20%	24%

Source: National Health Survey

Weight

Hype Alert: "Americans are getting fitter."

Think big—Americans are fatter than ever. Most Americans (64 percent) are overweight, the highest percentage ever—plus, 20 percent of those who are overweight do not think they are. *Prevention.* About 35 million Americans need to lose 30 pounds or more. *National Center for Health Statistics.* Almost one-third of children 6 to 11 years old are obese. *University of California, Adweek's Marketing Week.* And two-thirds of children between 6 and 17 can't pass a basic fitness test. *President's Council on Fitness and Sports.*

Hype Alert: "More and more dieting."

Fewer Americans are dieting today. Only one in four adults say they are on a diet, down 26 percent from 1986. People's perception of dieting has changed; dieting is now looked upon as a "weight-control effort of limited duration, rather than a permanent change in eating behavior." When people say "diet" nowadays they mean two weeks on a protein drink, not a lifetime of good eating habits. *Calorie Control Council.*

Exercise down, protein drinks up. As the exercise boom slows, people are turning toward methods that were the least popular in 1986—toward liquid/protein/fast diets, hospital/physician sponsored programs, diet soft drinks, diet books and low-cal microwaveable foods, and away from exercise clubs and diet pills. It is estimated that there are 65 million dieters in America today, with

18 percent of the adult population constantly dieting. Americans spend more than $29 billion a year to lose or maintain their weight. The 1989 estimate is $32 billion, and 1995's is $51 billion. *Marketdata Enterprises.*

Drugs

Hype Alert: "The drug situation just gets worse."
Truth: Casual use is down, and chronic use is up. About 14.5 million Americans over age 12 (7 percent of the population) were current drug users in 1988 (used drugs in the preceeding month). That's a 37-percent decrease since 1985, when 12 percent of the population were current users. However, crack and cocaine abuse is increasing. There has been a five-fold increase in medical emergencies due to cocaine abuse since 1984, and cocaine-related deaths have more than doubled in the same period. *National Institute on Drug Abuse.*

Hype Alert: "Drugs are only a problem of the underclass."
More people from upscale households report knowing someone seriously affected by drugs and knowing a person or place where drugs are sold than do people in downscale homes. More people from the top income bracket (34 percent of those in $50,000+ households) report having tried illegal drugs than from any other income group.*New York Times/CBS News Poll.*

Illicit drug use is less fashionable among youth today. A University of Michigan Institute for Social Research study finds that drug use is becoming more unfashionable among the mainstream of young Americans. Moreover, the likelihood of a college or high school youth actively using illicit drugs is only about half of what it was a decade ago.

Education works. The decline in drug use is not a reflection of the current "crackdown" on drug dealers, but rather an increased awareness of the dangers of drugs. The proportion of young people who say they have fairly easy access to various drugs has remained the same or increased over the last few years, while the percent who view drugs as harmful has increased.

Trends in perceived harmfulness (% saying great risk in trying once or twice), availability (% saying drug would be "fairly easy" or "very easy" for them to get) and 30-day prevalence (% having used once in past 30 days) of marijuana and cocaine among high school seniors

	1978	1980	1982	1984	1986	1988	1989
Marijuana: *harmfulness*							
marijuana/hashish	8.1%	10.0%	11.5%	14.7%	15.1%	19.0%	23.6%
availability							
marijuana/hashish	87.8%	89.0%	88.5%	84.6%	85.2%	85.0%	84.3%
30-day prevalence							
marijuana/hashish	37.1%	33.7%	28.5%	25.2%	23.4%	18.0%	16.7%
Cocaine: *harmfulness*							
cocaine	33.2%	31.3%	32.8%	35.7%	33.5%	51.2%	54.9%
availability							
cocaine	37.8%	47.9%	47.4%	45.0%	51.5%	55.0%	58.7%
30-day prevalence							
cocaine	3.9%	5.2%	5.0%	5.8	6.2%	3.4%	2.8%

Source: University of Michigan, Institute for Social Research

Brand-name prescription drugs will decrease in popularity. In the coming years expect to see a decrease in the number of brand-name drugs purchased as their patents expire and more generic drugs come onto the market. It's estimated that between 1991 and 1995, patents will expire on brand-name prescription drugs that have an estimated $10 billion in annual sales. *The Wall Street Journal.*

Americans have found new ways to buy drugs. Since 1985, mail-order drug distribution, health maintenance organizations, and doctors dispensing their own prescriptions (an estimated 10 percent of all doctors now sell medicines), have been eroding the retail pharmacist's share of the prescription drug market. In 1988, 15 percent of the nation's prescription drugs were sold by mail order, doctors, or HMOs. *The New York Times.*

Rehabilitation industry expected to grow. The drug and alcohol rehabilitation industry has grown from $1.5 billion in 1983 to $3.6 billion in 1988, and is projected to reach $6.2 billion in 1992. This is based on the number of admissions rising at 5 percent per year. *Marketdata Enterprises.*

Health Care System

Americans are dissatisfied with the heath care system. Most Americans (89 percent) feel that the U.S. health care system needs fundamental changes in its direction and structure. Only 55 percent of Americans are very satisfied with their last physician visit. Compare this to 73 percent of Canadians and 63 percent of Britons. The majority of Americans (61 percent) say they would prefer the Canadian health care system (totally government funded). *Health Management Quarterly.*

Quicker, more efficient service demands. Members of the health care community, hospitals, physicians, health maintenance organizations and others will be pressured for quicker, more efficient services. Hospitals will begin service training for their employees, and the emphasis will be on better service delivery and performance. *The Keckley Report on Health Care Market Research.* People need more convenience in health care because they are busier—expect more at-home medical tests and visits on weekends and evenings. *Market Intelligence Research Corporation.*

Costs and Insurance

Health care costs will continue to rise. America spends more than any other industrialized country on health care—11 percent of GNP (gross national product) in 1986. *National Center for Health Statistics. Health care costs will continue to rise into the 1990s*, with the latest government estimates projecting that spending could reach $600 billion at the end of 1989 and triple to $1.5 trillion by the year 2000 (15 percent of GNP in 2000). Health care expenditures were $1,900 per capita in 1987 and are expected to rise to $6,000 by 2000. There have also been projections that for the year 2005 the federal budget for Medicare will be greater than for Social Security. *The Conference Board.* In 1988, 13 percent of Americans said they did not receive needed medical care, with the majority (58 percent) citing lack of money/insurance/could not afford it as the reason. Of these 58 percent, almost two-thirds (64 percent) had insurance, meaning that their insurance was not adequate to allow them to receive needed medical attention. *Health Management Quarterly.*

Hype Alert: "A quarter of the nation has no health insurance."

In 1988 there were 37 million Americans who were uninsured, 15 percent of the population. *The Conference Board.* About one out of seven (4.6 million) adolescents age 10 to 18 are not covered by health insurance in 1987, this is up 25 percent from 1979 to 1986. *Office of Technology Assessment.*

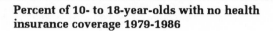

Percent of 10- to 18-year-olds with no health insurance coverage 1979-1986

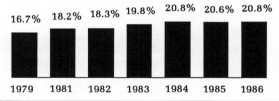

16.7%	18.2%	18.3%	19.8%	20.8%	20.6%	20.8%
1979	1981	1982	1983	1984	1985	1986

Source: Office of Technology Assessment

Long-term care insurance is increasing in popularity. Americans, fearing the financial strain that long-term care presents, are purchasing long-term care insurance, which is growing faster than any other type of insurance. There are now more than one million active policies, and more than half of these have been started in the past three years. By the year 2000, up to 30 percent of all working and retired adults could have long-term care coverage. *U.S. News & World Report.*

Marketing Health Care

Healthcare advertising is increasing. In 1984, $104 million was spent on health care advertising, increasing to $500 million in 1986 and $1 billion in 1987. But health care marketers had better use caution when advertising their services to cynical Americans—only 23 percent of Americans think health care providers advertise to help people. Fifty percent say they advertise to make money, 21 percent say to get rich, and 7 percent say to improve their image. *Healthcare Marketing & Communications Inc.*

Consumers' preferred ad scenario

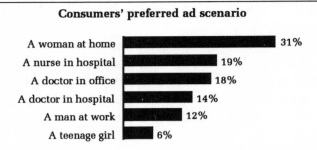

A woman at home	31%
A nurse in hospital	19%
A doctor in office	18%
A doctor in hospital	14%
A man at work	12%
A teenage girl	6%

Source: Healthcare Marketing & Communications Inc.

Consumers' preferred ad topic

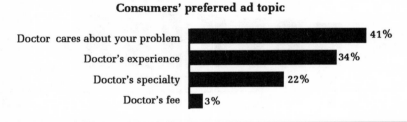

Doctor cares about your problem	41%
Doctor's experience	34%
Doctor's specialty	22%
Doctor's fee	3%

Source: Healthcare Marketing & Communications Inc.

Hospitals are paying doctors for patient referrals. The occupancy rate of hospitals has dropped 14 percent in the last decade. Because of this decrease in the patient pool some hospitals are actually paying money to doctors for their patient referrals. *The Wall Street Journal.*

Demographics

Women exert a powerful influence on health care. Women are the health care decision-makers for more than two-thirds of households in the U.S. Because they are better educated than in the past, they are demanding more information about health care services—procedures, alternative treatmentsand so on—and are relying less on physician advice as their sole source of health care information. *Market Intelligence Research Corporation.*

Blacks are 19 percent more likely than whites to have a personal physician or a hospital preference, and are 16 percent more likely to participate in an HMO. *Deloitte & Touche/Impact Resources.*

Baby Boomers are more health conscious and are more likely to use preventative care. Since cost and convenience are two areas of primary concern to Boomers, expect to see increased use of birthing centers, ambulatory care facilities, and surgery centers. *Market Intelligence Research Corporation.*

Mature Americans. In general, the majority of mature Americans are healthy and are not as limited in activity as has sometimes been assumed. A 1986 study by the National Center for Health Statistics reveals that 70 percent of mature persons (65+ers) living in the general community describe their health as excellent, very good, or good compared with others their age. The remaining 30 percent describe their health as fair or poor. *The Mature Market, Probus Publishers.* Though this does not include those 65+ers who are institutionalized, it is a good indicator of the older population's general state of health. Only one-eighth of persons 65+ are disabled, and half of those disabled are mildly so. *Find/SVP.*

The health care field will become more ethnically aware. As minority groups increase in size in America (it's estimated that only half the population will be caucasian by 2040), the health care industry will need to increase its sensitivity to and awareness of customs and mores of different cultural and ethnic groups. Health care organizations will need staffs that are able to relate to these burgeoning minority groups, and in some jobs multilingual skills will be required. *The Keckley Report on Health Care Market Research.*

The affluent are healthier than average Americans. The affluent ($50,000+ household income/year) are more likely than the general public to eat healthier foods and reduce consumption of fat, salt, and high-cholesterol foods (four-fifths vs. nearly three-quarterspercent of the general public). They are also willing to pay more for foods without additives in them (62 percent for affluents vs. 55

percent for the general public). And they exercise more than the general public (60 percent of affluents perform some kind of regular exercise vs. 52 percent of the general public). *Cambridge Reports' Trends and Forecasts.*

Food
Serving Up the Facts

Consumers are talking a lot about healthy eating habits, but they're not doing as much as we'd like to think. Where food is concerned, health and convenience are very much on their minds, but there are trade-offs between the two. On the health and nutrition front, so many conflicting claims have come out that many consumers are becoming cynical, turning off to claims and heading back to taste. People were frightened by alar on apples. Fish oil was replaced by oat bran, which is now being replaced by psyllium and rice bran as the latest quick fix. Studies introduced good and bad cholesterol, and made decaf coffee a no-no. Yet all the while, superpremium ice cream and fast food were growing more popular than ever. High-nutrition, low-fat foods and fat and sugar substitutes are getting their share of lip service (literally). Convenience will continue to be important to consumers in the '90s, and there will be a growing demand for foods that require minimal, if any, preparation. Half of all food dollars are now spent on food eaten away from home. Take-out will continue to eat up a larger share of the food dollar. And by 1992, you may see microwaves in cars.

Foods

Hype Alert: "Americans are eating healthy."

Americans' eating habits are schizophrenic. People will order a tofu burger for lunch, and eat a Snickers bar for a late afternoon snack. While more than half of adult Americans say they have reduced their consumption of red meat, cholesterol, sodium, and fried foods, a majority also say they can't resist the urge to eat ice cream. *Wall Street Journal Centennial Survey.* Perhaps people's inconsistent eating habits are understandable, considering all the contradictory health findings the "experts" are coming out with every day.

Percentage of people who have given up or cut back on these products, and the percentage who would gladly go back to them if new research showed they weren't at all bad for one's health

	given up	cut back	would go back to*
Tobacco products	16%	14%	4%
Bacon	8%	48%	13%
Liquor	6%	26%	2%
Fried foods	5%	60%	13%
Salt or sodium	5%	59%	9%
Beer	4%	21%	3%
Coffee and other caffeine beverages	4%	36%	9%
Eggs	4%	55%	18%
Ice cream	4%	38%	13%
Sugar and sweets	4%	55%	15%
Cheese and other dairy products	2%	31%	9%
Foods with preservatives	2%	45%	3%
Red meat	2%	53%	18%

*Respondents could make two or three choices.

Source: Wall Street Journal *Centennial Survey*

Percent of Americans who say they are making no effort to cut down on:

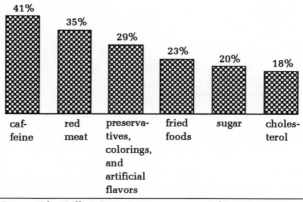

Source: The Gallup Organization, as reported in USN&WR

Food is a source of comfort for many Americans. Forty-seven percent of people find solace in food when they're depressed, and the most comforting foods are ice cream (21 percent of people eat it when depressed) and chocolate (13 percent). *Wall Street Journal Centennial Survey.*

Hype Alert: "Advertising a product's health benefits generates sales."
"Advertisements touting the health benefits of food products . . . have had limited success in changing diets. Only 21 percent of [people] who saw such ads said health claims made a difference in deciding whether to buy the product." *Wall Street Journal Centennial Survey.*

Concern about chemicals. Worries over pesticides and other chemical contamination of food have reached the top of the scary list. Consumers don't trust food retailers to protect them—only 2 percent think their favorite storekeepers will check for chemical contamination. *Food Marketing Institute, as cited in Adweek's Marketing Week.* In 1989, only 35 percent of Americans said the good effects of pesticides outweigh the bad (48 percent in 1987). *the Public Pulse, the Roper Organization.*

Has the safety of the the produce you eat improved, stayed the same, or declined in the past year?
(figures rounded)

	Total	Male	Female
Improved	24%	23%	25%
Same	52%	55%	47%
Declined	17%	15%	19%
Don't know	8%	7%	9%

Source: Maritz Ameripoll, Nov. 29, 1989

Is the federal government doing too little, just the right amount, or too much to ensure the safety of our food?

	Total	Male	Female
Too little	62.6%	62.6%	62.6%
Just right	26.4%	27.4%	25.4%
Too much	3.8%	4.0%	3.6%
Don't know	7.2%	6.0%	8.4%

Source: Maritz Ameripoll, Nov. 29, 1989

Hype Alert: "Only aging Hippies eat organic foods."

In 1990 most Americans (73 percent) believed fewer pesticides and other chemicals should be used, even if this results in higher food costs. Now almost half of Americans surveyed (45 percent) say they often or occasionally buy organic products. *Newsweek.* If organically grown produce was available at the same price as non-organic food, 84 percent of people would buy it. Of that group, 58 percent would buy it even if it were more expensive. The affluent and highly educated are more likely to have tried organic food. *Organic Gardening/Louis Harris/ as cited in Adweek's Marketing Week.* More than 30 percent of respondents to an *Organic Gardening* /Louis Harris poll say they have changed their eating habits in the past year in response to reports on pesticide use; 19 percent of respondents have bought organic produce for the first time in the past year. Almost 30 percent look for produce grown organically or with limited use of chemicals. *Organic Gardening /Louis Harris as cited in Adweek's Marketing Week.*

Women tend to respond to health warnings more quickly than do men. Women are more concerned about preservatives than are men (54 percent vs. 45 percent), and they are more apt to cut back on foods thought to be unhealthful, such as those high in fat or sugar. More than half of both men (61 percent) and women (67 percent) are cutting back on butter—the food product decreasing fastest in popularity. *Parade.*

Gourmet . The niche segment that enjoys designer food is still growing, though not quite as rapidly as during the beginning of the '80s. It is projected that 1989 sales of gourmet/specialty foods will increase 10 percent above the estimated 1988 level of $20 billion. Annual growth of this product area ranged between 15 percent and 20 percent during the early 1980s. The market is projected to rise 10 percent annually through 1995. *Packaged Facts.*

Hype Alert: "Only dieters eat light foods."
Of the 78 million adults who purchase light (containing less than the average amount of a specific ingredient such as salt or sugar) or low-calorie food products, 34 million are non-dieters. Both younger (25-34) and older (35-49) Baby Boomers are the most likely of all age segments to buy light foods (23 percent and 21 percent, respectively). People with higher education and income are also more likely to buy light. While women are still the largest consumers of light and low-calorie food products (62 percent are bought by women), men have doubled their purchases since 1978. Sales of these products are expected to grow at an annual rate of about 7 percent until 1993. *Packaged Facts.*

Use of selected low-cal foods by non-dieters and dieters	% of users	
	nondieters	dieters
Light beer	83%	17%
Light or low-calorie margarine	65%	36%
Diet soft drink	61%	39%
Sugar substitutes	59%	41%
Low-calorie salad dressings	58%	42%

Source: The NPD Group; Packaged Facts

High-fiber is still hot. In 1988, 54 percent of persons surveyed purchased high-fiber products, a 3 percent increase over the previous year. Of those cognizant of fiber importance, 85 percent picked cereal as their fiber source. High fiber consumers are mostly better educated Easterners between the ages of 40 and 64. *Prevention, as cited in the Lempert Report.* Sales of cereals with oat bran increased 215 percent, to $100 million between 1988 and 1989. *SAMI as cited in the Lempert Report.*

The perennial sweet tooth. The worldwide sweet tooth remains more demanding than the capacity to satisfy it. Production lags well behind demand—the average of the three most recent forecasts suggests sugar production could soon fall behind demand by 1.7 million metric tons annually. *The Wall Street Journal.* The American sweet tooth shows no sign of going away—use of sugar and other sweeteners is up to 168.2 pounds per person annually. *Census Bureau.*

Red meat consumption is still high, but Americans are eating smaller portions. While a comparison of consumption of meats by retail weight shows Americans eating more chicken than beef, a boneless weight comparison finds 41 percent more beef being swallowed than chicken (66 lb. per capita vs. 47 lb.), and a comparable amount of pork being eaten (44 lb.). We are still eating nearly twice as much red meat as poultry. *National Food Review.*

Teen health concerns. Teens are still eating foods now deemed unhealthful, even though they are aware of the need for good eating. Fewer than half of teens try to avoid foods they are aware can contribute to high cholesterol levels, even though 87 percent say they make a personal effort to maintain a diet they think is good for them. *The Gallup Organization.*

Beverages

Cola is still king. Out of the 46 gallons of soft drinks chugalugged by the average American last year, 32 gallons were cola-flavored. *Wall Street Journal.* By 2000, Americans will be gulping down 65 gallons of soda a year. *Adweek's Marketing Week.*

Bottled water sales flow upward. Sales are currently $1.9 billion a year, and growing at an annual rate of 10 percent to 15 percent.

Thirty-nine million American adults drink bottled water; per capita consumption is 7 gallons. The drinkers are typically age 25 to 44, well-educated, and living in a suburb in the Northeast or West. *Mediamark Research as cited in the Lempert Report.*

Annual per capita consumption of liquor was down to 1.6 gallons in 1988, from 2.0 in '81. Only vodka and tequila showed increases in 1988 (4 percent and 3.5 percent, respectively). *Jobson's Liquor Handbook as cited in Advertising Age.*

Hype Alert: "College students are drinking less alcohol."
They may be buying less, but they certainly aren't drinking less. There have been no major changes in the drinking habits of college students since the 1930s, despite the recent nationwide increases in minimum age for alcohol purchase. *Indiana University, department of Applied Health.* In bars, beer is increasing its share among men, rising to 27 percent of orders in 1988, up 21 percent from 1987. *Beverage Media.* Among beer drinkers, 46 percent prefer to eat Mexican food with their beer, 23 percent want American, and 7 percent enjoy Chinese. *Golin Harris Communications.*

Mealtime

Take-out breakfasts. Take-out breakfasts showed 18 percent growth between 1982 and 1987. In 1987, persons aged 25-34 accounted for the highest percentage of any demographic group for breakfast take-outs (30 percent). Behind them were 35- to 49-year-olds (26 percent). Households with incomes of $30,000-$40,000 and $40,000+ represented 48 percent of the take-out breakfast market, similar to the figures for take-out lunch and dinner. Take-out breakfasts showed strongest consumption by affluent singles, and on weekends. *Restaurants USA.*

Eat-out lunch. "Marketers are now zealously competing for the microwaveable lunch dollar . . . sales for frozen microwave sandwiches for the 52-week period ended March 1988 totaled just under $21 million." *Find/SVP.*

Teens eat like teens. The drive to incorporate more fruits and vegetables in the diet is largely ignored by teenagers at lunch-time—traditional noontime foods such as lunch meats, burgers, and pizza account for 79 percent of the lunches eaten most often by teens. *The Gallup Youth Poll.*

Take-home dinner. Busy lifestyles, especially for people under 50, are changing dinner preparation habits. Of the 86 percent of Americans who dine at home on weeknights, only about half now prepare the meal from scratch. The rest eat prepackaged or take-out food. The most frequent users of ready-to-serve and take-out food are 18- to 29-year-olds—25 percent of this age group eats this type of food on weeknights, compared to 16 percent of 30- to 49-year-olds and just 10 percent of 50+ers. *The Gallup Poll.*

Minorities and fast-food consumption. Minorities are just as short on time as their white counterparts—there is increased dining out by blacks, and Hispanics are dining out at about the same rate as whites. In general, younger, working, male, educated, upscale Hispanics are dining out most frequently. They are slightly more likely to eat fast food than are whites (41 percent of 1987 meals, vs. 37 percent for whites), and in a cafeteria (17 percent, vs. 11 percent of whites). They are less likely to go to a family restaurant than whites (32 percent, vs. 41 percent of whites). Hispanic 25- to 34-year-olds are eating over half (52 percent) their meals in a fast food place. Blacks are consuming half of all the meals they eat out at fast food spots—60 percent of the meals eaten out by 18- to 24-year-olds, and 66 percent of the meals for blacks without a high school diploma. While married and college-educated blacks predominate in family-style restaurant dining, households with higher incomes do not—under $15,000/year households eat 38 percent of their meals out at family restaurants, while only 32 percent of $30,000+ers do so. *The Gallup Organization.*

Convenience Continues

Less cooking time. According to a study by the University of Michigan, the amount of time spent cooking decreased by about one hour a week between 1965 and 1985. Women spent an average of 8.4 hours a week preparing meals in 1965, compared to only 6.9 hours in 1985. (Men spent more time cooking in 1985 than in 1975).

Microwave ovens are now in three-quarters of American homes—career women buy more microwave foods than other women (62 percent vs. 55 percent overall), and they are buying more frozen entrees than they did three years ago. *Conde Nast.*

Microwave use. Across all demographic groups, Americans use the microwave oven to prepare 20 percent of their heated food, a percentage unchanged since 1983. Although older retired consumers are least likely to own microwave ovens, those seniors who do have them consume microwaveable foods and beverages at a rate 52 percent above the national norm. Dieters are more likely than non-dieters to use microwaves, and they show preferences for small items such as popcorn, muffins, and baked potatoes. *MRCA Information Services.* The single heaviest consumers of microwave foods are infants. *Information Counselors, Inc.*

Cooks as you open it. One firm is testing thermal packaging. The contents of room-temperature soda cans and sandwich boxes will respectively cool down or heat up when the containers are opened. Special heat-exchange material is placed inside the packages. *The Lempert Report.*

Scratch is out. The kind of food preparation *decreasing* the fastest is cooking from scratch. The kind of food preparation increasing the fastest is no cooking. In 1987, 56 percent of all food and beverages consumed at home needed no heating. *NDP Group, as cited in the New York Times.*

Grocery stores adding services

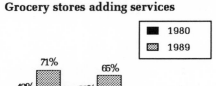

| | 1980 |
| | 1989 |

71%

65%

42%

39%

18%

10%

delis   bakeries   catering

Source: The Lempert Report

Carried foods getting left behind. Americans are brown bagging less today than five years ago. Per capita eating of carried items declined by 5 percent over the five-year span between 1981/1982 and 1986/1987. Although lunch remained the primary occasion for eating carried food, with more than 70 percent of 1986/1987 lunches being eaten from brown bags, other occasions for eating carried foods increased—snacks, in particular. Carried snacks expanded by nearly five points during the five-year period, to comprise 18 percent of all brown bag eatings. The most avid eaters of carried foods and beverages were children between the ages of 6 and 12, followed by adults aged 35 to 54. *MRCA Information Services.*

Shelf-stable foods are catching on. In 1989, sales of shelf-stable microwave food reached close to $90 million. Within six years, these products could grab 50 percent of the prepared canned foods market, with 1994 sales hitting $3.6 billion. Projections are that within 10 years, sales of refrigerated microwave items will reach between $1.2 billion and $1.7 billion. Currently, the market has sales of $15 million. *Find/SVP.*

Frozen foods. Frozen breakfasts, sandwiches, and pasta are new favorites. Sales of frozen breakfast products for 1988 were $1.21 billion, a gain of 12.5 percent over the previous year. *SAMI, as cited in the Lempert Report.* Frozen sandwiches saw the greatest growth in supermarket dollar sales last year. The 42-percent increase brought sales to $148 million. *The Lempert Report/Supermarket Business.* The frozen pasta dish market grew 133 percent between 1982 and 1988. *Find/SVP.* Frozen pasta dinners gained 21 percent in 1988 over the preceding year (sales totaled $793 million), and will gain 6 percent annually through 1998. *Business Trend Analysts.*

Snacks. Health consciousness is evident in between-meal eating. In the snack food category in 1988, microwaveable popcorn sales were 27 percent above 1987 levels. Although granola snack sales have dropped 32 percent from 1982 to 1988, fruit snacks have gone up 15 percent in the same period. *Advertising Age.*

Ice cream. Sales of superpremium (extra fat) ice cream will grow only 5 percent over the next five years. *Ice Cream Reporter.* Of all ice cream dessert products, ice cream is the preferred type (15.3 qt. per capita), followed by ice milk (5.4 qt.), sherbet (.82 qt.), water ices (.80 qt.), and vegetable fat and tofu-based products (.16 qt.). *International Ice Cream Association.*

Supermarkets. Time-crunchers are going to supermarkets for foods already prepared or easy to design into sandwiches. In supermarkets, the runaway leaders in dollar increases have been the delis. In 1988, deli sections had an increase of $1.64 billion in sales, or 20 percent over the previous year. Delis accounts for more than 3 percent of grocery sales. *The Lempert Report/Supermarket Business.* Fifteen percent of supermarkets now have sit-down eating facilities, up from 4 percent in 1980. *Parade.* Supermarkets are responding to the needs of dual-career families by offering a wide array of services: 51 percent are open 24 hours a day; 37 percent have automated teller machines; 36 percent offer self-service food bars. *Nielsen Marketing Research.*

Restaurants and Carry out

"On any given day, about half of the American population eats at a restaurant or buys carryout food." *FutureScope by Joe Cappo.*

Hype Alert: "The restaurant biz is booming."

Yes, but it's not what you may think. Restaurant sales have soared from $22 billion in 1970 to $72 billion in 1980, reaching an estimated $150 billion in 1990. However, this increase is fueled largely by growth in the fast-food sector, not in sit-down restaurants. *Demand for carryout foods will increase.* "In the next decade there will be a growing demand for dinner food that requires little or no preparation. Restaurants will battle supermarkets to become the main source of carryout food, and both will reap the benefit of this trend." *Future Scope by Joe Cappo.*

More adults are eating at fast food restaurants. In 1987, 88 percent of adults ate at fast food restaurants, up from 84 percent in 1984. *Mediamark Research, Inc.*

The meal we're most likely to eat at a fast-food restaurant
(percentage citing)

Lunch	49%
Dinner	32%
Snack	10%
Breakfast	8%
Don't know	2%

How often we eat at fast food restaurants times per week

1-3 times	45%
Never/don't know	21%
Less than once	23%
7-9 times	3%
10+	1%

Source: Maritz Ameripoll

Restaurants' share growing. Restaurants had a 32-percent share of the food market in 1988, compared with supermarkets' 68 percent. But restaurants continue to beat stores in growth. Restaurants enjoyed a real dollar sales increase of 2.6 percent, compared with supermarkets' 1.2 percent, factoring in 4-percent price increases for both. *The Lempert Report/Supermarket Business.*

Entrees show more variety. An analysis of changes in 150 restaurant menus between 1982 and 1988 shows that entrees are greater in number and variety. More seafood is being offered, and there is an increase in the number of salad entrees. *National Restaurant Association.* You can expect this trend to continue steadily throughout the 1990s.

Restaurant food more nutritious. Fifty-nine percent of adult consumers are very interested in having restaurants offer items for the nutrition-conscious, and they are getting what they want. The proportion of table service restaurants featuring healthy food has risen substantially (40 percent in 1988, up from 25 percent-33 percent in 1986). *National Restaurant Association.*

Ranking of features consumers are interested in at table service restaurants
(percent responding; 5=very important; 1= not at all important)

	5	4	3	2	1
Separate section for smokers	74%	4%	8%	2%	11%
Menu items for the nutrition conscious	59%	17%	13%	3%	7%
Children's menu	59%	8%	11%	4%	16%
Self-service salad or food bar	53%	18%	11%	6%	12%
Baking done on premises	49%	16%	13%	7%	13%
Daily menu changes	44%	16%	22%	6%	10%
Seasonal menu features	43%	19%	20%	6%	10%
Display cooking	40%	13%	18%	11%	16%
Dessert display	34%	18%	18%	11%	18%
Live entertainment/music	34%	14%	18%	12%	21%

Source: National Restaurant Association

In upscale restaurants, nutritious menu items are of interest to 76 percent of customers. Other items of interest to upscale restaurant patrons are separate smoking/no smoking sections (78 percent), children's menu items (67 percent), and self-service salad or food bars (71 percent). *National Restaurant Association.*

Children under 12 in restaurants. Children under the age of 12 are included in a substantial number of parties who patronize specific restaurant types. Children under 12 are present in:

- 40 percent of all parties where dinner food was delivered;

- 40 percent of parties where dinner was eaten inside a fast food restaurant;

- 39 percent of parties where a meal is carried out of a fast food restaurant;

- 28 percent of parties where a meal is eaten at a sit-down restaurant (and the average check is less than $10 per adult);

- 17 percent of parties where a meal is eaten at a sit-down restaurant (and the average check is $10 or more per adult). *National Restaurant Association.*

Kids' influence in restaurant decisions. More than half of children aged 7 to 17 have a say in choosing where the family goes to dine. *USA Today/Roper Organization in the Public Pulse.*

Cook-it-yourself. The jury is still out on the potential of a new angle in restaurants—cook-it-yourself. Some success has been reported by restaurants that invite customers to cook their own steaks. *Insight.*

Gourmet take-out meals. Apricot-glazed leg of lamb on a bed of mushroom and sherry rice to go, please. Upscale restaurants are going after the home market. The latest trend in the food industry is delivered gourmet food. *Newsweek.* Take-out can also be a major income generator at table service restaurants. *National Restaurant Association.*

Restaurants reported a 33-percent increase in appetizer offerings between 1982 and 1988. Seafood cocktails are the appetizer of choice for East Coast persons, aged 35-49, with household incomes of $30,000+. Women ages 25-34 and 50+ prefer soup. *The Lempert Report.*

Meat is appetizing. Although restaurant menus showed a decrease in beef and egg entrees—along with an increase in pasta, salads, and poultry last year—red meat dishes were gaining as appetizers. *National Restaurant Association.*

Tidbits

Gallup's recent poll on dining habits shows:

- **Men cook.** While nearly three-quarters of women say they do most of the shopping and cooking, there are signs of change. Younger men today are more likely to help with cooking than are men aged 50+. Nearly a third of men under 50 say they do at least half of the cooking.

- **Weeknight dining.** Among those who dine at home in the company of others, nearly four in ten watch TV, study, work, or read while eating. The figure rises to 71 percent among those who typically dine alone.

- **Quality concerns.** The large majority of adults claim their diets are very (44 percent) or somewhat (48 percent) healthful. But many are worried about the quality of their diet. More than six in ten say they worry a great deal or a fair amount about the quality and healthfulness of the food they eat. And the people with the healthiest diets are the ones who worry the most about what they eat.

- **Three squares a day.** Only a slight majority (56 percent) eat all three meals on a typical weekday. One in three adults skips breakfast on a typical weekday morning, and nearly one in five skips lunch. Very few miss dinner (7 percent).

- **The rich eat alone.** Affluent adults and those under 50 years of age are eating together and eating homemade meals even less often than others.

- **Label reading.** One in four (26 percent) adults say they read the list of ingredients or nutritional contents on the label of packaged foods every time they buy a new type or brand.

- **Processed veggies.** Although consumption of fresh vegetables is up, people continue to use processed vegetables more often than fresh.

Percent change in per person vegetable consumption, 1975 to 1988

	pounds 1988	% change '75-'88
Mushrooms	3.7	+85%
Broccoli	5.8	+65%
Cauliflower	3.6	+40%
Onions	16.3	+24%
Potatoes	118.7	-1%
Asparagus	1.0	-17%
Peas	3.7	-21%

Source: United Fresh Fruit and Vegetable Association

Youth

Teens are preparing more meals at home these days, both for themselves and for their families. More than eight out of ten teens prepare at least some of their own meals at home, and 59 percent sometimes cook for the whole house. Seventy-nine percent of teenagers report home baking, and 38 percent do so at least once a month. The vast majority (84 percent) of teens' family kitchens include microwave ovens, and more than three-fourths of teenagers prepare something in the microwave oven at least once a day. *Scholastic, Inc.*

Teens are making grocery decisions. Teens are going grocery shopping, but only 45 percent of them made their own grocery lists last year, down from 62 percent the year before. Think point-of-purchase. *Food & Beverage Marketing*

Dorm room pantry. Don't overlook college students, a group now 60-percent more involved with buying and preparing food than students in the past—64 percent of college students go food shopping, and they spend an average $34 per week on it ($41 for those living off-campus on their own). Sixty-nine percent of students report preparing at least some of their own meals. Of the 70 percent of college students who have access to microwave ovens, 97 percent use them, most frequently for popcorn (56 percent), microwaveable entrees (54 percent), and soup (40 percent). *Campbell Soup Company.*

Pre-teen cooks. More than half of children under the age of 13 (62 percent) prepare one or more meals in the kitchen. *American Frozen Food Institute.*

Demographics

Mature people take their time. Mature consumers perennially cite the need for healthy eating, and they are taking more time to cook than younger people. Prepackaged ingredients or food mixes are only half as likely to be used by adults over 50 (11 percent) as by younger ones (22 percent). *The Gallup Organization.* The most likely Americans to think they eat a well-balanced diet are older adults aged 50 to 65 (70 percent say they do), men (60 percent), and married people (60 percent). Singles are the least likely to believe they eat a well-balanced diet. More than 50 percent of consumers 50 to 65 have limited their consumption of foods high in cholesterol, and 55 percent of them are eating more fiber (40 percent of persons under 34 have increased fiber intake). *Parade.*

Minorities' food buying habits. When food shopping for the home, Hispanics' grocery bags generally contain less in the way of frozen food than the population at large, in line with their lower microwave oven ownership. With the exception of instant potatoes (39 percent in Latino homes, 45 percent elsewhere), Hispanic consumption levels of packaged products like rice mixes, sugar and salt substitutes, brownie and cookie mixes, granola bars, and pizza mixes are about half the rate reported in non-Hispanic homes. *Strategy Research Corp.*

Affluents eat out and eat healthy. Affluents (household income $40,000+) direct approximately 40 percent of their total food expenditures to food eaten away from home. This percentage falls with income to about 25 percent for those in households with incomes between $10,000 and $14,999. In comparisons of food spending among income groups at the grocery store, among the lowest ranking items for affluents were ham and eggs, cereal, and oil. Affluents do, however, fill their carts with fruits, vegetables, seafood, and dairy products (other than milk and cream). *The Food*

Institute. Persons with annual household incomes of $45,000+ base their dining-out decisions on convenience—impulse decisions made by the stressed and tired. The most popular outside-the-home dinner choice among affluents is a sit-down meal costing more than $10 per person. *National Restaurant Association.*

Environmentalism
It's Not Easy Being Green

On Earth Day 1, April 22, 1970 young activists made mediagenic warnings about environmental degradation. On Earth Day 20, in 1990, 200 million people around the globe held the largest demonstration in human history, establishing environmentalism as the fastest growing trend of our time. Earth Day 30 (in the year 2000) will find pro-environmental lifestyle changes widespread in the U.S. and all industrialized nations.

Groundwater pollution, toxic waste, tainted food, radon, air pollution, acid rain, and so forth have shaken John and Jane Doe out of their traditional apathy. Not only do they now spout pro-environmental attitudes and practice new, eco-friendly habits (like recycling and buying "green" products), they are also prodding government and industry on the issue, forcing them to catch up and do their part. Businesses are gearing up to address consumers' concerns, but we are still talking more than doing. No one has measured the guilt vs. convenience struggle—planetary health vs. hectic lives. Products that satisfy both needs will thrive. Making "green" easy will make both marketers and consumers happy.

Public Awareness and Action

It's not a fringe movement anymore. "Protecting the environment is so important that regulations and standards cannot be too high, and continuing improvement must be made regardless of cost" is the opinion of an overwhelming 80 percent of respondents in a June 1989 *New York Times Poll*. Just eight years prior, only a minority of the population (45 percent) agreed with those sentiments. *New York Times Poll*

- Most (62 percent) Americans now believe that environmental pollution is a very serious threat to our country—that is a 41-percent increase in just four years. *The Public Pulse, the Roper Organization.*

- Almost every American (97 percent) thinks more should be done about environmental degradation by both public and private sectors. *Louis Harris and Associates.*

- The number of people recognizing the threat of environmental contamination has increased substantially—in 1988, 88 percent of those polled thought air pollution was a serious problem, up from 68 percent in 1980. Eighty-two percent indicated water pollution was a serious problem, a jump from 69 percent in 1980. Also in 1988, 65 percent of those asked thought the global warming greenhouse effect was a serious issue, up from just 37 percent four years before. *The Public Pulse, the Roper Organization.*

Ranking the threats. Of eight potential environmental threats, highest public concerns are about water quality (80 percent), air quality (78 percent), and pesticides (66 percent). *Opinion Research Corporation.* Concerning those issues the public thinks should be taken care of immediately, 63 percent want "urgent action" on waste disposal, 52 percent on drinking water pollution, 43 percent on ocean pollution, 43 percent on acid rain, 43 percent, deforestation, 39 percent, global warming, and 32 percent, air pollution. *Media General/AP.* Most people think the environmental situation in this country is bleak. By 64 percent to 35 percent, the American people rate the environment in this country as negative; 81 percent think the world will be worse in 50 years. *Louis Harris and Associates.*

Public ranking of environmental threats: percent calling the problems "very serious."

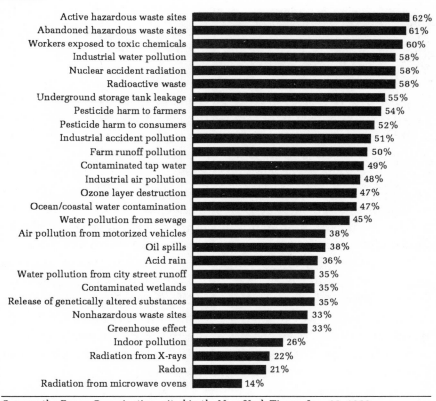

Active hazardous waste sites	62%
Abandoned hazardous waste sites	61%
Workers exposed to toxic chemicals	60%
Industrial water pollution	58%
Nuclear accident radiation	58%
Radioactive waste	58%
Underground storage tank leakage	55%
Pesticide harm to farmers	54%
Pesticide harm to consumers	52%
Industrial accident pollution	51%
Farm runoff pollution	50%
Contaminated tap water	49%
Industrial air pollution	48%
Ozone layer destruction	47%
Ocean/coastal water contamination	47%
Water pollution from sewage	45%
Air pollution from motorized vehicles	38%
Oil spills	38%
Acid rain	36%
Water pollution from city street runoff	35%
Contaminated wetlands	35%
Release of genetically altered substances	35%
Nonhazardous waste sites	33%
Greenhouse effect	33%
Indoor pollution	26%
Radiation from X-rays	22%
Radon	21%
Radiation from microwave ovens	14%

Source: the Roper Organization, cited in the New York Times, *Jun. 22, 1989*

Health problems from pollution. As many as 15 percent of the population may already have EI—Environmental Illness—also known as Multiple Chemical Sensitivity and Total Allergy Syndrome. This severe combination of allergic symptoms results from chronic exposure to commonly used chemicals. *Utne Reader.*

Hype Alert: "Everyone is worried about radon."

The truth is there has yet to be a groundswell on radon. Americans show an ambivalence about radon—27 percent do not feel radon is a serious problem, and 15 percent have no opinion; 46 percent feel homes should have radon testing. Interestingly, desire for mandatory testing declines as income rises. *ICR Survey Research Group.* Although the EPA estimates that 10 percent of the nation's 90 million homes have unsafe levels of radon gas, only 2 million homes have so far been tested. *Insight.* When it's time to sell the house, radon/energy issues arise. Radon and energy efficiency are now big concerns among home sellers and buyers. *National Association of Realtors.*

Hype Alert: "Plastics are the environmental bogeyman."

The hard fact is that paper constitutes a far greater percentage of landfill volume. In fact, recent estimates place the percentage of household trash that is plastic at only 5 percent-7 percent by weight, less than 12 percent by volume. In contrast, paper constitutes about 37 percent of the household trash, and waste from the yard more than 20 percent. *Browning Ferris Industries. The public is misinformed about plastics' harmfulness.* In a Roper poll asking the public to name the most important contributors to the solid waste problem, out of 13 refuse items, the leaders in blame are plastic bottles and plastic packaging (each picked by 37 percent), way ahead of disposable diapers (20 percent), newspapers (13 percent), and paper packaging (12 percent). *Adweek's Marketing Week, March 27, 1989.* These public impressions are just plain wrong, since most of the stuff in landfills is paper. The 1989 joint study by Franklin Associates andthe Garbage Project of the University of Arizona finds that just 18 percent of the volume of municipal solid waste is made up of plastic products. The dominant materials in municipal solid waste, paper, and paperboard, represent 38 percent by volume. Metals make up 14 percent, glass accounts for 2 percent, and other materials comprise 28 percent. Packaging in one form or another accounts for about a third (34 percent) of the total volume of municipal waste. Plastic packaging represents 27 percent of the total volume of packaging in municipal solid waste, while paper and paperboard account for 46 percent. Metals make up 15 percent and glass 7 percent of packaging in municipal solid waste. *Estimates of the Volume of Municipal Solid Waste and Selected Components, Executive Summary, Franklin Associates Ltd., October 19, 1989.*

Hype Alert: "Everyone is an environmentalist."

Be careful of those who claim to be environmentalists. The following table and chart show the percentage of Americans who say they are environmentalists—and the percentage who actually perform activities that help preserve the environment.

Do you consider yourself to be an environmentalist? If yes, would you say you are a strong environmentalist, or not?

	strong environmentalist	not strong environmentalist	not an environmentalist
National	41%	35%	20%
Age			
18-29	31%	38%	28%
30-49	39%	40%	18%
50 & over	49%	28%	17%
Education			
Coll. grad.	43%	36%	19%
Coll. incmpl.	42%	39%	18%
HS grad.	41%	37%	19%
Not HS grad.	38%	24%	27%
Household Income			
$50,000 & over	38%	41%	19%
$30,000-49,999	43%	43%	14%
$15,000-29,999	42%	31%	22%
Under $15,000	42%	28%	22%

Source: The Gallup Organization 1989, report #285

According to Gallup:

- Environmentalist identity tends to increase with education, income, and age.

- Gender and political affiliation show little influence on environmentalism.

- Residents of the South are the least likely to identify themselves as strongly environmentalist (36 percent) and the most likely to identify themselves as not environmentalist (23 percent).

Most (57 percent) Americans say they have made changes in their daily behavior due to environmental concerns. Among the sixth of the U.S. population that identifies itself as strongly environmentalist, 80 percent have made pro-environmental changes in the way they live their daily lives. *The Role of Plastics in American Society, a presentation by Gene Pokorny, President of Cambridge Reports.*

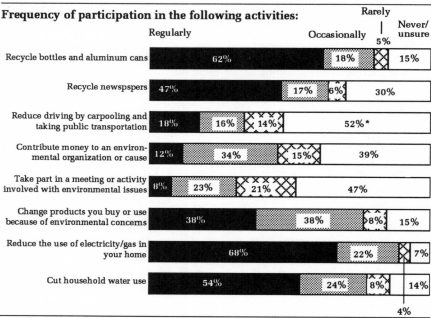

Frequency of participation in the following activities:

	Regularly	Occasionally	Rarely	Never/unsure
Recycle bottles and aluminum cans	62%	18%	5%	15%
Recycle newspapers	47%	17%	6%	30%
Reduce driving by carpooling and taking public transportation	18%	16%	14%	52%*
Contribute money to an environmental organization or cause	12%	34%	15%	39%
Take part in a meeting or activity involved with environmental issues	8%	23%	21%	47%
Change products you buy or use because of environmental concerns	38%	38%	8%	15%
Reduce the use of electricity/gas in your home	68%	22%		7%
Cut household water use	54%	24%	8%	14%

4%

* Includes 11 percent to whom the question does not apply.
Source: NBC News/Wall Street Journal poll, #169, April 27, 1990

Hype Alert: "Individuals alone can save the planet."
Sure, individual efforts can help—it would be a good step if many consumers turned off lights when they left their living rooms, and

put fluorescent bulbs in their lamps, and became attentive to their electrical usage. However, in 1987, residential energy consumption accounts for only 7 percent of U.S. energy usage. Over a third of the nation's energy usage is for transportation, and yes, it would be a help if people drove less, and carpooled, yet only a third of transportation energy usage is for private cars. *"The Trouble with Earth Day," in The Nation, April 30, 1990, by Kirkpatrick Sale.* In total, the energy used by individuals accounts for only a bit over a quarter of all energy consumption in the nation. This pattern is also true for pollution, for toxic waste, for loss of wetlands, soil erosion, ozone depletion, rain forest destruction, and so forth— consumer efforts are only a part of the overall solutions. Institutions create the majority of the problem. As this message seeps into the public mind, attitudes toward government and industry will grow more stern. As Jay Leno says, "Why do we look to Congress to clean up the air? Isn't that like asking the pigeons to clean up the statues?"

NIMBY. "Not In My Back Yard—I know we need to get rid of all this garbage, but don't toss it where I live." Most people who recognize that solid waste disposal is a serious local problem would still oppose a landfill in their community. The likelihood of individuals opposing facilities to convert waste to heat, and the likelihood of describing such a facility as an "incinerator," increases with the closeness to the facility. *Opatow Associates.* We anticipate both NIMBY and NIABY (Not In Anybody's Back Yard) activism to grow in regard to many of the solutions proposed for waste and toxic waste disposal.

Will They Pay Green for Green?

Hype Alert: "Consumers won't pay more for environmentally sound products."

Actually, they will—three-quarters of Americans (74 percent) are more likely to buy a product whose packaging is degradable or recyclable, and nearly eight in 10 Americans (78 percent) are willing to pay extra for such packaging. Eighty-four percent say there should be federal legislation requiring manufacturers to use degradable or recyclable packaging. *Penn & Schoen.* During 1989, environmentally sound packaged goods grew 30 times faster than all new packaged goods. *New Packaged Goods Go Green, Marketing Intelligence Service.* Think of 15 percent as the bottom line. Consumers could be convinced to switch from convenient plastic to breakable glass packaging if a 15-percent tax were imposed on plastic. Also, most consumers would be willing to pay at least 5 percent more for a recyclable or degradable package. However, fewer than a quarter of people would switch to environmentally sound packaging if the greener product cost as much as 15 percent more. *Gerstman+Meyers.*

Packaging loyalty of plastic soda bottle users; consumer behavior if there were a tax increase of 5 percent or 15 percent

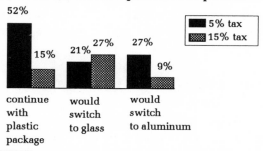

Source: Gerstman+Meyers

Putting money where your mouths and lungs are. Eighty-one percent of adults would be willing to pay higher taxes, if the money would go to protect the environment. *Louis Harris and Associates.*

Percent willing to accept a lower standard of living if it means a cleaner environment, by annual household income

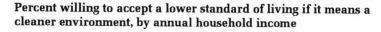

Source: USA Today *poll, March 1990*

Environment over economic growth. Americans "overwhelmingly" favor helping the environment over promoting economic growth. *The Los Angeles Times Poll.* Forty-nine percent think no tradeoff is necessary between environmental improvement and economic growth, but if some kind of a tradeoff were needed, a majority of Americans (52 percent to 21 percent) think the nod should go to the environment at the expense of growth. *The Role of Plastics in American Society, a presentation by Gene Pokorny, President of Cambridge Reports.*

Most consumers are willing to pay more to clean up the environment:
Would pay 15% more if all groceries were packaged for recycled use:

Would pay more	57%
Would not pay more	37%

Would pay an additional 15% in taxes to reduce pollution significantly:

Would pay more	60%
Would not pay more	33%

Would pay $50 more a month for electricity:

Would pay more	42%
Would not pay more	50%

Would accept a lower standard of living for a cleaner environment:

Yes	63%
No	26%

Have stopped buying products made by a company thought to be polluting the environment:

Have stopped buying	52%
Have not stopped	46%

Source: USA Today *poll, April 1990*

"Protecting the environment is so important that requirements and standards cannot be too high, and continuing environmental improvements must be made REGARDLESS of cost."

	9/81	9/82	4/83	1/86	7/88	4/89	Total 6/89	Women 6/89	Men 6/89
Agree	45%	52%	58%	66%	65%	74%	80%	80%	80%
Disagree	42%	41%	34%	27%	22%	18%	14%	13%	14%
Don't know/ No answer	13%	7%	8%	7%	13%	8%	6%	7%	6%

Source: The New York Times *Women's Poll, June 1989*

Who's To Blame?

Public/private sector officials are not trusted. A large majority of the public (85 percent) worries about how well people in commerce and government are doing with regard to the safe disposal of dangerous chemical waste. The majority (97 percent) thinks an inadequate job has been done by both public and private sectors to curb and to protect against pollution. *Louis Harris and Associates.* Among all adults asked how they would rate the job being done by the federal government on keeping the environment clean, 51 percent said only fair, and 32 percent said poor. Local governments were rated poor by 27 percent and fair by 44 percent. *Media General/AP.* By 48 percent to 46 percent, a plurality denies that a good job is being done to protect people from radiation from nuclear power plants. A majority, 54 percent vs. 42 percent, is not convinced that a good job is being done on maintaining trees and forests. *Louis Harris and Associates.*

Have environmental protection laws and regulations gone too far, not far enough, or have they struck about the right balance?

	1989	1982	1981	1980	1979	1977	1976	1975	1974	1973
Gone too far	11%	16%	21%	25%	24%	20%	15%	20%	17%	13%
Not enough	55%	37%	31%	33%	29%	27%	32%	31%	25%	34%
About right	27%	38%	38%	33%	36%	39%	35%	37%	44%	32%
Don't know	7%	9%	10%	10%	11%	14%	18%	12%	15%	21%

Source: The Roper Organization, as cited in The Public Pulse, *March 1990*

How green is the President? Although TV spots showing a cruddy Boston harbor may have helped the President into office, they won't keep him there. When asked in early 1989 if George Bush would be able to improve the environment significantly, 41 percent of the public said he would and 54 percent said he would not. By September 1989, 56 percent said he would not and only 35 percent said he would. *New York Times/CBS News Poll.* At the end of the first calendar quarter of 1990, pollsters found only one-fourth of the public believes Bush is progressing on the environment. *U.S. News & World Report, March 19, 1990.* The majority trusts Bush's point of view on environmental issues (57 percent think he would make the right decisions), but they think he creates more hot air than substance. As of April 1990, 68 percent felt that he had mainly talked about the issues, while only 18 percent felt he had made progress. *The New York Times Poll, conducted March 30-April 2, 1990.*

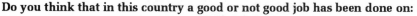

Do you think that in this country a good or not good job has been done on:

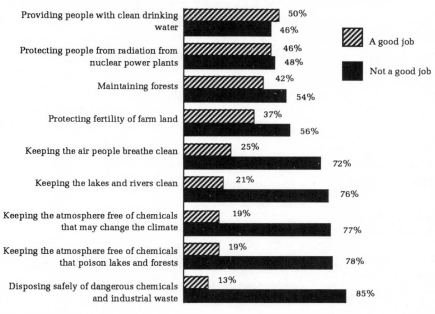

Providing people with clean drinking water — 50% / 46%

Protecting people from radiation from nuclear power plants — 46% / 48%

Maintaining forests — 42% / 54%

Protecting fertility of farm land — 37% / 56%

Keeping the air people breathe clean — 25% / 72%

Keeping the lakes and rivers clean — 21% / 76%

Keeping the atmosphere free of chemicals that may change the climate — 19% / 77%

Keeping the atmosphere free of chemicals that poison lakes and forests — 19% / 78%

Disposing safely of dangerous chemicals and industrial waste — 13% / 85%

A good job

Not a good job

Source: Louis Harris and Associates 1989, #21

Hype Alert: "Post-Reagan America still favors deregulation."
Americans now want more regulation. Growing concerns over threats to public health (such as medical wastes on beaches, oil spills, plane crashes, and so on), have made Americans ready for more government regulation. Following the deregulatory policies of the Reagan administration, Americans now favor increased monitoring of the environment—three-quarters feel there is not enough regulation of air and water quality. *Roper Organization as cited in Adweek's Marketing Week.*

Percent of Americans who feel the following areas need more regulation

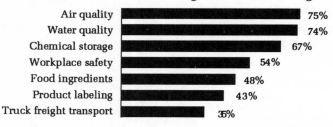

Air quality	75%
Water quality	74%
Chemical storage	67%
Workplace safety	54%
Food ingredients	48%
Product labeling	43%
Truck freight transport	35%

Source: Roper Organization as cited in Adweek's Marketing Week

Is there too much government regulation, not enough government regulation, or about the right amount of government regulation of:

	Too much	Not enough	About right	Don't know	Not enough 1984	1980
How chemicals are used and stored	7%	67%	20%	6%	65%	58%
Nuclear energy	10%	53%	28%	9%	50%	50%
What ingredients can be used in food	10%	48%	37%	6%	40%	30%

Source: The Roper Organization, as cited in The Public Pulse, *March 1990*

Business is doing a poor job. Just 36 percent of the public thinks business is fulfilling its responsibility to control pollution satisfactorily. *The Public Pulse, The Roper Organization.* Put another way, 42 percent said business was doing a poor job, and 36 percent said fair. *Media General/AP Poll.*

Environmental indifference will cost businesses money. Public relations officers and investment analysts take note: more than three-quarters of Americans (77 percent) say their purchase decisions are affected by a company's reputation with regard to environmental issues. *The Michael Peters Group telephone survey conducted by Penn & Schoen.* Corporate public image will become a critical issue during the 1990s. An anti-environmental label on a company may damage sales profoundly, while earning an eco-star will be a modest boon. A strong and public corporate commitment to pro-environmentalism is one of the best long-term image builders for the 1990s and beyond. Already the movement is strong enough in the mass market that eco-activism by itself will not garner a company a liberal image. The eco-image is a slow-growing seed that will eventually tower over other corporate images. The tuna industry was well aware of the damage that a million boycotting children could do to their image, so they wisely adopted expensive "dolphin-safe" policies *before* they were mandated.

Green Products and Industries

Consumers want to know what products are greenest. The move made by Wal-Mart stores—green-labeling pro-environmental products—may become as much a national assumption as the Underwriters Laboratories' seal is now. West Germany's Blue Angel eco-label has been in force for a decade, and Japan and Canada have recently introduced national eco-labeling plans. There is talk of similar plans in the U.S., but don't look for one to be in force before 1993.

Convenience is still most important. People do not think take-out containers are enough of an environmental problem to give up the convenience of leak-proof, heat-retaining packages. The packaging that people describe as "trash" today differs from what they cited 20 years ago. Now they associate litter with take-out food, whereas soft drink and beer containers were the culprits in the '60s. *Opatow Associates.* McDonald's is said to be considering a return to paper cups, but is reportedly afraid consumers will resist because of leakage. Mc D's is understandably a little sensitive on the subject of environmentalism after a series of ups and downs. Ups: a good eco-image, and a popular program to use recycled materials in their redecorating plans. Downs: a flap about a recycled label on unrecycled hash brown wrappers, and cosmetic early attempts to promote recycling of their clam shell plastic containers.

The question of terminology. Products claiming to be environmentally safe may be the next battleground between legal prosecutors and marketers. This is because terms like "recyclable" and "degradable" have no fixed definition. *Advertising Age.* Some plastic called "degradable" is in fact "photodegradable," meaning that in order to break down it has to be in direct sunlight—a rare occurence when buried under tons of debris. *Newsweek.* As consumers become sophisticated about environmental claims, their tolerance for questionable claims will diminish. This has already happened—the claims of "photodegradeability" of Hefty trash bags were removed when consumers objected.

Natural farming will increase in the next two decades. Beneficial insects and other organisms are being used increasingly by farmers to control pests—sales of such insects have tripled in the past five years. *The Wall Street Journal.*

Beach pollution fuels the medical waste disposal industry. The bad news of medical waste washing up on beaches has led to some positive action. The medical waste disposal industry is booming, fueled by several states passing strict disposal laws. Currently the market generates revenues estimated between $800 million and $1.4 billion. It is expected to increase to $5 billion by 1995. *Find/ SVP.*

Giving the diaper problem the powder. Disposable diapers do not decompose for 500 years, and U.S. landfills receive 16 billion diapers each year—an amount that would reach to the moon and back seven times. So far, the cloth diaper movement has barely made a dent in the market, but it can be expected to grow, according to the Environmental Action Foundation. Hospitals are increasingly returning to cloth diapers. *The New York Times.* Manufacturers of disposables are far from giving up. At least one recycling firm has begun recycling plastic diapers, and one major manufacturer has begun extracting baby poop from disposable diapers for reprocessing into compost. *Utne Reader.*

Recycling
Recycling is not yet a full-fledged trend. Regardless of public support for recycling, some municipal paper recycling efforts have had to be cancelled because of a paper glut. Although only 20

percent of the country now lives in areas where recycling of household refuse is required, 87 percent of those not presently required would support such a measure. *Media General/AP Poll.*

Local lawmakers are moving aggressively with recycling laws. More than 800 pieces of recycling legislation were introduced this year, with 134 new laws enacted in 38 states and DC; recent acts include efforts to build markets for recycled materials. *The Wall Street Journal.*

Plastic: a mixed blessing. A trend that may be ecologically sound for one target of environmental concern can be a curse on another. In part to make cars lighter (and therefore less polluting), the use of plastics in auto exteriors will increase from 125 million pounds today to 220 million lb. in 1993. *The New York Times.*

Growth in wrapping material is projected to favor non-degradables. Converted flexible packaging materials' (plastics, paper, and aluminum foil) forecasted growth is set at 3.6 percent annually through the year 2000, to more than 6 billion pounds. Converted flexible film (cellophane) packaging will lead the industry, at 5-percent annual growth in consumption as a result of new technologies, moderate price increases, and new market opportunities. Of traditional flexible packaging materials, aluminum foil will remain the chief competitor of plastic films through 2000. *Leading Edge Reports.*

Recyclable packaging. The increase in environmentally sound packaging may mean increased recycling. Products in packaging that helps consumers cut down on solid waste, pollution, and degradation of non-renewable resources are growing 30 times faster than all new packaged goods. *Marketing Intelligence Services.*

Priorities by Income Groups

Eco-activism increases on the upscale side of society. Higher education levels and higher income levels generally mean greater concern about environmental issues, as well as greater willingness to participate in solutions. *The Role of Plastics in American Society, a presentation by Gene Pokorny, President of Cambridge Reports.* However, the socioeconomic disparities are not great. For example, upper-middle-class Americans ($35,000-$49,999/yr household income) and affluents ($50,000+) are somewhat more likely (80 percent of $50,000+) than lower income groups (68 percent of $15,000-$24,999) to support pollution controls on power plants even if it means higher utility bills. The $15,000-$24,999 group has the largest percentage (25 percent) opposing such controls. *Media General/Associated Press Poll.* Lower income Americans are, unsurprisingly, sensitive to pocketbook solutions for environmental problems. Fees and increased taxes (like gas taxes) hit lower-income groups disproportionately hard and so are less popular. Even though they support environmental improvement, the less affluent are wary of many environmental solutions assuming that most solutions will hit their already strained family budgets.

It is worth noting, however, that middle- and lower-class Americans still support a range of proposals, even ones that hit them in their wallets. Just as the less-wealthy give a higher proportion of their income to charitable organizations than do the wealthy, so they seem willing to bite a larger share of the bullet to address environmental needs. There is a curious, possibly semantic difference in responses between income groups in describing how immediate the crisis is. In most categories of ecological threat, upper middles and affluents are the most likely to want "prompt" remedial action, although lower income groups are more likely to call for "urgent" action. *Media General/Associated Press Poll.*

The environment is a top priority for the powerful. Those lucky people described as "Influential Americans" (opinion leaders who are the most politically and socially active 10 percent of the population, as named by the Roper Organization) rank the environment as the top priority for more government spending. Seventy-six percent of them, up from 59 percent in 1988, think more should be spent to improve and protect the environment. This is considered a more important issue than helping the poor or the homeless, or dealing with drug addiction. *The Public Pulse, The Roper Organization.* A psychographic group known as "Achievers" (the materialistic younger people zooming up the ladder of success) are very afraid for the Earth's health—82 percent say they are worried about the environment. *Backer Spielvogel Bates Worldwide.*

Minorities

Minorities, while concerned about the environment, are more worried about economic issues. While most Americans think laws against polluters are too weak, Hispanics are more likely than whites (34 percent vs. 19 percent) to say the current laws are about right. The differences in responses of minorities may stem from the feeling of futility that is the concomitant of being disenfranchised, or the justified fear that environmentally sensitive products cost more (they usually do), thereby hitting lower-income consumers harder.

Over the last 20 years, the percentage of people of all ethnic groups who felt they could personally do something about pollution fell from 90 percent to 60 percent. *Opatow Associates.*

While more blacks and Hispanics than whites rate the environment in the U.S. as fair or poor (71 percent and 64 percent vs. 63 percent, respectively), and minorities show higher levels of concern about environmental issues in the future (see chart below), *the job issue, a persistently critical one for minorities, will not be pushed to the side by environmental concerns.* Choosing between industrial development, which would provide a better standard of living but with health risks, or a lower standard of living, but with many fewer health risks, only 12 percent of whites choose industrial development, compared to 24 percent of both blacks and Hispanics, who are willing to risk their health in the name of economic progress. *United Nations Environment Program/Louis Harris and Associates.*

Percent responding "very serious" danger in next five years

	Whites	Blacks	Hispanics
Drinking water that makes people sick	54%	68%	73%
Air that is polluted and makes breathing more difficult	60%	75%	67%
Climates that are too hot or too cold	19%	34%	27%
Land that will not produce enough food to feed the people who live there	44%	62%	51%
More land turning into desert	31%	50%	28%
Fewer birds, insects, wild animals, and plants	47%	46%	51%
Lakes and rivers more polluted each year	73%	84%	85%
Oceans and seas more polluted each year	68%	79%	82%

Source: United Nations Environment Program/Louis Harris and Associates

---

Minority groups tend to have priorities somewhat different from those of whites on environment-related constraints that would effect their everyday lives.

Would you support or oppose a community requirement that you separate and recycle household glass, cans, and paper?

	Support	Oppose	Don't know/no answer
White	87%	9%	4%
Black	90%	8%	2%
Hispanic	75%	10%	15%

If curbside pickup service were provided, would you support or oppose it? (Asked of those who opposed above)

White	45%	30%	25%
Black	65%	15%	19%
Hispanic	17%	22%	61%

Would you support or oppose a ban on household aerosol products?

White	75%	16%	9%
Black	67%	27%	6%
Hispanic	74%	14%	13%

Would you support or oppose a ban on non-radial tires, which release more rubber into the air?

White	*58%*	*25%*	*17%*
Black	55%	31%	14%
Hispanic	65%	32%	3%

Would you support or oppose a ban on gasoline-powered garden appliances?

White	32%	62%	7%
Black	50%	45%	5%
Hispanic	50%	41%	8%

Would you support or oppose parking restrictions in cities to discourage the use of cars?

White	44%	46%	10%
Black	39%	54%	7%
Hispanic	30%	59%	12%

Would you support or oppose strict pollution controls on oil- and coal-burning power plants, even if that would raise the price of electricity?

	Support	Oppose	Don't know/no answer
White	73%	19%	8%
Black	63%	33%	3%
Hispanic	59%	30%	12%

Source: Media General/AP poll #26

Youth

Young people are environmentalists, too. Young people concur with their elders' environmental perceptions, and that has already affected career choices. Out of 20 possibilities, a plurality of people aged 14-21 put the environment as the top problem facing the country. *Seventeen.* One college reports that the number of students enrolled in environmental studies has more than doubled in the last three years. *The Wall Street Journal.* College freshman are increasingly interested in "becoming involved in programs to clean up the environment"—26 percent now list this as a very important goal in life, up from 16 percent in 1986. This represents a 63-percent increase in interest in just three years. *UCLA.*

Percent of college freshman who say:

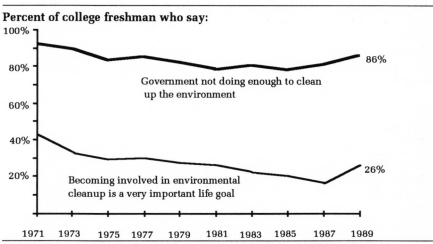

Source: The American Freshman: National Norms for Fall 1989, *UCLA Higher Education Research Institute*

Work 2000
New Workers, Flextime, Flexplace

Although the USA has always worn the "melting pot" moniker on its sleeve, the visible members of its workforce on a career path have until now been overwhelmingly males of European stock. No more. As we approach 2000, immigration and social changes will cause the entering workforce to continue its rapid ethnic and female growth skew. The increase of immigrants, coupled with the shrinkage of the entry-level labor pool (a result of Baby Busters coming of age), will worsen what has recently come to be called the "skills gap."

The feminization and ethnicization of the market will coincide with the ongoing shift to a service economy. We see an increase in a part-time and short-term intensive workforce, partly as a result of a wish or need for "flextime" to enable workers to attend to family responsibilities.

Labor Market

Hype Alert: "There was a job boom in the '80s, and it continues."

The labor force is expected to expand by nearly 21 million, or 18 percent, over the 1986-2000 period. However, this represents a slowdown in both the number of workers to be added to the labor force and in the rate of growth from the previous 14-year period when the labor force increased by almost 31 million, or 35 percent. The slow growth trend is already underway. The projected slower economic growth for the remainder of the century is a continuation of a trend that started in the late 1970s. *Bureau of Labor Statistics.*

Projected population and labor force growth by age group, 1986 to 2000

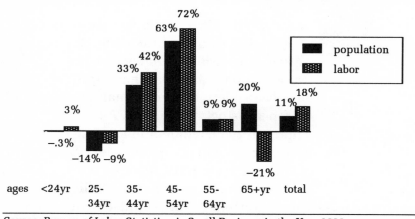

Source: *Bureau of Labor Statistics, in* Small Business in the Year 2000

The labor force is projected to become increasingly heterogenous. The white labor force is projected to increase less than 15 percent between 1986-2000, while the black labor force is expected to grow by nearly 29 percent, or 3.7 million workers—more than 17 percent of the projected total labor force increase. The Hispanic labor force is projected to grow by approximately 6 million, and to account for nearly 29 percent of the labor force growth. The category of "other races" (Asians, Native Americans, Pacific Islanders) is expected to grow by nearly 2.4 million, and account for more than 11 percent of labor force growth. Blacks, Hispanics, Asians, and other races are projected to account for a total of 57 percent of labor force growth. If non-Hispanic white women are included, these groups' combined share of future growth reaches more than 90 percent. *Bureau of Labor Statistics.* By the end of the 1990s, only 8 out of 100 new workforce entrants will be white males. *Dr. David Bloom of Columbia University, as cited in Industry Week.*

Labor force growth by race or ethnic origin. Percent of growth each group will account for 1986-2000

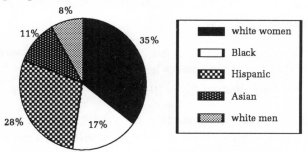

Source: *Bureau of Labor Statistics, in* Small Business in the Year 2000

Current and estimated projections of the makeup of the workforce

Year	white male	white female	Hispanic	black	Asian
1986	45%	35%	7%	11%	3%
2000	39%	35%	10%	12%	4%

Source: The Hudson Institute

There will be a slowdown in the rate of occupational growth for men in the rest of the century, affecting all major job levels. Top-level managerial growth jumped 74 percent between 1972 and 1986, but it is projected to inch up only 29 percent between the late 1980s and the year 2000. Gross mobility patterns for men will be very different in 2000 from patterns of the early 1960s. About half of all men were upwardly mobile in 1962, but only about one-third will be moving up in 2000. Roughly equal proportions of the other two-thirds will be immobile and downwardly mobile.

Over half of the men on their way down the career ladder in the year 2000 will be sons of white-collar fathers. Trends in equality of opportunity are not promising. Access to higher level jobs by sons of higher level and lower level fathers became more equal between the early 1960s and the late 1980s, but will become less equal between now and 2000. *Tadeusz Krauze, Hofstra University.*

The "skills gap" will worsen. More than half the jobs in the U.S. will soon require education beyond high school, and the skills of workers have not kept pace with occupation changes. *Immigrant population will exacerbate the skills gap.* Given the skills shifts implied by the occupational projections, many immigrants may not possess the job skills that are in high demand in the economy. *Bureau of Labor Statistics.*

Low pay. In 1985, 44 percent of all newly created jobs were low-wage jobs (full-time at $7,400 or less). *National Commission on Working Women of Wider Opportunities for Women.*

Average age of workers will increase. In sync with an aging population, the average age of the working population will increase from 35.3 years in 1986 to 38.9 in the year 2000. *Bureau of Labor Statistics.*

Hype Alert: "We're gaining against child labor violations."
Violations of child labor laws are on an upswing. The General Accounting Office reports that violations of laws limiting how long, and and under what conditions children work have increased 150 percent since 1983. Restaurants and grocery stores are the worst offenders. *USA Today.*

Employment Trends

More people are moonlightling. A higher proportion of the workforce is moonlighting than at any time in 30 years of record keeping by the Labor Department—6.2 percent of all employed people were working two jobs in May 1989, up from 5.4 percent in 1985 and 4.9 percent in 1980. Forty-four percent of Americans took a second job to meet routine living expenses and pay off debt, while 41 percent cited those reasons in 1985 and 37 percent in 1979. Incomes have simply failed to keep pace with lifestyle expectations. "Wages by and large have been pretty stagnant since the early 1970s. Things get better very slowly. Some people have been raised on very high aspirations in terms of consumption and what they're entitled to. Working a second job is one way to stretch incomes to meet what it takes to lead the middle-class life," says Frank Levy, an economist at the University of Maryland School of Public Affairs. *Wall Street Journal.*

Multiple job-holding rate (moonlighting),* sex and race differences					
year	total	men	women	white	black**
1970	5.2%	7.0%	2.2%	5.3%	4.4%
1974	4.5%	5.8%	2.6%	4.6%	3.8%
1978	4.8%	5.8%	3.3%	5.0%	3.1%
1985	5.4%	5.9%	4.7%	5.7%	3.2%
1989	6.2%	6.4%	5.9%	6.5%	4.3%

*Multiple jobholders as percent of all employed persons in specific group.
** Beginning in 1977, data refer to black workers only; data for prior years refer to the black-and-other population.
Source: Bureau of Labor Statistics

Unemployment for some segments will decline. The projected decline of jobseekers ages 16 to 19 offers an opportunity for lowering the unemployment rate for this labor force group that historically has had a high rate. The technicians and related support workers category is projected to grow faster than any other major occupational group (38 percent) between 1986 and 2000, or more than twice as fast as total employment. There will not be as much of an increase of paperwork staff. The number of administrative support workers, including clerical, will grow more slowly (only 11 percent) than the average for total jobs from 1986 to 2000. *Bureau of Labor Statistics.*

Expansion of service industries will shrink some unemployed groups. The projected large employment increases in eating and drinking places, retail sales, and many service industries that

typically employ first-time jobseekers also will ease unemployment for the 16- to-19-year-old age group. Growth will be very
strong for most of the service-producing industries, particularly
health services, business services, and trade. *Service-producing
employment will constitute about 80 percent of all wage and
salary jobs by 2000. Bureau of Labor Statistics.*

Largest job growth
(numbers in thousands)

| | employment | | change in employment 1986-2000 | | |
| | | | *increase* | | |
Occupation	1986	*projected* 2000	*in* number	*percent* change	*% job* growth
Salespersons, retail	3,579	4,780	1201	33.5%	5.6%
Waiters and waitresses	1,702	2,454	752	44.2%	3.5%
Registered nurses	1,406	2,018	612	43.6%	2.9%
Janitors and cleaners	2,676	3,280	604	22.6%	2.8%
General managers and top executives	2,383	2,965	582	24.2%	2.7%
Cashiers	2,165	2,740	575	26.5%	2.7%
Truck drivers	2,211	2,736	525	23.8%	2.5%
General office clerks	2,361	2,824	462	19.6%	2.2%
Food counter and related workers	1,500	1,949	449	29.9%	2.1%

Fastest growing jobs
(numbers in thousands)

| | employment | | change in employment 1986-2000 | | |
| | | | *increase* | | |
Occupation	1986	*projected* 2000	*in* number	*percent* change	*% job* growth
Legal assistants	61	125	64	103.7%	0.3%
Medical assistants	132	251	119	90.4%	0.6%
Physical therapists	61	115	53	87.5%	0.2%
Physical and corrective therapy assistants and aides	36	65	29	81.6%	0.1%
Data processing equipment repairers	69	125	56	80.4%	0.3%
Homemaker-home health aides	138	249	111	80.1%	0.5%
Podiatrists	13	23	10	77.2%	0
Computer specialists analysts	331	582	251	75.6%	1.2%
Medical record technicians	40	70	30	75.0%	0.1%

Source: Bureau of Labor Statistics, as cited in the 1990 Information Please Almanac

Hype Alert: "Temps were a trend of the 1980s."
They certainly were, but they won't be going away in the '90s—now nine out of ten businesses use some kind of temporary workers, and 62 percent of temporary workers are women. *National Commission on Working Women of Wider Opportunities for Women.* The number of temps will increase. During the 1980s, over half (52 percent) of job growth has come from the contingent workforce (temps, part-time, subcontractors, consultants, leased workers, and life-of-contract workers). The biggest growth was among temp workers, up 75 percent. In the past decade, the temporary service industry has grown three times faster than the service sector overall. Near-term growth in the temp sector shows almost all (85 percent-95 percent) companies employ temporary workers, and employment in the temp industry will experience a 6.7 percent average annual growth from 1988 to 1995. *Temps are more productive.* The Deptartment of Labor finds that temporary workers are productive 90 percent of the time, compared to only 65 percent-85 percent for permanent staff. *Marketdata Enterprises.*

Business

All in the family. More than 75 percent of companies in America are family owned or controlled. One third of Fortune 500 companies are family firms. *Family businesses* generate 60 percent of the U.S. gross national product. *Family Business magazine, Corporate Bloodlines, as cited in Newsweek, Winter/Sping 1990.*

Hype Alert: "Business failures continue to set records."
Business failures actually continue to decline. The number of business failures is the U.S. declined for the third consecutive year in 1989, an impressive achievement considering the continued increases in the number of new businesses. Between 1988 and 1989, the number of business failures declined 12.9, percent from 57,099 to 49,719. Between 1987 and 1988, the decline was 6.6 percent. *Small Business Administration.*

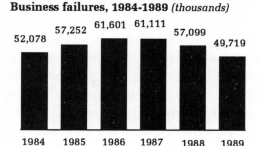

Business failures, 1984-1989 *(thousands)*

52,078 57,252 61,601 61,111 57,099 49,719

1984 1985 1986 1987 1988 1989

Source: adapted by the Small Business Admin. from
The Dun & Bradstreet Corp., Business Failure Record

More entrepreneurs in the future. Several demographic and business factors suggest an increase in the number of U.S. entrepreneurs in the '90s:

1. **The aging of the labor force.** Older, more experienced workers tend to start businesses more frequently, and tend to be more successful. The increase in the number of 35-to 54-year-old workers will significantly increase the number of potential entrepreneurs.

2. **Middle manager squeeze.** The demands for (and salaries of) many middle managers decrease as companies continue to merge and downsize. Entrepreneurship becomes an attractive option, as it lets them use their skills and maintain (or increase) their earnings.

3. **Higher education.** The most successful entrepreneurs are those who have college degrees. If the U.S. continues to produce more high school and college graduates, the numbers of business owners should increase.

4. **Teaching entrepreneurship.** In the last 10 years, colleges have shown an increased emphasis on teaching entrepreneurial skills. A larger proportion of business schools are gearing grads towards entrepreneurship. *Small Business in the Year 2000, Small Business Administration.*

The share of women-owned businesses will increase. Not only did the number of women-owned businesses (nonfarm proprietorships exclusively) increase 135 percent between 1977 and 1987, from 1.9 million to 4.4 million, but during the same period, the share of businesses owned by women also increased from 22.6 percent to 30.6 percent. This trend is expected to continue into 2000, with the percent of women-owned businesses increasing, while the share of male-owned businesses declines. Please keep in mind that while these businesses are not necessarily small, the overwhelming majority can be classified as small businesses (less than 500 employees). *Small Business Administration.*

Share of nonfarm sole proprietorships to the year 2000 by gender
(percentage)

Year	female-owned	male-owned	jointly-owned
1977	22.59%	74.34%	3.07%
1987	30.61%	65.69%	3.50%
2000	36.72%	58.87%	4.06%

Source: U.S. Small Business Administration, based on IRS data

Hype Alert: "Women only own a third of all small businesses in the U.S."

While the IRS estimates (see above data) that women own only one-third of small businesses in the U.S., please remember that this estimate *only* includes women who are sole proprietors as business owners. It does not report on the ratio of male- to female-owned partnerships, corporations, and other types of businesses. A study of women in professional associations nationwide finds that 52 percent of respondents who own business are sole proprietors, but an additional 17 percent are involved in partnerships, 14 percent own corporations, 11 percent have S-corporations, and 6 percent other forms not identified. *The Business Women Leadership Media, Inc.*

How women business owners define success. *The Avon Report: A National Attitude Survey on Successful Women Entrepreneurs* (based on the results of 450 in-depth surveys completed by applicants for Avon's Women of Enterprise Awards over a three-year period) estimates there are 4.1 million women business owners in the U.S. (very close to the IRS estimate of 4.4). The majority (68 percent) of Avon's entrepreneurs own service businesses. Success isn't just sales to these women. Though the number-one goal for most of these women is to increase sales, they say that the feelings of happiness, self-fulfillment, achievement, and challenge they experience make them feel successful.

Entrepreneurial women's personal definition of success at different revenue levels, *(figures rounded)*

gross sales	happiness self-fulfillment	sales/ profit	helping others	achievement challenge
<$100K	24%	23%	23%	24%
$100K-$499.9K	35%	41%	30%	29%
$500K+	41%	36%	46%	47%

Source: Avon Report

Characteristics of minority businesses, by ethnic group
(Census Bureau 1986)

	Business ownership as a % of group	Number of firms (thousands)	Firms with employees (thousands)	Percentage of firms with employees	Employees per firm
Asians	5.5%	256	49	19%	4.7
Koreans	9.0%	32	8	25%	3.1
Asian Indians	7.1%	26	6	25%	3.2
Japanese	7.0%	49	7	14%	4.7
Chinese	6.6%	53	14	28%	6.5
Filipinos	3.4%	26	3	11%	2.7
Vietnamese	2.0%	5	2	44%	2.0
Hispanics	1.7%	248	40	16%	4.8
Cubans	4.6%	37	5	14%	4.3
Mexicans	1.6%	143	24	17%	4.4
Puerto Ricans	0.7%	15	2	12%	3.3
Blacks	1.3%	339	39	11%	4.3

Source: Ethnic Entrepreneurs, *Sage Publications*

Hype Alert: "The 'Glass Ceiling' will crack in the 1990s."

That assessment is too optimistic. This metaphoric invisible barrier that keeps women out of the top echelons of corporate management will recede during the 1990s, and will shatter in isolated cases, but there will still be an enormous disparity between the number of men and women at the top by the year 2000. There are three reasons for this:

1. Women execs start the decade at such a numerical disadvantage. In 1990, only 3 percent of senior executives in Fortune 500 companies are women, a miniscule 1-percent increase since 1985. Only three *Fortune 500* companies have a female CEO. *Regina Herzlinger, Harvard University.*

2. It takes about 35 years of experience to earn one's way to the top, and in the late 1950s and early 1960s, comparatively few women entered business with the kind of singular focus needed to climb the ladder that brings managers to the very top. *Regina Herzlinger, Harvard University.*

3. Old prejudices persist against women as good managers. A Catalyst poll of Fortune 1000 CEOs found that 81 percent believe that male prejudices and preconceptions are major blocks to women reaching the top; and 49 percent feel that management is reluctant to take risks with women in management positions that lead up the corporate ladder. *Catalyst.*

Franchising

The number of U.S. franchise companies, which doubled in the '80s, will triple in the '90s, to a total of 9,000. The pool of prospective franchise buyers will increase as the Baby Boomers age and come into their franchise buying years. Stereotypical blue-collar "Mom and Pop" businesses are giving way to savvy, lucrative franchises, with older and more affluent Boomers at the storefront. Today's franchise buyers are better educated, wealthier, and have more business savvy than past buyers—the typical franchisee has a college degree and an average annual income of $67,356. These upscale Boomer franchisees will be more demanding than franchise buyers of the past—they will thoroughly research deals before committing and will require more legal assurances and documentation from sellers. Franchise sellers have found that franchise buyers, compared to five years ago, have higher incomes (80 percent of sellers said their buyers' incomes were higher than five years ago), higher net worth (83 percent), and are better educated (61 percent). *DePaul University and Francorp, Inc.*

The Feminized Workforce

Hype Alert: "The working mother spiral continues up and up."

There are more working moms in today's work force, though the rate of growth is slowing. Today 65 percent of women with children under 18 are in the workforce; this number has almost tripled since 1960. By the year 2000, though the rate of growth will slow, it's estimated that 75 percent of children will have working moms. The fastest growing segment of the workforce is married moms with children under the age of two (3.1 million). Today, over half of new moms are back to work before their baby's first birthday, a jump of 60 percent in one decade. *National Association of Working Women.*

Working poor women. Women account for half the working poor (4.5 million in 1986), and more than half of those women have children. Three out of five minimum wage earners are women. *National Commission on Working Women of Wider Opportunities for Women.*

Young vs. old women. In 1987, 6.2 million (20 percent) of women age 55+ were in the labor force. Participation rates for today's younger women start high and continue to rise during childbearing years; their labor patterns more closely resemble those of their fathers. Two-thirds of women age 55+ are employed in traditionally female job categories (sales and administrative support). Only half of those aged 25-34 are employed in those types of jobs. Not only are there strong employment differences between older black women and older white women, there are also striking differences between older and younger black women. Older black women are three times more likely than older white women to be employed in service occupations. In 1987, 33 percent of black working women age 65+ worked as cooks, servants, or cleaners, compared to 1 percent of black women age 25-34. *Family Economic Review.*

Hype Alert: "Most career women say they have experienced job discrimination."

While almost half of female executives (46 percent) feel there are separate company standards for men and women, and a third (32 percent) feel that talented women do not have a fair chance to reach top levels, most (84 percent) say they have never experienced job discrimination based on sex. *U.S. News & World Report.*

Women want success. Success in work is more important to women of the high school class of 1982 (77 percent) than it was to the class of 1972 (70 percent). *U.S. Dept. of Education. Lack of opportunity ousts women.* Age, rather than sex, and women's perceptions of the glass ceiling more strongly determine their intention to exit a company than do family-related conflicts. *Opinion Research Corp.*

Flexibility for All

The sandwich generation: people in their peak earning and spending years, having to care for elderly parents and growing kids. Most of this kind of unpaid labor falls upon the daughter/mother—who also happens to be a worker and a wife. The stress of juggling all of these roles is forcing changes in corporate America. Companies cannot afford to lose highly skilled workers, and families cannot afford to lose the income; something's got to give.

Expect to see more flexible work schedules in the 1990s, with flextime, job sharing, and home-based work becoming increasingly widespread, according to a study of senior human resource executives at 521 of the nation's largest companies. The majority of respondents (93 percent) say they offer at least one type of flexible work schedule—flextime, part-time work, job sharing, home-based work, phased retirement, or compressed workweek. Those most likely to have flexible schedules are female and are employed in a clerical, administrative support, or sales position.

Managers, professionals, and executives tend not to have flexible schedules. *Conference Board. Flextime is very important to working parents.* One-quarter of men and almost 50 percent of women have considered going to another firm offering more flexibility for family responsibilities. *Paternity leave will be common.* In the 1990s, new fathers will take one to two weeks parental leave, but longer parental leave will not become a dominant pattern. *Bureau of National Affairs Inc. Homework will continue to increase.* By 2000, up to 20 percent of the American workforce will opt to work at home. Among information workers, up to half will be able to work wherever they find it most convenient. American Renaissance, *St. Martin's Press. Increase in part-time.* One-third of all new jobs created since 1981 have been part-time (three-quarters of these workers would prefer full-time). *National Commission on Working Women of Wider Opportunities for Women.*

Child care
Time with kids remains a priority; leisure and chores get the ax among women—82 percent of working mothers say they must sacrifice personal time, and 75 percent say they must neglect housework. *Working Mother.*

Hype Alert: "Quality time."
Whether they say it's a priority or not, a study of business men and women finds that over half of working parents (53 percent) spend less than 2 hours a week looking after the kids, and 42 percent spend no time reading to the kids. *Priority Management.*

Offering maternity benefits keeps employees. Between 1981 and 1985, 71 percent of women with benefits returned to work within six months of birth, versus 43 percent of those without benefits. *Census Bureau.*

Only one in ten workers receives child care benefits. *Accounts on Call in USA Today.*

More "split-shift" parenting. Split-shift married couples with young children are on the rise, increasing parental childcare, including father care. The trend is expected to continue for two reasons: 1) the continuing and rapid increase in the number of married women with young children in the labor force; 2) the sector of the economy with the highest proportion of shift workers among dual-earner couples—the service sector—is the fastest-growing sector of the economy. *Harriet Presser, University of Maryland.*

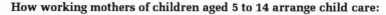

How working mothers of children aged 5 to 14 arrange child care:

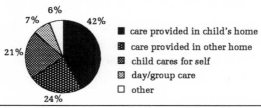

- ■ care provided in child's home
- ▨ care provided in other home
- ▨ child cares for self
- ▧ day/group care
- □ other

Source: Consumer Research Center, The Conference Board, as cited in NEA Today

Elder care
Hype Alert: "Eldercare will become a problem after the turn of the century."
Actually, eldercare is already a problem for many Americans. One-quarter of America's workforce *now* provides care for an elderly person, and almost all employees (93 percent) think this is difficult to do when putting in time at work. Almost all (85 percent) workers are concerned about their job performance while caring for an elderly person. Of the 37 percent of workers who have had the experience of caring for elders in the last two years, 51 percent have felt extra stress, 44 percent have had to be on the phone more, and 24 percent say they have been less productive. A third of all working men have undertaken elder care responsibilities in the last two years, while 43 percent of female workers have done so. Women put in more time caring for the elderly (15.4 hours each week vs. 10 for men). *Fortune.*

Work-at-home
Home workers are most likely to be dual incomers. One-quarter of all U.S. households have at least one person who works at home either regularly or occasionally. Half of all homeworkers have set

up an area specifically for doing work. Nearly three-quarters are in households with dual incomes. Home workers work an average of nearly 21 hours per week at home, and three in ten either own or plan to purchase typewriters, word processors, copy machines, telephones, fax machines, computer software, personal computers, and office furniture in the coming year. *Discount Store News.* The annual LINK Resources' National Work-At-Home Survey indicates that 4.2 million Americans began doing job-related work at home during the past year. A total of 26.6 million Americans now work at home, a 6.8 percent gain over 1988. Homeworkers are evenly divided between men and women, average 39 years of age, and tend to be part of dual-career households. Their total household income averages $42,000.

Satisfaction

Hype Alert: "Americans are fed up with their jobs."
Over half of workers (52 percent) enjoy work more now than five years ago (19 percent enjoy it less), even though most people say they are working harder over the last five years (51 percent harder, 15 percent less hard). Job demands are the main reason for the extra hard work (51 percent), above increased cost of living (20 percent) and improved living standards (12 percent). Forty-four percent find family and work equally fulfilling, 10 percent find work most fulfilling, and 46 percent say family provides most fulfillment. *Chivas Regal Report on Working Americans.*

Management is not in tune with the needs and concerns of workers. Though workers may generally be more satisfied than in the past, today's workplace is no utopia. In what is called an "aspiration gap," many issues described by workers as very important are not characteristic of their work environment. The majority of both workers and bosses (87 percent each) agree that honesty and ethics, the job attributes of highest importance to workers, are important, but 69 percent of execs say their company's management is honest, vs. only 39 percent of employees who think so. *Steelcase.*

Top executives' views on office characteristics: importance and prevelance

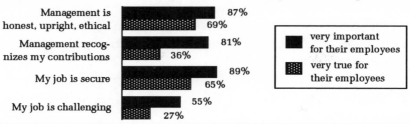

Source: Steelcase

Workers' views on office characteristics: importance and prevalence

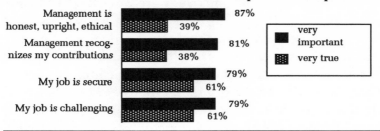

Source: Steelcase

Job satisfaction increases with age. Sixty two percent of workers age 50+ are satisfied, compared to 36 percent of those 18-29. *Accountants on Call.* Satisfaction varies with salary and job type— older and better-compensated office workers are more satisfied than others with their jobs. The general level of satisfaction is lower for unionized workers and for clerical/secretarial workers. *Steelcase Inc./Louis Harris and Associates.*

Managers are working harder. Sixty three percent of middle managers say they are working harder now than three years ago because of increased workloads resulting from heavy layoffs between 1984 and 1987. However, they are quite satisfied with their jobs because there has been an increase in the skills and talents required to do their jobs (72 percent say so) and more autonomy (59 percent) over the past three years. *Dunhill Personnel Systems Inc.*

Security up. Two-and-a-half times as many workers feel more job secure over the last five years than feel less secure (50 percent feel more; 19 percent less), particularly among younger workers age 25-34 (60 percent more; 30 percent less). *Chivas Regal Report on Working Americans.*

Retirement

Hype Alert: "The early retirement trend continues."
Older workers' participation in the labor force has dropped significantly in the last three decades, but is now increasing again. In 1950, almost half of all men 65 and over were working. By the late 1980s, only 16 percent of this group were working. Early retirement and a drop in self-employment explain the decline. Seventy percent of retirees say they are not interested in working; 60 percent of retirees consider their income from pensions and Social Security adequate. *The Mature Market, Probus Publishing.* However, some studies indicate that now and in the future, people will work longer, and may simply change careers rather than retiring. In 1989, there were 3.4 million workers age 65+, an increase from 2.9 million in 1986. About half of these seniors work part-time. *Bureau of Labor Statistics in the Wall Street Journal.*

Pension benefits strongly affect decision to keep working. Receipt of pensions and marital status are important factors in determining whether older women work. Women without pensions are three times more likely to work than women with pensions; seventy percent of divorced women age 55-59 work, compared to 45 percent of married women. After age 65, divorced women are three times more likely than married women to be in the labor force. *Family Economic Review.*

Business Travel

Hype Alert: "Business travel is booming."
Actually, it's status quo. Business travelers comprised 35 percent of the resort lodging guests in 1988, down from 40 percent in 1987, though the actual number of business travelers was the same during this period. *Laventhol & Horwath.*

Travel causes stress. Business travel interferes with the traveler's personal life after 5.2 days on the road. Women feel travel-related problems more than men do. But business travelers who have been on the road more than five years report feeling less stress than others. *Hyatt Hotels Corp.*

Can't leave home without it. The most important piece of equipment to a frequent business traveler is the credit card (89 percent), followed by a long-distance calling card (69 percent) and calculators/facsimile equipment (34 percent). *Erdos & Morgan/MPG.*

Favorite place to hang their hats. For frequent business travelers, Marriot is the hotel of preference (58 percent), followed by Hyatt (49 percent), Hilton (46 percent), and Sheraton (42 percent). *Erdos & Morgan/MPG.*

Ups and downs of traveling. Two-thirds of business travelers dislike being separated from their families, and 50 percent feel harried when traveling. However, 98 percent report a sense of accomplishment from business travel; 81 percent enjoy the exposure to new people and places; 70 percent revel in the break from routine. *Hyatt Hotels Corp.*

Health, Safety, Drug Testing

Looking out for women. Twenty percent of companies restrict women's work duties because of potential risk to their reproductive health. *Boston Deptartment of Public Health. Poor are undercovered.* Approximately two-thirds of all poor workers do not receive health insurance. *National Commission on Working Women of Wider Opportunities for Women.*

Hype Alert: "Life is stress."
Actually, work is stress—the top five causes of stress all come from the office, and stress-related illnesses and burnout are responsible for 75 percent of lost workdays in North America. Half of all business people experience stress daily. *Priority Management Systems Inc.*

There is twice as much disability among blacks. Fourteen percent of blacks, age 16 to 64, compared with about 8 percent for whites and Hispanics, had a work disability in '88. *Census Bureau.*

VDT use diminishes production. Heavy users of computer terminals (five or more hours a day) report they are somewhat less productive than workers using computers less often; 46 percent of heavy computer users say they do as much as they reasonably can vs. 49 percent of all office workers. *Steelcase Inc./Louis Harris and Assoc.*

Substance abuse surpasses AIDS as issue. Sixty-six percent of industrial relations executives say drug abuse is the number one problem in the workplace (83 percent cited AIDS as number one in 1987). *Jackson, Lewis, Schnitzler & Krupman.*

Hype Alert: "American workers say no to workplace drug testing."
Testing is considered okay. The "right" of employers to test employees for drug use is supported by a wider margin than three years ago—72 percent say drug tests are fair (68 percent in 1986) vs. 19 percent who say unfair (24 percent in 1986). Firing is okay—55 percent of employees say employers have the right to fire staff who refuse to take drug tests. Roughly half that number (28 percent) say bosses should not have that right. Although a clear majority of employees support drug testing, there is far less agreement that employers have the right to fire employees who test positive if there is no proof that drugs are used on the job or have impaired performance: 46 percent say the employers have that right, 38 percent say they do not, and 17 percent are undecided. *Cambridge Reports' Trends & Forecasts.*

Regulation

Hype Alert: "Free market Americans love deregulation."
They did; now they don't. They want things to work, and they are showing renewed willingness to have government handle the problems. But, they want results. They will be willing to pay

higher taxes for solutions to urgent problems (particularly the environment and infrastructure, but not the federal deficit), as long as they can see a direct linkage and results. You'll find solid support for re- (or increased) regulation in air travel, false-advertising and labeling, auto standards, job safety, consumer information, trash disposal, and securities transactions.

Business regulation is gaining appeal. In the last year there has been a 10-point decline in the percentage of people who feel U.S. businesses are generally over-regulated (now 26 percent think so vs. 35 percent last year). Now 35 percent say biz regulations should be increased, rather than simply maintained at current level; 52 percent say regulations have become too lax. *Cambridge Reports' Trends & Forecasts.*

Has deregulation of this industry been in the best interest of the country and consumers?

	Yes	No	Not sure
Airline industry			
1988	38%	48%	14%
1987	47%	35%	18%
1986	46%	40%	15%
1985	56%	24%	20%
Telephone/telecommunications industry			
1988	37%	51%	12%
1987	35%	52%	14%
1986	36%	52%	13%
1985	30%	56%	14%
Banking industry			
1988	41%	34%	25%
1987	40%	34%	26%
1986	42%	33%	25%
1985	45%	29%	27%

Source: Cambridge Reports' Trends and Forecasts

PRINCIPAL SOURCES

Advertising Age
220 East 42nd Street
New York, NY 10017

Adweek's Marketing Week
49 East 21st Street
New York, NY 10010

American Demographics
Post Office Box 68
Ithica, NY 14851

The American Forecaster
Almanac 1990
Running Press
125 South 22nd Street
Philadelphia, PA 19103

Cambridge Reports' Trends and Forecasts
675 Massachussetts Avenue, 4th Floor
Cambridge, MA 02139

The Census Bureau
Public Information Office
Room #2705-3
Washington, DC 20233

The Conference Board
845 Third Avenue
New York, NY

Find/SVP
625 Avenue of the Americas
New York, NY 10011

FutureScope
Dearborn Financial Publishing
520 North Dearborn Street
Chicago, IL 60610

The Gallup Organization
100 Palmer Square
Suite 200
Princeton, NJ 08540

Good Housekeeping
959 Eighth Avenue
New York, NY 10019

Louis Harris and Associates
630 Fifth Avenue
New York, NY 10111

Impact Resources
125 Dillmont Drive
Columbus, Oh 43235

The Lempert Report
Post Office Box 585
Montclair, NJ 07042

Link Resources
79 Fifth Avenue
New York, NY 10003

Management Horizons
570 Metro Place North
Dublin, OH 43017

The Mature Market
Probus Publishing
118 North Clinton Street
Chicago, IL 60606

National Center for Health Statistics
6525 Belcrest Road
Presidential Building, Room 1050
Hyattsville, MD 20782

The New York Times
229 West 43rd Street
New York, NY 10036

Nielsen
1290 Avenue of the Americas
Avenue
New York, NY 10104

The Public Pulse
The Roper Organization
205 East 42nd Street, 17th floor
New York, NY 10017

Seventeen
850 Third Avenue
New York, NY 10022

Simmons Market Research Bureau
380 Madison Avenue
New York, NY 10017

Teenage Research Unlimited
601 Skokie Boulevard
Northbrook, IL 60062

USA Today
1000 Wilson Boulevard
Arlington, VA 22229

The Wall Street Journal
200 Liberty Street
New York, NY 10281

Yankelovich, Clancy, Shulman
8 Wright Street
Westport, CT 06880

Research Alert is a bi-weekly newsletter, founded in 1983, that covers the latest trends among the American people. The staff collects virtually all of the market research studies about Americans, over a thousand studies each year, from every possible source. We analyze each study, extract the key findings, and write them into quick-reading articles— 15 to 30 of which appear in any given issue. Subscribers keep on top of the latest trends in lifestyles, attitudes and needs, as well as staying ahead of numerous demographic, psychographic and behavioral changes with our predictions. Our articles are 100% fact-based, 100% independent (we don't take any advertising), and include full contact information for every source for your convenience.

In addition to the bi-weekly *Research Alert*, Alert Publishing, Inc. publishes three monthly newsletters:
- *Affluent Markets Alert*
- *Minority Markets Alert*
- *Youth Markets Alert*

Alert Pulishing editors are also available to make speeches to various business and social groups. We also publish a series of business reports. Recent ones include:
- *The Affluence Explosion: The Real Affluents, The Real Impact*
- *Environmentalism & Americans: A Guide to the Most Important Trend of Our Time*
- *Environmentalism: What Every Marketer Needs to Know*

Please feel free to contact us should you want to:
- Obtain futher information about any of our publications
- Follow up on the information in *Future Vision*
- Submit a report for us to consider for coverage

Please contact us at:
Alert Publishing, Inc.
37-06 30th Avenue
Long Island City, NY 11103